Japan Against Russia
in the Skies of Nomonhan

Japan Against Russia in the Skies of Nomonhan

Col Prof Dimitar Nedialkov PhD

Crécy Publishing Limited

Japan Against Russia in the Skies of Nomonhan
Col Prof Dimitar Nedialkov PhD

First published by Propeller Publishing, Sofia, in 2005
This edition published in 2011 by Crécy Publishing Limited

A CIP record for this book is available from the British Library

ISBN 9 780859 791526

Printed in Malta by Gutenberg Press

Crécy Publishing Limited
1a Ringway Trading Estate, Shadowmoss Road, Manchester M22 5LH
www.crecy.co.uk

CONTENTS

Glossary and abbreviations

Russian

AG	*Armeyskaya Grupa*, Army Group
Aviapolk	Basic tactical unit
Aviozveno	Flight of up to six aircraft
BAE	*Bombardirovochnaya Aviaeskadrilya*, Bomber Squadron
'Chayka' ('Gull')	Nickname for I-153
Eskadrilya	Squadron (plural *eskadrily*)
IAE	*Istrebitelnaya Aviaeskadrilya*, Fighter Squadron
IAP	*Istrebitelnyi Aviapolk* Fighter Air Regiment
'Ishak' ('Donkey')	nickname for I-16
Kantogun	Kwantung Army Operations Bureau
Komandarm	Army Commander
Kombrig	Brigade CO
Komdiv	Divisional CO
Komkor	Corps CO
KON	*Korpus Osobogo Naznacheniya*, Special Assignment Corps
MBBR	*Motobronevaya Brigada*, Motor-Armoured Brigade
MSD	*Motostrekovaya Diviziya*, Mechanised Infantry Division
MSP	*Motostrelkovoy Polk*, Motorised Infantry Regiment
Narkom	*Narodnay Komisar Abaronay*, People's Commissar of Defence
Palk	*Palkovnic*, Colonel
Podpolkovnik	Lt Colonel
RKKA	*Rabocheye-Krestyanskaya Krasnaya Armiya*, Workers' and Peasants' Red Army
SABR	*Smeshannaya Aviabrigada*, Mixed Air Brigade
SB	*Skorostnoy Bombardirovshchik*, High-Speed Bomber
SBABR	*Skorostnaya Bombardirovachnaya Aviobrigada*, Fast Bomber Air Brigade
SBAP	*Skorostnoy Bombardirovacnoy Aviapolk* High-Speed Bomber Regiment
SBAP	*Smeshennyi Bombardirovochnyy Aviapolk*, Mixed Bomber Air Regiment
SP	*Strelkovay Polk*, Infantry Regiment
St Lt	*Starshy Leytenant*, 2nd Lieutenant
TBR	*Tankovaya Brigada*, Tank Brigade
VNOS	Aerial Monitoring, Warning and Liaison
VVS	*Voyenno Vozdushnye Sily*, air force

Japanese

Chutai	Squadron
Hiko Shidan	Air Division or Air Brigade
Hikodan	Two or more *sentai* under a joint command
Koku-Heydan	Joint Air Command
Sentai	Basic combat unit
Shutai	Wing

1

Tension grows

The years immediately preceding the colossal armed conflict later called the Second World War saw the successive preparation by the Great Powers for yet another redrawing of the world map. Striving to attain strategic superiority, each of them launched into a complete militarisation of its economy. Those that had dictated the conditions of the last peace strove to retain the post-Great War status quo. Others strove for revenge and a strategic release of pent-up aspirations. Thus, as early as the start of the 1930s, statesmen no longer asked if, but rather when, the accumulation of armed power would lead to the subsequent large-scale conflict.

To test new weapons systems taken on strength by their armies and play out operational changes dictated by the technical superiority of those weapons, different corners of the world witnessed what at the time were known as 'small wars' – today's local armed conflicts. Europe was again expected to be the stage upon which revenge would be sought for a final resolution of the tensions of Versailles, yet the first flames erupted along its peripheries – Africa, South America and Asia.

The bloody Spanish Civil War erupted in 1936. This was to continue for three torturous years and bring enormous misery to the millions directly or indirectly affected by its internationalisation. In April 1939 this war led to the establishment of yet another repressive and totalitarian regime in Europe.

It was between General Franco's entry into Madrid and the start of the Second World War that a conflict that remained somewhat unnoticed by analysts, yet was far from random, took place. This had its prehistory, and left a lasting imprint on the progress and outcome of important events to come. Soviet military historiography calls it 'the Khalkhin-Gol River Incident', while Japanese historians call it the 'Nomonhan Incident'.

Stalin foresaw the coming clash and appreciated the significance of a victory in the East. Naturally, he did not intend to give up a single handful of territory. Contemporary Soviet military doctrine, specifically regarding its air force, emphasised the creation of an army and navy capable of repelling any aggression, regardless of whether waged by a single adversary or a coalition of states acting on several fronts. The Civil War had shown that this was the only way in which the world's sole socialist state could survive amid global militarism by relying on its enormous territory and unique natural riches. Border reinforcement measures included engineering works at key sites, and forced dispersal and movement. As part of this, the Red Banner Far Eastern Army began to be boosted from the mid-1930s, and positions along the commanding Sheng-Kyu-Feng (Zaozernaya) heights were reinforced; these heights are at the conjunction of the Manchurian, Korean and Soviet borders. Well aware of the area's significance, the Japanese decided to capture it, thus wresting control of the source of the Tyumen River. Japan's attack was well organised. On 30 July 1938 two 19th Infantry Division regiments rapidly overcame weak Soviet border posts, and captured the Bezimyannaya and Zaozernaya heights. The Soviet command launched a counter-strike between 6 and 9 August, employing two infantry divisions and a mechanised brigade. By 11 August, when combat ended, Russia had restored the integrity of the border. The *Kantogun* (Kwantung Army Operations Bureau) was left with a loss of face, as well as about 500 troops killed and 900 wounded.[1]

A decisive factor in the rapid and decisive Soviet victory was played by the Red Army's aviation component. The Japanese Imperial Headquarters had not included any genuine air support in planning for such regional operations, and air action was sporadic (or, rather, symbolic), involving about seventy combat-ready aircraft mainly based at Changchung and Harbin airfields. At the same time, Soviet ground forces were backed by the 48th *Shturmovaya* ('Strike', with R-10, SSS and R-5 aircraft), the 69th *Iztrebitelnaya* ('Fighter', with I-15bis and I-16s), and the 25th *Skorostnaya Bombardirovachnaya Aviabrigada* ('Fast Bomber Air Brigade'), as well as several separate reconnaissance R-Z *eskadrily* (squadrons), several independent air detachments and specialised aviation units supported by the Pacific Navy Air Force and the Third Special Army air components. The latter included units with heavy four-engined TB-3 bombers and new DB-3s, which were barely entering service.[2] Yet, regardless of its numbers, the potential of Soviet air power was not optimised due to the Stalin purge, which in 1937 had changed the entire commanding tier of the Red Banner Far Eastern Front. Young and inexperienced officers were appointed to the newly vacant command posts following the purge. Despite this blow to its staff, Soviet combat aviation had complete superiority in the air above the conflict zone, its only adversary being the sparse Japanese anti-aircraft artillery (AAA).

The operation was a success for that hopelessly obsolescent symbol of 1930s Soviet air power, the four-engined TB-3. Forty-one TB-3RNs had led the Soviet air armada towards the heights on 6 August 1938 at the start of the offensive operation. The battle order comprised a core strike group (the forty-one TB-3s and eighty-nine SB-2s), a group aiming at the enemy's anti-aircraft defences (thirty I-15bis), and a close cover group of twenty-five I-16s.[3] Fog disrupted the schedule, with strike echelons appearing over the field of battle only at 15.30. A total of 1,592 air bombs of various calibres and a total weight of 122 tonnes was delivered, and some 37,985 rounds were expended in fire on Japanese positions. Despite the sandy ground reducing the effectiveness of large-calibre high-explosive bombs, and area bombing methods leaving many targets intact, the air strikes crushed the morale and physical resistance of the entrenched adversary, allowing Soviet forces to attain their operational aims. The brief overall period of combat saw Soviet air force units complete 1,029 combat sorties (forty-one with the TB-3, 346 with the SB, fifty-three with the SSS, twenty-nine with the R-Z, 534 with the I-15bis, and twenty-five with the I-16).[4]

As mentioned above, Japanese aircraft were practically absent above the key border heights. The ability of Soviet strategic aviation to reach practically any point on Japanese or Korean territory was probably an inhibiting factor. The Red Army VVS (*Voyenno Vozdushnye Sily* – air force) had more than eighty four-engined TB-3s in the Pacific Military District alone. Armed with incendiary bombs, such a group could deliver a massive strike on the Japanese capital with its largely light, inflammable buildings. Japanese fighter forces were not yet ready for action at night, and air defences were relatively weak.

Naturally, the Japanese Army and Navy Air Force Commands could launch a retaliatory strike using limited numbers of the new G3M bombers, Ki-21-Is, Type Is (Fiat BR.20s) and H6K flying boats, but Moscow was too far even for the latter, and the numbers of these aircraft were a mere token against the Bolshevik state's air power.[5] The potential inherent in their long-range bombers freed the hand of Soviet air commanders at operational and tactical levels. They completed their missions with minimal losses (only one SB-2 and one I-15bis downed, eighteen I-15bis, seven SBs and four TB-3s damaged by anti-aircraft fire, and two I-15bis lost away from combat[6]). Air power had again showed its decisive importance in the progress and outcome of combat.

The long arm of the Bolshevik state: TB-3 heavy bombers over the Far Eastern Military District.
(MoD Archives, Bulgaria)

Regardless of this, there could hardly have been a less opportune time for the Soviet leadership to embark upon larger-scale open conflict with the Empire of the Rising Sun. The moral loss of Spain, the defeats of Soviet defence ally Czechoslovakia, and the rapidly worsening European crisis called as never before for Red Army forces to concentrate in the country's western regions. In early 1939 the Soviet armed forces lacked their erstwhile authority as the ultimate symbol of the Bolshevik state. They were weakened by Stalin's continuing repressions, and this was no secret in the West. Perhaps this was among the reasons for the unsuccessful progress of Soviet defence negotiations with military missions from the United Kingdom and France for a common front against Nazi Germany.

Imperial Japan also faced difficult issues at this time. It was bartering conditions for cooperating with Germany and Britain. The war in China was not progressing as well as expected, and losses among the most combat-ready Japanese Army and Navy units were becoming ever more significant. Of the Army and Navy aviation component alone, combat involved more than 900 aircraft[7] and the best crews, many of whom met their deaths fighting Soviet 'volunteers'. With such limitations, despite the country's very aggressive foreign policy, the commencement of a parallel armed conflict, which would divert significant military and economic resources from the major theatres of war in China, was against Japanese interests.

Despite their difficulties, both the Soviet Union and Japan had to demonstrate their combat-readiness to future potential allies, despite the fact that the major players in the world political arena showed serious doubts as to whether either of them could be regarded as a reliable partner in future coalitions whose configurations were as yet unclear. In this regard, the maturing conflict (formally a quadripartite one between Mongolia and the USSR on the one side, and Manchu-Kuo and Japan on the other) offered not only an opportunity to resolve an otherwise petty territorial squabble, but also a significant raising of military and political prestige on the international stage.

The difference in the names the two sides gave the conflict was purely geographical and reflected the main force concentration areas. Nomon-Han-Burd-Obo was a village of some 80 yurts (circular collapsible skin-covered tents) and tents east of the Khalkhin-Gol River and the main base of raids into Mongolia.[8] These raids grew more frequent, especially since Japan occupied three provinces in north-eastern China and large parts of Inner Mongolia in the early 1930s. The border dispute was a formal conflict engendered by the use of different maps by two satellite nations: Soviet protégé Mongolia on the one side, and the Manchu-Kuo entity created in the territory of Manchuria by Japan on the other. Until the end of 1939 the 740km (440-mile) Mongolian-Chinese border in the area was marked by a mere thirty-five signs, none of which were in the proximity of the Khalkhin-Gol River. The Japanese General Staff's 1934-issue maps showed the border as lying on the river's eastern bank, whereas 1920s-vintage Chinese maps, as well as those used by the Kwantung Army Command, put it rather further east. Mongolian political and military leaders adhered to the latter demarcation.

In reality this was wild, sparsely inhabited country of little interest to ether side. The disputed zone was a semi-desert, save for a waterlogged portion irrigated by an intermittent river that sprang from the Buir-Nur Lake and was home to clouds of mosquitoes. The differences in demarcation had nevertheless led to two serious border clashes on 24 and 31 January 1935, when Japanese units had attacked Mongolian border posts. First blood was drawn. This led to formal negotiations in Manchuria between representatives of Mongolia and Manchu-Kuo with a view to renewing the border demarcations. From the outset, their positions were entirely at odds with one another. The dispute failed to be resolved by diplomatic means due to the unwillingness of either side to make compromises, and negotiations ended in November of that year.[9]

These events coincided with the return to Mongolia after study in a Soviet military academy of former Mongolian People's Revolutionary Army Commander-in-Chief Horolgiyn Choybalsan. He installed an authoritarian regime, killing more than 1,000 Communist party and state leaders, and turning his country into a de facto Soviet republic.

The renewed sporadic shootings along the disputed border served as a pretext for the 12 March 1936 signing of a Mongolian-Soviet Mutual Assistance Protocol.[10] This bound the two nations to afford all aid, including military, to each other in the event of aggression against one of them. Mongolia had been dependent on the Soviet Union economically and politically from as long ago as the 1921 revolution, and the Protocol was a next step in furthering this status. The Japanese ambassador to Moscow was duly advised of the signing of the document. The new Soviet ally then built camps for the confinement of Stalin's victims, and Beria's security apparatus took measures to purge the Mongolian leadership. At the close of 1937 Mongolia's Prime Minister, Pelzhidiyn Genden, was arrested and shot as an enemy of the people. The same year saw the suspicious death of the Mongolian defence minister, and the arrests of his deputy, the head of the army staff, and a number of senior military figures, including Air Force Commander (CO) Shagrin Surun and his Chief of Staff Munko. They were declared counter-revolutionary plotters and shared the fate of their Soviet colleagues.[11]

Under the Protocol's clauses, a limited contingent of Soviet forces moved into Mongolia from September 1937. This was later to be designated the 57th KON (*Korpus Osobogo Naznacheniya*, or Special Assignment Corps). The Corps' Staff was established in Ulan Bator, *Komdiv* (Divisional CO) Nikolay Vladimirovich Feklenko being appointed as its head. This highly mobile unit comprised the 36th MSD (*Motostrekovaya Diviziya*, or Mechanised Infantry Division), the 11th TBR (*Tankovaya Brigada*, Tank Brigade), and the 7th, 8th and 9th MBBR (*Motobronevaya Brigada*, Motor-Armoured Brigade) – almost 27,500 personnel, some 5,000 vehicles of various types, 284 tanks, 370 armoured vehicles and 200 guns with calibres of more than 45mm. The arrival of this none-too-numerous force, however, did not represent a barrier to Japanese ambitions in the region, since it was some 400-700km (240-400 miles) from the Mongolian-Manchurian border, concentrated mainly around Ulan Bator.[12]

Nevertheless, the changed military and strategic situation did encourage Mongolian border units to attempt to establish a lasting presence east of the Khalkhin-Gol River and conduct regular patrols in the area. For their part, the Japanese changed their passive stance and decided to move west and hold the disputed territory.

In 1950, *Marshall* Georgiy Konstantinovich Zhukov – a major figure in the conflict and the architect of its final outcome – expressed the opinion that the Japanese aim had been to conduct large-scale combat reconnaissance. The moment was exceptionally propitious for gaining an understanding of whether the Manchurian-based Japanese Army was capable of overcoming the resistance of its principal and most powerful regional adversary. Apart from this, the Japanese Headquarters' Action Plan No 8[13] of 1938-39 foresaw

The Khalkhin-Gol River from the air.
(MoD Archives, Bulgaria)

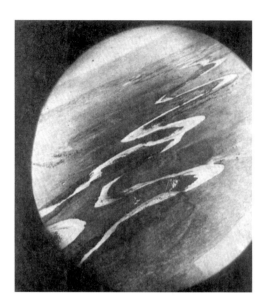

offensive action directed at the Baykal hinterland and the Usuti and Amur regions. The Nomon-Han-Burd-Obo area was also earmarked to accommodate the Halun-Arshaan-Gandjur-Miao railway, which would supply units acting against Mongolia and the Soviet Baykal hinterland.

The Japanese had more to gain from an escalation of the conflict in the disputed region from the level of occasional shooting. Their aim was to fix the border permanently at the Khalkhin-Gol River, thus offering more reliable protection for the strategic railway. At the same time, it must be noted that the Japanese military and political leadership did not foresee further moves to occupy Mongolia and parts of the Baykal hinterland.

In fact, the Tokyo Imperial Army General Staff was principally opposed to any diversion of forces away from the major front against China to the south. Thus it is reasonable to view the advance to the river as a regional action instigated by the Kwantung Army Command as a local operation, from which the Imperial capital consciously detached itself. Even assuming success, the realistic short-term objectives were merely to force the Soviet side to redraw the Mongolian-Manchurian border.

The operational region was significantly more favourable to the Japanese Command. It was supplied from the Manchurian side by two railway arteries, one 125km (75 miles) away and the other a mere 60km (35 miles) distant, at Khandagay. The Japanese Command took every opportunity to study and reconnoitre the area. This involved aerial reconnaissance, which covered not only the border area but also the Mongolian interior. The commands of the units assigned to the action conducted a series of command and staff exercises involving incursions into the locality using excellent specially prepared maps. These exercises in turn grew to involve army units, thus acclimatising them to the future combat theatre.[14]

The closest railhead to the Soviet and Mongolian forces lay at Borzya, some 750km (450 miles) away. Stretched lines of communication and the practical absence of prepared roads would greatly hinder force concentration, logistic support and reinforcement in the event of serious military conflict. In early 1939 a Mongolian border corps did patrol the Khalkhin-Gol River, but in practice its command did not have permanent monitoring posts beyond the eastern bank, relying instead on sporadic cavalry recces. The Command of the 57th KON made no effort to study the area and reconnoitre the border region. A Staff group surveyed the wild area in early 1939, but this marked the beginning and end of Corps efforts to acquire the necessary information and plan any action in the event of an enemy attack.

2

Potential of the region's air components

At that time, of the 766 Soviet aircraft in the Far East, the 100th SABR (*Smeshannaya Aviabrigada*, or Mixed Air Brigade) was located close to the theatre. This was a tactical unit for close air support and comprised the 150th SBAP (*Smeshennyi Bombardirovochnyy Aviapolk*, Mixed Bomber Air Regiment) led by *Mayor* (Major) Mikhail Burmistrov and equipped with twenty-nine SB-2 fast medium bombers in three *eskadrily*, and two *eskadrily* with seventeen recce and assault R-5Sh. Its base, code-named 'Leningrad', was near Bain-Tumen, some 300km (180 miles) from the disputed area.

The 70th IAP (*Istrebitelnyi Aviapolk*, or Fighter Air Regiment), initially with thirty-eight I-15bis, later re-equipped with more modern I-16s (the numbers at the start of hostilities were twenty-four I-16 Type 5/6 and fourteen I-15bis), was commanded by Major Vyacheslav Zabaluyev. The regiment had obsolete equipment, lacking Polikarpov's later armour, and with little life left in it. Only thirteen I-16s and nine I-15bis were airworthy. The rest were stored to rot away in the open in the expectation of possible overhauls. They were based at the five-runway airfield near Tamsag-Bulak (code-named 'Kiev'). Brigade CO was *Podpolkovnik* (Lt Colonel) Viktor Yefimovich Nyestyertsyev.[15] To this establishment may be added the three Mongolian squadrons with thirty-six R-5s and R-5Sh biplanes for recce and ground-attack duties.

To gain an idea of the degree of completeness of these units, we must refer to the Soviet military theory of the late 1930s. The *Aviapolk* was a basic tactical unit. A *Bombardirovachnyi Aviapolk* had to comprise five twelve-aircraft BAE

Soviet fighter pilots from the 70th IAP conducting a debriefing in July 1939. *(MoD Archives, Bulgaria)*

(*Bombardirovochnaya Aviaeskadrilya*, or Bomber Squadrons) plus two machines in a staff flight (sixty-two bombers in total)[16], and an *Istrebitelnyi Aviapolk* had to comprise four fifteen-aircraft IAEs (*Istrebitelnaya Aviaeskadrilya*, Fighter Squadrons) plus three machines in a staff flight.[17] From this, it followed that the practical degree of completeness of the 150th SBAP was 74 per cent. The technical situation at the 70th IAP was significantly more critical, the regiment having just 60 per cent of its combat aircraft establishment, while technical combat-readiness was running at below 35 per cent of establishment levels.

In the event, the fighter regiment crews were still getting used to their mounts, with pilots having flown between a mere 60 and 120 hours in them.[18] Many had yet to execute complex manoeuvres, target practice and dogfighting with their demanding new aircraft. This was particularly so with regard to the I-16 crews, the aircraft's unforgiving handling having led to high accident rates. Only 40 per cent of pilots were engaged in handling and combat exercises, with the rest absent on sickness or other leave. Conditions were primitive and requests for relocation back to the homeland were routine. The position with the just-delivered SB-2s was even less favourable. Despite the proximity of the China conflict, not one pilot in the RKKA (*Rabocheye-Krestyanskaya Krasnaya Armiya*, The Workers' and Peasants' Red Army) units had any combat experience. Apart from this, the location of the Khalkhin-Gol River rendered Soviet aerial reconnoitring exceptionally arduous. To the east of the river the terrain offered cover to the potential aggressor, and to the west the sandy plain, devoid of natural cover and points of reference, hampered aerial sighting and navigation.[19]

After a reorganisation of Japanese army aviation in July and August 1938, the *sentai* emerged as the basic combat unit. This was equivalent to an aviation grouping or regiment (depending on the system being compared) and comprised three *chutais*, or squadrons. The latter comprised three *shutais* (wings) of three aircraft each. Together with the staff wing (the *sentai hombu*) and back-up aircraft, which could be up to 30 per cent of the regular establishment number, the number of aircraft could be some forty-five per fighter *sentai* and some thirty per recce and bomber *sentai*. Two or more *sentai* under a joint command comprised a *Hikodan*, a formation with the rank of an air brigade; two or more *Hikodans* plus additional *chutais* comprised a *Hiko Syudan*, or air brigade.

Japanese aviation closely linked with the theatre of war in the area was spread around airfields in Manchuria and Korea. It comprised 274 aircraft (105 Ki-27 fighters, thirty Ki-10 fighters, twelve Ki-21 'heavy' bombers, eighteen Fiat BR-20 'heavy' bombers, sixteen Ki-15 recce machines, fifty recce/strike Ki-30s, twenty-eight Ki-32 light bombers, six Ki-36 and nine Ki-4 reconnaissance aircraft) within the 2nd *Hiko Syudan* (Air Division) operational unit commanded by Lt Gen Tetsuji Giga. This in turn comprised five *Hikodans* (wings) with five fighter, two bomber, three light bomber and two reconnaissance *sentai* (Air Groups), or some thirty-five *chutais* (squadrons).[20] As with the Soviet units, those of the Japanese were not up to wartime strength, but maintained high levels of technical readiness. Japanese pilots in these units had considerable combat experience acquired in the ongoing China war, and the morale of conquerors of the Far East. Most of them had around 1,000 hours in the air and were completely at ease with their units' equipment.[21]

Everyday activity on a Japanese airbase in Manchuria. *(MoD Archives, Bulgaria)*

Running ahead somewhat, it is important to note that the coming combat would be entirely limited to dogfights and aerial battles, yet their scale was often unparalleled even during the Second World War. Such an operational concept of the use of aerial power in the struggle for air superiority was not devoid of logic. It was linked with the purposeful attrition of aircraft – and much else. Each of the adversaries' air groupings could rely on well-developed industrial bases capable of making good technical losses within relatively short periods. Human losses were not so easy to replace, and combat squadrons could not rely on sufficiently rapid replacement of missing personnel. Two years' flying training was considered the norm at that period to enable combat pilots to feel confident in the cockpits of their machines, as mentioned above. Naturally, the overall formation of air potential also depended on the quality of the aircraft, the basic item in the military aviation system. Hence it is essential to assess the main combat aircraft types that took part in this local conflict, the fighters above all.

Biplanes were still widely used on both sides of the emerging front line. The oldest of them was the Japanese Kawasaki Ki-10 or Type 95 Fighter (the 95 stood for the 95th year of the Meiji era in deference to Japanese tradition), which had first flown in February 1935. In tests, it attained 400kmph, a record for a biplane at the time. It was seen as one of the most capable and highly manoeuvrable fighters of the period. Thanks to its high power-to-weight ratio, it remained manoeuvrable throughout its altitude envelope and enjoyed a reasonable rate of climb. The Type 95 also had a relatively low wing loading, helping its horizontal agility and endowing it with a high operational ceiling. The otherwise all-metal structure had cloth-covered wings, empennage and aft fuselage. Thanks to the smooth surfaces and clean aerodynamic shapes, aerodynamic drag was low, assisting the overall excellent flyability. The quality of workmanship, modest maintenance and operational needs of the type, the easy access it offered to all its assemblies and the engine, and its docility, made it a favourite among Japanese pilots and technicians in China. To the Chinese, armed with I-15bis and Curtis Hawk IIs, the new type came as an unpleasant surprise.

However, combat use showed up some defects: a poor forward stability, which particularly affected aiming and shooting, the need for relatively long field lengths, which called for airfield expansion, and the relatively poor armament of twin 7.7mm Vickers machine guns. The latter's delivery of 0.32kg per second and 90kW muzzle power was less than sufficient for success against modern all-metal bombers. (Incidentally, this applied to all Japanese fighters until the renowned Zero.) A certain improvement was achieved through increasing the areas of the upper wing and fin. The developed machine was significantly better suited to Japanese strategic doctrines, with an emphasis on manoeuvrability in air combat to attain air superiority. Some 280 Ki-10-IIs were rapidly built, and went on to give Japanese military aviation its Chinese successes in 1938. On

A Ki-10 taxiing after a scramble. *(MoD Archives, Bulgaria)*

encountering the new I-15bis on 25 March, the 2nd Fighter *hiko-daitai* (a temporary operational unit or two to three *Chutais*) downed twelve of the Soviet-built machines at the expense of two fighters damaged and a wounded pilot.[22] Prior to the start of the Nomonhan Incident, thirty Ki-10-IIs armed the 33rd *Sentai* within the area covered by the 8th *Hikodan*.

China was also the testing ground for the Soviet fighters. The first I-15s delivered badly failed to live up to expectations due to their poor directional stability, low top speed, over-sensitive controls and insufficiently sturdy structure. The aircraft had been produced in 1935 and its ills were being remedied relatively slowly, and entailed a root-and-branch rethink. The gull wing at the top was made straight, improving forward view and fine aiming, but increasing profile drag. Armament was boosted to include four synchronised 7.62mm PV-1 machine guns, doubling the delivery per second. The structure was beefed up and the engine cover changed to allow installation of the 20 per cent more powerful M-25V[23] engine.

However, the modifications, which cost 300kg in weight, cut manoeuvrability and rate of climb. The fighter could now outshoot its Japanese adversary, but in other ways (excluding rate of climb below 10,000 feet) it was inferior. As the I-15bis (I-152) entered large-scale production in early 1938, it was already hopelessly obsolete by the standards of modern air combat.[24]

The major Soviet biplane fighter: an I-15bis (I-152) before a test flight. *(MoD Archives, Bulgaria)*

The I-15bis chief designer, Nikolay Nikolaevich Polikarpov, was known as the 'King of Fighters' because of his long association with this class of aircraft. He was at the peak of his career and quickly became aware of his biplane's problems. As early as 1937 his design office prepared an outline project for a highly manoeuvrable fighter designated the I-153. Using the same engine, the upper wing reverted to a gull design to cut profile aerodynamic drag, while the main landing gear was retractable. In addition, the structure was strengthened, and the machine guns were replaced by faster-firing ShKAS units (1,800 shots per minute), improving delivery per second by more than 150 per cent.

The first I-153 was test-flown in 1938, being approved by a state commission in November after demonstrating between 41 and 45kmph higher speeds than the I-152.[25] The first mass-produced machines appeared in early 1939, yet problems with the new M-62 engine and the variable-pitch twin-bladed prop delayed deliveries to units, which began only when the Khalkhin-Gol conflict was already under way.[26] Combat experience from Mongolia and China, where the major adversary was the Japanese Type 97, showed Soviet strategists the error of pouring money and effort into obsolescent biplanes. Major Stepan Danilov, a pilot from the I-153 'Chayka' *eskadrilya* that fought above the Khalkhin-Gol River, recalls his dogfights with Nakajima Ki-27s thus: 'We had problems with our Chaykas there. Certainly fewer than with the Bis [I-15bis], but still problems. We had no speed! In addition, no manoeuvre is helped when you have no speed. Spin as long as you like, and they will still attack you from above...'

The Nakajima Ki-27 monoplane was the most numerous Japanese aeroplane east of Nomon-Han-Burd-Obo. It was designed to an air force commission and

An I-153 'Chayka' ('Gull'). One of the few biplane designs with a retractable undercarriage, the 'Chayka' did not fulfil Soviet hopes of a qualitative leap in technology. *(MoD Archives, Bulgaria)*

first flew in October 1936. Production of the 'Type 97' began the following year, with 3,386 built by the start of the 1940s, a Japanese record until the Second World War. The aircraft was rather similar to its carrier-based Type 96 cousin, designed a year earlier, but had a developed structure, more powerful 650/710hp engine and an enclosed cockpit. Japanese designers demonstrated a fine sense for disposable weight versus power in the Type 97. Its wing was larger than the Type 96, yet the overall weight was increased by only 120kg, giving a relative wing loading of just 85kg per square metre – a biplane figure. This gave the machine the manoeuvrability of a biplane, yet its superior aerodynamics gave it significantly higher speed.[27]

Major Stepan Danilov, 56th IAP CO. *(MoD Archives, Bulgaria)*

Pre-flight checks on a Ki-27 fighter.
(MoD Archives, Bulgaria)

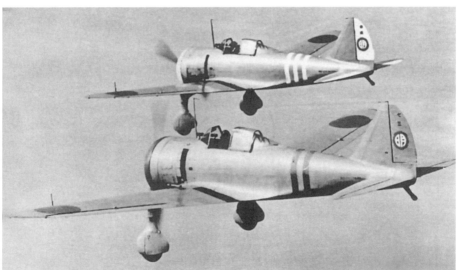

A training group flight of Ki-27's. *(MoD Archives, Bulgaria)*

A principal characteristic of the Type 97 was the engine reductor. Although this lowered the top speed to an extent, it allowed a larger propeller to be fitted, increasing low-speed thrust and hence giving faster acceleration and climb. This, combined with easy handling even for inexperienced pilots, made the Ki-27 an exceptionally dangerous adversary, combining biplane manoeuvrability with monoplane speed.[28] Japanese pilots rapidly took to the machine, not least because of its phenomenal take-off and landing ability. Where a Type 97 landed at 90kmph, rolled to a stop in 120 metres and needed only a 256-metre field for take-off, the I-15bis and I-16 tip 5 (Type 5) needed 105 and 116kmph, 90 and 257 metres, and 270 and 380 metres respectively.[29]

The new fighter's combat debut was on when three aircraft, accompanied by twelve Ki-10s, were on patrol. The group intercepted thirty Chinese I-15bis and within half an hour had downed twenty-four Bis for the loss of one pilot and two aircraft.[30]

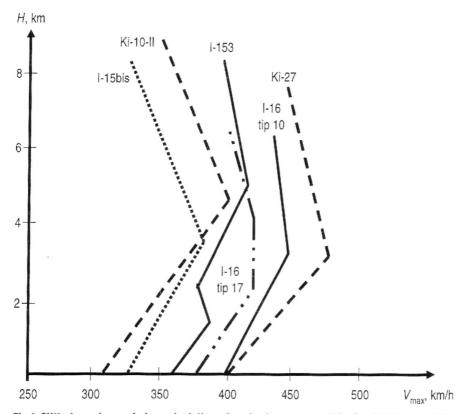

Fig.1 Altitude and speed characteristics of main Japanese and Soviet Fighters in 1939

The fighter's major shortcomings also emerged in combat. The desire to pare down weight had cut structure strength and survivability. The lack of any armour plating and the unprotected fuel tanks led to major and unnecessary losses in encounters with equal opponents, more and more of which were being produced in many countries. The engine lacked any damping, leading to constant vibration in flight. This, together with the structure's limitations, cut dives to no more than 500-700 metres, and was the type's greatest shortcoming. Japanese pilots taken prisoner testified that when diving away from pursuing fighters, vibrations increased to a degree where parts of the wing tore off, and the engine overcooled rapidly. Poor armament was another weakness, as in the Ki-10. The platform for the twin machine guns was more stable and offered grouped fire, but muzzle power harked back to older times. Despite this, the Type 97 remained a serious adversary to the basic Soviet fighters of the time, the I-16 tip 5 and the new I-16 tip 10.[31]

The I-16 fighter was one of the most remarkable of 1930s aircraft. It was among the first retractable-undercarriage high-speed fighters to go into service and had an advanced design for its time. Initially flown in 1934, in early 1936 it was re-engined with the M-25A and was widely produced. The mixed structure had good strength for its time. The enclosed cockpit, armour-plated seat (for series subsequent to the tip 10), the unmatched top speed, excellent dive acceleration and the superb twin ShKAS machine guns left the opposition disheartened at its combat debut over Madrid in late 1936. Soviet pilots could play 'like cats with mice' with German He-51s and Italian Fiat CR.32s. Thanks to these fighters, the Republican side retained air superiority until mid-1937.

Unit operations highlighted a number of weaknesses. The intentional placing of the centre of gravity aft in order to attain high manoeuvrability made the aeroplane a handful for pilots. The blunt-nosed and fat monoplane was unforgiving of errors and was hard to get used to, even by reasonably experienced pilots, which explains the high rate of attrition. In its early combat months in Spain, more than half of the losses of the 'Moscas' (the Spanish affectionately called the aeroplane 'the fly') were non-combat ones. Undercarriage retraction – requiring fifty-two turns of a lever and taking too long – gave trouble, as did high landing speeds (drooping ailerons proved to be ineffective and landing speeds remained high). The VVS RKKA insisted on this high-speed fighter and had to lengthen fields and subject them to careful levelling. Frequent crashes and the loss of even experienced pilots in freak accidents led to an order for twin-seat trainers (the so-called 'Sparkas', after the Russian for twinned or dual) with which flyers could be introduced to this 'strict master'. The average annual number of hours flown by Soviet fighter pilots at the time barely exceeded 70, extremely inadequate in view of the approach of war, and far below the real needs of contemporary aircraft.

The difficult struggle with the I-16's 'infantile disorders' (as the Soviets called early design defects) and the appearance in Spain and China of adversaries such as the Bf-109B and A5M or Type 96 led to a fevered reworking of the emblematic symbol of Soviet air power. The improvement in flyability was achieved by means of the new and more powerful M-62 engine, and firepower was to grow with two ShKAS units above the engine, in addition to the two original wing-mounted units. The I-16 tip 17 (I-16P) had two wing-mounted 20mm ShVAK cannon in place of the wing machine guns. They exacted a terrible price from bombers and scantily protected ground targets. Any comparisons with Japanese aircraft machine guns were misplaced. The four ShKAS spat out 7,200 bullets per minute, or 1.43kg per second, with a muzzle power of 480kW, while the cannon's figures were 2.56kg and 950kW respectively.[32] Yet the I-16 in all its incarnations remained an unsteady platform that rendered aiming difficult. This wasted a great deal of ammunition, especially in dogfighting, massively cutting the effectiveness of the otherwise powerful armament.

The extent to which these efforts were successful became apparent in the Spanish Civil War and later over the Khalkhin-Gol River. It was clear that the improvements were short-lasting and the VVS RKKA had to seek more radical solutions. In the latter conflict, however, and in the hands of experienced Soviet pilots who had fought over China and Manchuria, the small and manoeuvrable 'Ishaks' ('Donkeys') saw their last days as equal contenders and represented the essential symbol of Soviet air power.

Tactical and technical data for Soviet and Japanese fighter aircraft in 1939

Type (country)	Length (m)	Wing span (m)	Wing area (sq m)	Engine output (hp)	Gross weight (kg)	Max speed (kmph)	Ceiling (m)	Time to 5,000m (min)	Range (km)	Armament (mm)	Combat potential
I-15bis (USSR)	6.27	10.2	22.5	1 x 750	1,730	379	9,800	6.6	520	4 x 7.62	1
I-153 (USSR)	6,18	10.00	22.14	1 x 800	1,765	426	11,000	5.7	560	4 x 7.62	1.15
I-16 tip 10 (USSR)	6.07	9.0	14.5	1 x 750	1,716	448	8,470	6.7	525	4 x 8	1.25
I-16 tip 17 (USSR)	6.07	9.0	14.5	1 x 750	1,810	425	8,240	8.9	417	2 x 8, 2 x 20	1.15
Ki-10-II (Japan)	7.55	10.0	23.0	1 x 850	1,740	400	11,500	8.4	1,100	2 x 7.7	1.1
Ki-27 (Japan)	7.53	11.35	18.61	1 x 780	1,790	468	10,400	5.3	1,790	2 x 7.7	1.75

While there was relative parity between the two sides in fighters, things were not as even-handed as regards bombers and reconnaissance aircraft. The Red Army's basic medium bomber was the SB (an abbreviation of the Russian for High-Speed Bomber, *Skorostnoy Bombardirovshchik*), the prototype of which had flown on 30 December 1934. The results of its tests exceeded all expectations. Its maximum speed at 5,000 metres (an altitude the twin-engined machine reached in 9.4 minutes) was 404kmph, at the limits of the capabilities of even contemporary fighters. The Tupolev design bureau spent two years developing the aircraft before beginning tests of the first pre-production example, fitted with more powerful M-100 engines and some 20kmph faster still. With a 600kg bomb load, the strike aircraft had a 700km combat range. Some of the first production-batch machines underwent combat testing in Spain and China, initially flown by Soviet crews, with foreign pilots successfully converting to them. The appearance of the new high-speed bomber was a genuine surprise. Enemy fighters could not intercept it, and it needed no fighter cover. However, this was only at the beginning – later, Messerschmitts and naval Type 96s gave it a hard time. In fact, pilots had already endured hardships in its tight and uncomfortable cockpit with spartan equipment and unsatisfactory field of view. The gunner's workstation was the worst, affording him a severely limited ability to protect the rear hemisphere. The lack of armour and the unprotected fuel tanks rendered the bomber easy prey to fighters, and the small warload meant that more aircraft had to fly each given task.[33]

Checking an M-100 engine before start-up. *(MoD Archives, Bulgaria)*

Things were even worse as regards the Soviet light bombers. They were based on the R-5, a wooden biplane designed by Polikarpov as long ago as 1928. Though improved many times to the R-Z mark, in production since 1935, with its 316kmph maximum speed, by the second half of the 1930s it was an easy target, as proved in the Spanish Civil War when 'Natashas' (as the Spanish nicknamed them) could only hope to fulfil their tasks with solid fighter escort, suffering significant losses in all other cases.[34]

Similar aircraft equipped the Soviet reconnaissance forces, explaining their low effectiveness and the frequent recourse to I-16 fighters and SB bombers for tactical and operational aerial reconnaissance.

Naturally, if the description of VVS RKKA air potential in the theatre is to be complete, the heavy TB-3s that were later to be brought into the conflict must also be mentioned. They flew special missions and occasionally bombed enemy sites, but only at night, when the fighter threat was minimal.[35] A small number of reconnaissance R-10s also made their way to Mongolia. They arrived at Tamsag-Bulak airfield by rail and were assembled in short order by a team of factory workers, yet their presence again did not affect local Soviet air potential greatly.[36]

After the start of the Chinese war, the Imperial Headquarters paid especial attention to the arrival of new 'heavy' (as classified by the Japanese) bombers. The twin-engined Mitsubishi Ki-21, first flown in December 1936, was among the first proposals. The bomber was faster than the Soviet SB, carried a greater bomb load and had a greater operational range, yet was also poorly protected from fighter attacks and lacked armour. In the theatre, the 61st *Sentai* was armed with twelve combat-ready such bombers.[37] The slow production debut of the machine forced shortfalls to be made up by imports. The choice fell on the Italian Fiat BR.20, eighty-five of which were bought. They too had better combat potential than the SB, but just eighteen machines in the 12th *Sentai* were on hand in Manchuria.[38]

A formation flight of Ki-21s above the clouds. *(MoD Archives, Bulgaria)*

The qualitative superiority of Japanese aviation was most clearly evident in light bombers and reconnaissance aircraft. They largely comprised the all-metal Mitsubishi Ki-15, Ki-30 and Kawasaki Ki-32. Entering production in 1937 and 1938, these types had superior performance even to Soviet monoplane fighters, despite their fixed undercarriages. This meant they could only be intercepted by I-16s that had sortie in good time. The Japanese types' considerable operational range allowed their use at relatively distant field airstrips, which were unreachable by most Soviet tactical bombers. Their structures allowed diving at up to 60° to be employed as the major bomb-delivery method, this significantly improving precision. Their disadvantages were mostly to do with weak defensive armament (two 7.7mm machine guns apiece), small combat loads that called for greater numbers, and the lack of any armour or fuel tank protection.[39]

Ki-30s in formation: this light multi-role aircraft was the main Japanese close air support aircraft in the late 1930s. *(MoD Archives, Bulgaria)*

Tactical and technical data for Soviet and Japanese bomber and recce aircraft in 1939

Type (country)	Length (m)	Wing span (m)	Wing area (sq m)	Engine output (hp)	Gross weight (kg)	Max speed (kmph)	Ceiling (m)	Time to 5,000m (min)	Range (km)	Armament	Combat potential
SB-2 (USSR)	12.57	20.33	56.7	2 x 860	5,730	423	9,500	8.8	1,500	4 x 7.62 mm, 600kg bombs	2.3
SB-2bis (USSR)	12.57	20.33	56.7	2 x 960	7,880	450	9,300	8.4	1,600	4 x 7.62 mm, 1,500kg bombs	2.5
TB-3 (USSR)	24.4	39.5	230.0	4 x 730	17,150	198	3,800	14 (3000m)	1,380	8 x 7.62mm, 2,000kg bombs	1.92
R-5 (USSR)	10.56	15.30	50.20	1 x 680	2,805	244	6,100	23.7	800	2 x 7.62mm, 400kg bombs	1
BR.20 (Japan)	16.17	21.56	74	2 x 1,030	9,900	432	7,600	17.56	3,000	5 x 7.7mm, 1,600kg bombs	2.25
Ki-21 (Japan)	16.0	22.5	69.6	2 x 950	10,610	486	10,000	14	2,700	5 x 7.7mm, 1,000kg bombs	2.7
Ki-30 (Japan)	10.34	14.55	30.58	1 x 950	3,322	432	8,570	10.6	1,700	2 x 7.7mm, 450kg bombs	1.9
Ki-32 (Japan)	11.65	15.0	34.0	1 x 850	3,760	423	8,920	10.8	1,965	2 x 7.7mm, 450kg bombs	1.9
Ki-36 (Japan)	8.0	11.8	20.0	1 x 510	1,660	348	8,150	11.8	1,235	2 x 7.7mm, 150kg bombs	1.45
Ki-15 (Japan)	8.5	12.0	20.36	1 x 750	2,300	481	8,600	10.5	1,800	2 x 7.7mm, 250kg bombs	1.65

While discussing aircraft combat potential, a few words should be added on crew conditions: cockpit ergonomics, equipment, visibility and fitness for all-weather day and night operations. The Japanese again had the upper hand here. Their better navigational equipment enabled all-weather use, and their breathing equipment allowed them to attain superior altitudes, affording them initial tactical superiority. Radio was inevitably fitted to all Japanese strike aircraft. The leader aircraft of the Ki-10 and Ki-27 type fighters (flight CO equivalent and higher) were fitted with radiotelephones, with their charges having radio receivers. This improved communication as significantly as it improved the effectiveness of control by direct superiors. Soviet pilots in the confined open cockpits of their 'Chaykas' and 'Ishaks' could only communicate by visual signals at close visual range. Control from the ground was by means of arrows and other signs, which harked back to the First World War. This disadvantage became pivotal in the negative results from many a dogfight in Europe and Asia.

Any assessment of the initial air potential of the two sides in the Khalkhin-Gol conflict, in terms of crew preparedness and aircraft performance, must inevitably conclude that the Japanese enjoyed superiority. This could only be overturned at the expense of numerical superiority and the transfer of experienced pilots from elsewhere.

A group flight demonstration of five Soviet fighter aircraft. (*MoD Archives, Bulgaria*)

3

The conflict begins

By early 1939 exchanges of fire between Mongolian and Japanese/Manchurian patrols were almost routine. By late March they began to escalate into open warfare employing heavy military equipment. In one case a Mongolian R-5 strafed and dispersed a cavalry unit. On 31 March seven Japanese Army Ki-30 bombers supported an attack on the Adik-Dolon border post, having relocated several days earlier from the Manchurian interior to an airfield near Haylar. This did not help the invaders, however, for after regular Mongolian Army units became involved, the advancing column of seventy-two vehicles loaded with troops and armaments and accompanied by twelve light tanks withdrew in disarray. A dozen Japanese were taken prisoner of war. Later, all prisoners were exchanged with Manchu-Kuo authorities at the Kerulen River for twelve Mongolian troops taken prisoner by the Japanese at the Bulun-Dersu border post some time earlier.[40]

These incidents left eastern Mongolia tense. Military terminology refers to clashes in such open and almost unpopulated regions as 'combat reconnaissance', but it was accompanied by frantic planning for the coming combat on the part of the Japanese. With a view to this, as early as March the Japanese High Command sent three exceptionally well-prepared staff officers to the Kwantung Army Staff: Col MasaoTerada, Lt Col Takushiro Hitori and Major Takeharu Shimanuki from the Planning Department. The result of their work was reflected in Order No 1488 by Kwantung Army CO Gen Kenkichi Ueda in late April 1939, which defined the order of battle for Japanese armed units in the border area. Their commanders had the right to define the border in areas where it was indistinct, using as reference their units' locations (Paragraph 4). This encouraged even junior commanders to make incursions into disputed territory east of the mouth of the Khalkhin-Gol River. Alongside the escalation of border clashes. New railways were laid through Greater Hingan, running parallel with the Mongolian border between Salunia, Halun-Arshaan and Gandjur-Miao.[41]

On 10 May Japanese fire hit not only Mongolian border guards but also cattle farmers who had crossed the river's eastern bank. There were casualties. The following day, a Mongolian cavalry squadron crossed the river to chase away the aggressor, subsequently receiving reinforcements. The Burgud cavalry (Manchurians in Japanese service) threw its 300-troop strength into battle, supported by seven armoured vehicles and aircraft, managing to quell the Mongolian squadron's resistance and that of the Nomon-Han-Burd-Obo border guards, and reaching the eastern bank of the Khalkhin-Gol River.

The Kantogun used the escalation of the conflict as a welcome pretext to avenge the Hasan Lake defeat. Despite Tokyo's directives not to become involved, the Headquarters of the occupied Chinese province decided to react in force. Active measures began as early as 11 May 1939. This time, the *Kantogun* took into account the bitter lessons of the recent clash, and one of its first measures was to decree on 12 May that Lt Gen Tetsuji Giga set up a temporary tactical unit from the 2nd *Hiko Syudan*, which would support the land units in the conflict area. The new *Rinji-Hikotai* comprised the 10th *Sentai* (six Ki-30 bombers and six Ki-15-I recce aircraft) and the 24th *Sentai* (twenty Ki-27 fighters). On 13 May they relocated to field airstrips near Haylar (160km north-east of Nomonhan) and Gandjur-Miao (on the Nomonhan Plateau). 10th *Sentai* CO Col Noboru Tazoe was appointed senior commander of the unit. On the very next day, the 14th, Japanese aviation was launched into action. It was unopposed, with fifty-two bombs of various types being delivered to the Dungur-Obo border post. On 15 May light single-engined bombers attacked the Hamar-Daba border post[42], continuing in subsequent days to make incursions, undertake reconnaissance, and strafe border posts and units fighting the Japanese/Burgud cavalry.

Commanders from the 24th *Sentai*: (l-r) Lt C Kojiro Matsumura, Capt Saiji Kani and Lieutenant Hyoe Dainaga. *(MoD Archives, Bulgaria)*

The escalation of the conflict and the start of Soviet eastward relocation made the Japanese 23rd Infantry Division commander, Red Army specialist and former military attaché to Moscow Lt Gen Michitaro Komatsubara, decide to throw his division into battle east of the river. His subordinate, Col Yamagata Takemitsu, set up a detachment of a little over 2,000 troops, ten Type 94 tanks and light artillery. Close air support was also provided. The detachment's offensive was planned for 21 May. Forward Japanese units moved west and reached the Khalkhin-Gol River in three days. Their objectives were to take the ground between the border and the river (a front of 70km and a depth of 20km), transfer forces from the interior, and 'destroy Outer Mongolian forces in the Nomonhan area'. The People's Republic of Mongolia had insufficient forces to repel the attack, and Soviet forces began to relocate to the conflict area alongside Mongolian cavalry units. By the close of the month, a frontal clash was being played out, the ferocity of which grew with each passing day.[43]

The same period saw serious Soviet diplomatic efforts to defuse the growing crisis. On 19 May the People's Commissariat of Foreign Affairs in Moscow urgently summoned Japanese Ambassador Sigenori Togo, to whom Vyacheslav Molotov personally handed a Soviet declaration with the unambiguous warning that Soviet patience was at its end. The document package made its way to Tokyo the same evening, but the Japanese did not even bother to reply. Their reasons were certainly sound, since on 20 May Japan took the fateful decision to join the German-Italian Axis.[44] In the circumstances, Japan's soldiers needed to deliver a real success, though perhaps not on a very large scale, thus pressing still-wavering Japanese politicians and reassuring a none-too-enthusiastic Germany. The means to achieve this was the ultimate trump – force of arms.

Japanese aviation launched its planned Mongolian offensive the same day. The first aerial clashes also began. At about 18.10 on 20 May three 24th *Sentai* 1st *Chutai* Ki-27s led by unit CO Lt Col Kojiro Matsumura encountered a pair of I-16s that were covering a recce R-5 over the Khalkhin-Gol River. Japanese pilots 1st Lieutenant Syoichi Suzuki and Master Sergeant Kiyoshige Tatsumi attacked six times, downing the biplane[45]; its burning remains marked the start of the air war over Mongolia. Documents of the 100th SABR do not mention the case and mention no losses for the day.[46] The 2nd *Chutai*, led by Capt Shigenobu Marimoto, scored a victory the next day by downing another R-5 that had sortied on a liaison mission with the 6th Mongolian Cavalry Division. Pilot Suprun died, the first casualty of the growing aerial conflict.[47] 1st Lt Chiyoji Saito claimed the second victory of the Incident.[48] On the same afternoon Cap Saiji Kani's 1st *Chutai* scored a further three victories in a dogfight with I-15bis[49], this again being omitted from Soviet records.

Japanese fighter pilots from the 24th *Sentai* awaiting the take-off signal near a mobile starting machine in June 1939. *(MoD Archives, Bulgaria)*

On 22 May 1939 the strong afternoon sun was baking the Mongolian countryside and gusting winds had cleared all cloud. Three silver-doped I-16s and two standard-camouflaged I-15bis were patrolling at 5,000m.[50] The five machines were from the 70th IAP and the bright five-pointed stars on their wings contrasted well with the sharp, golden horizon. Such views are balm to the soul of any pilot, especially if he is young and at the controls of a manoeuvrable and fast machine. Today's patrol had a serious mission, but over the previous two months patrols over the Mongolian-Manchurian border had become routine. The five pilots therefore felt calm as they slid their blunt-nosed machines over the familiar monotonous landscape.

Soviet fighter pilots after a patrol flight over the conflict region. *(MoD Archives, Bulgaria)*

The sky failed to warn them of anything unusual or alarming. Yet five silvery dots had appeared to the east. They rapidly grew in size until their wings and spatted fixed wheels were clearly visible. The Soviet pilots had heard many a tale of such encounters from returning China volunteers, but this was for real. After a short period of indecision, pilot Lysenko attacked first. His Japanese adversary banked steeply and avoided his fire. The attacker became disorientated; his training had only taught him to fire at a cone in straight and level flight. Dogfight manoeuvres had also been practised, yet without anyone playing the adversary. He instinctively pulled back on the column and banked steeply to the left. His adversary had already slowed down and the 'Ishak' was now ahead of him. Using his excellent low-speed manoeuvrability and his better propeller thrust, M Sgt Tatsumi kept to the inside of the turn, carefully increasing power to close on his quarry. The roar of the two fighters was soon joined by the crackle of the twin synchronised Vickers machine guns. Tracer rounds sank into the stumpy monoplane's fuselage, sawing it in half from engine to tail. The coming tragedy was first heralded by a small flame between cockpit and engine. This grew fast, taking hold in the wooden aft end. The torched aircraft was now entering a steepening dive, from which it did not recover before hitting the ground and exploding.[51]

The hellish carousel of firing aircraft continued to hang in the sky. Soon a second machine left it, this time with red stars, leaving a thick silver trail as it made off to the east. It was probably Yutaka Kimura's fighter, hit twenty-one times, several bullets puncturing the fuel tanks, which started to leak.[52] Then everything went quiet, with only the burning remains of the fighter and the smashed body of its young pilot serving as reminders of the drama.

Both sides in the conflict began to appreciate the importance of aviation in attaining their forthcoming operational objectives, and a constant effort began to facilitate its contribution. The Trans-Baykal Military Region urgently sent the 22nd IAP commanded by Major Nikolay Glazikin. He was from the 23rd SABR commanded by *Palk* (*Palkovnic*, Colonel) Timofey Kutsevalov, which also included the 38th SBAP (*Skorostnoy Bombardirovacnoy Aviapolk*, or High-Speed Bomber Regiment) with its fifty-nine SB-2s commanded by *Kapitan* Vladimir Artamonov, which also relocated a short while later. By 26 May all four *eskadrily* with sixty-three airworthy fighters (thirty-five I-15bis and twenty-eight I-16 tip 10s) first ferried across to an airstrip near Bain-Tumen, then to Tamsag-Bulak, which was significantly closer to the epicentre of the emerging conflict.[53] The ferry flight claimed pilot Gusarov and his I-15bis, which disappeared without trace. Though equipment was significantly better, crew and command experience remained insufficient, especially as regards combat preparedness.[54] The fear of accidents and incidents had crippled training missions. A major reason for this was that the hitherto elite Soviet air forces had gone through the mill of Stalin's purges and were now commanded by young and inexperienced cadres.

On the other side, together with ever more frequent recce and strike missions by the 10th *Sentai* against the Soviet 57th KON, 11th *Sentai* CO Col Yujiro Noguchi was ordered to relocate the 1st and 3rd *Chutais*' twenty Ki-27 fighters from Harbin to the Nomonhan Plateau. The silver-doped monoplanes were successfully ferried across by late on 24 May. This did not affect air force ratios significantly, since the Japanese command could still call upon the entire resources of the Kwantung Army.[55]

By 25 May the Japanese began to concentrate the significant 23rd Infantry Division and Manchurian cavalry forces around Nomon-Han-Burd-Obo. They were part of a combined detachment commanded by 64th Regiment CO Col Yamaguta. By daybreak on 27 May the region hosted almost all components of this unit (lacking just two battalions), the 23rd Infantry Division Reconnaissance Detachment, the entire 8th Manchurian Cavalry Regiment, and parts of the 1st and 7th Cavalry Regiments.[56]

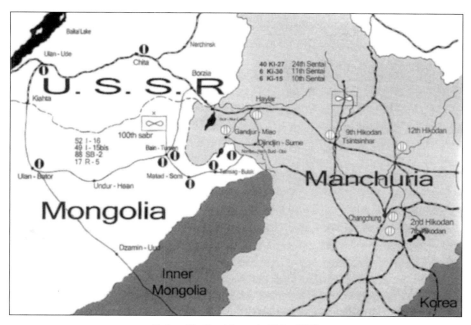

Order of battle at the end of May 1939

Amid these preparations for action on the ground, the situation in the air was becoming tenser, too. On 25 May alone, Soviet fighters flew some sixty combat sorties. Patrols from the 24th *Sentai* reported encounters with enemy fighters and recce aircraft. *Aviapolk* CO Major Vyacheslav Zabaluev personally led a mixed biplane and monoplane support group, yet the enemy still had the initiative and reaped all successes. The tally was three downed I-15bis and an I-16, and one damaged R-5.[57] The 11th *Sentai* pilots had time to overfly the theatre. The new Nakajima Ki-27, the aggression and skill of the Japanese pilots, and their ability to coordinate their actions using radio came as unpleasant surprises to the young and inexperienced Soviet commander and his subordinates.

The following two days made matters worse. On 27 May eight 1st IAE (22nd IAP) I-16 tip 10s departed from their Tamsag-Bulak base to Hamar-Daba (height 752m) near the Khalkhin-Gol River and lay in wait there. Should enemy aircraft appear, their job was to scramble into the air and destroy them. The leader was the acting 23rd SABR Palk Timofey Kutsevalov. Before departure he warned his subordinates not to cross the border even in hot pursuit of enemy aircraft.

The ferry was successful and did not involve unexpected encounters or incidents. For some time the group flew along the emerging front line, before turning west and landing by a dry lake bed some 30km from the forward enemy units. A fuel bowser and engine starter awaited them on site. The same day saw three group sorties in pursuit of enemy invaders, none leading to any result. As the technicians refuelled and flight-checked the aircraft for further sorties, a wing of three Japanese fighters appeared overhead, and flew undisturbed over Mongolian territory at 2,500m.[58]

The *Palkovnic* rapidly scrambled his pilots. None of them had any combat experience, and most saw the unfamiliar silvery silhouettes as curiosities rather than as enemies who had to be caught and engaged. However, they quickly took up their places in the confines of the 'Ishaks' and fastened their belts. The *eskadrilya* leader attempted to start his engine first, but his nine cylinders categorically refused to come to life. Thus his charges were forced to depart from the steppe leaderless, and without another of their comrades, whose engine had also refused to start. The six flew east without having formated for combat, merely following each other in the order of departure. They managed to climb to 2,000 metres by the time they encountered the adversary, two flights from the 1st *Chutai* with a total of six Nakajima Ki-27s led by Capt Kenji Shimada.[59] The Japanese attacked in a tight combat formation, diving from superior heights of about 1,000 metres, and moving faster. They had the tactical advantage, despite the Soviet numerical superiority. The latter in any case turned out to be short-lived, since the three fighters that had been spotted initially were soon joined by their comrades. Having clearly played the role of bait, they now attacked from the rear. Deputy *eskadrilya* CO St Lt (*Starshy Leytenant*, 2nd Lieutenant) Nikolay Cherenkov, who now led the grouping, tried to formate his red-starred machines in a defensive

There were smiles on the faces of many Japanese fighter pilots at the beginning of the Nomonhan conflict. *(MoD Archives, Bulgaria)*

circle. Their engines worked at their limits, yet their situation remained extremely poor. Even worse, two Soviet pilots were forced to leave the encounter with failing engines. They made use of the superior dive speed of the 'Ishak' and left westwards, landing in the steppe without reaching their airstrip. As their pilots left their cockpits to signal that all was well, they instead witnessed Cherenkov's demise. His aircraft was fatally hit by Warrant Officer Hiromiti Shinohara and left a black smoke trail on its way to impact and explosion.

Attempting to flee their Japanese 11th *Sentai* adversaries, the remaining 'Ishaks' dived nearly to the ground. A Type 97 got rather too close for effective aiming, but was nevertheless attacked by *Kap* Savchenko. The two ShKAS machine guns tore part of the fuselage and control surface covering and hit the fuel system, and the Japanese fighter began to trail smoke as it made off. Yet Savchenko did not have time to rejoice. His engine began to lose power. At the extremely low level, the pilot had no chance of any manoeuvring. As he landed, his blunt-nosed machine flipped over, killing him instantly.

Not far away, another Soviet pilot was attempting to flee the Nakajima Ki-27s that had attacked from behind. His aeroplane was a mess of bullet holes and only its forgiving structure and the 9 millimetres of armour behind the pilot's seat allowed wounded Lt Aleksandr Pyankov to belly-land. As he did so, the last of his diving attackers strafed him. Though covered by armour, a 7.7mm bullet glanced across his face. He managed to keep his cool despite the second wounding, jumping clear after the last adversary had flown past, and using the

A group of Nakajima Ki-27s in a waiting zone over the Khalkhin-Gol River. *(MoD Archives, Bulgaria)*

moment to run from his burning machine. He then faced three exhausting days in the steppe before coming across an armoured column, which rescued him.[60]

Thus the 1st IAE was almost completely wiped out. Only a shot-up I-16 (with twelve bullet holes) returned from the hapless encounter. Two pilots died, one was wounded, and the unit was left with no airworthy aircraft within a day. Gaps in tactical dogfighting skills and the lack of coordination and knowledgeable leadership were fatal in the struggle against a clearly able adversary who had grown used to the taste of gunpowder. Adding the technical failures caused by poor fuel quality makes the picture even sadder. That day the 57th KON CO had an unpleasant telephone conversation on the hotline to *Narkom* (*Narodnay Komisar Abaronay*, People's Commissar of Defence) Kliment Voroshilov concerning Soviet air losses.[61]

Amid the drama, the situation wasn't analysed calmly and explained to other *eskadrily*. This may well have been the reason for the defeat of Soviet fighter forces the next day, 28 May. On that day Japanese forces launched a surprise offensive in line with Lt Gen Kamatsubara's plan. Fierce battles erupted on the ground. Overcoming the resistance of the Mongolian 15th Cavalry Regiment and a company of Soviet infantry, Japanese strike forces surrounded the left flank of the Soviet-Mongolian grouping to the east of the Khalkhin-Gol River, threatening its sole foothold ahead of the natural barrier of the river. The poorly led Red Army units withdrew in disarray, taking up a defensive position some 2-3km from the river bank.

Japanese strike and reconnaissance aircraft covered by fighters supported the infantry and cavalry offensive. At daybreak forty aircraft appeared above the course of the Khalkhin-Gol River and struck Soviet and Mongolian forces there. This led to an order for the 70th IAP to bring two *eskadrily* of twenty aircraft into readiness at Tamsag-Bulak. They were scrambled, but the scramble was rescinded after a single *aviozveno* (flight) of I-15bis had sortied. The three biplanes went off towards the distant crackle, never to return after encountering nine Ki-27s.[62] Another three Soviet pilots' lives had been claimed by the 11th *Sentai*.[63]

A similar standby order was received at the same airfield by the 22nd IAP. *Aviopolk* CO Major Nikolay Glazikin led ten I-16 tip 10s and as many I-15bis in parade-like formations, but failed to find the adversary. On their return, as technicians began readying the aircraft for a further sortie, they were scrambled again. The monoplanes were always first to be made ready, so the commander could only scramble them. The ten I-15bis of the 4th IAE led by Deputy *Aviopolk* CO Major Pavel Myagkov were 25 minutes late in the air. Thus, tactical coordination was damaged at the very outset of the coming encounter. Errors in ground directions and the lack of radios meant that they lost the opportunity of finding the Japanese, and their limited fuel forced them to return after a short patrol.[64]

Left without the cover of the fast monoplanes, the ten I-15bis were surprised from above by eighteen Ki-27s led by 11th *Sentai* CO Col Yujiro Noguchi. The Japanese had not only numerical superiority, but also tactical advantages in speed and height. Meeting the Soviets head-on, they first set the leader, Major Myagkov, alight. He dived for the ground and managed to put out the flames, but as he levelled off his pursuer caught up with him and shot him dead.

Eskadrilya CO *Kap* Balashov was also shot. His head wound caused him to lose consciousness for an instant, but seconds before impact he came to and summoned the strength to bring his stricken machine to the airfield. Left leaderless, the Soviet fighters scattered in an attempt to flee their Japanese pursuers. The Type 97 was almost 100kmph faster than the I-15bis; now it proved itself its equal in manoeuvrability, too. The encounter was turning into a rout for the Soviets. Four of their pilots died, one was missing in action, two were wounded, one was forced to bale out from his burning aeroplane, rejoining the unit after four days, and a sole survivor managed to bring his shot-up machine to the airfield. The Japanese returned with the loss of a single Ki 27, when Lt Sadayoshi Mitsutomi baled out and landed in hostile territory. 2nd Lt Tomoari Hasegawa flew him out – the very first occasion when such a rescue was undertaken during the Incident.[65]

The aircraft of the Empire of the Rising Sun had uncontested control of the skies above the 80km of front line. In just two days they had downed fifteen Soviet fighters, killing eleven pilots for the loss of one of their own. (Other sources claim seventeen combat and four non-combat Soviet losses: five I-16s, twelve I-15bis, two R-5s and an SB lost when overflying the 38th SBAP).[66] Its strike component could not only hit military targets, but also deliver part of its bomb loads over the towns of Bain-Tumen and Undur-Haan.[67] Admitting as much, *Komdiv* Nikolay Feklenko reported to RKKA Chief of General Staff Boris Mikhaylovich Shaposhnikov: 'Enemy aircraft have air superiority… Our aircraft are unable to cover ground forces…' This would continue until 16 June.[68]

This could not fail to evoke a strong response in Moscow. At stake was the very authority of Soviet combat aviation. A second fiasco hard on the heels of the recent defeat of the Spanish Republican air force was unthinkable. VVS Command summoned twenty-two of the most experienced Soviet pilots and commanders, all veterans of the Spanish Civil War and the China air war. Selection was thorough indeed, bearing in mind that these two conflicts had produced no fewer than forty-nine airmen Heroes of the Soviet Union (thirty-five from Spain[69] and fourteen from China[70]). The group gathered outside the office of the VVS Head of Command, Second Degree *Komandarm* (Army Commander) Aleksandr Dmitrievich Loktionov. On ushering them in, he intimated that the order had in fact emanated 'from higher up'. Each of the aces was then further checked before meeting People's Commissar of Defence Kliment Yefremovich Voroshilov.

After briefing the special group on the situation along the Mongolian-Manchurian border, Voroshilov set down details of their schedule. On 29 May 1939 forty-eight pilots, navigators and engineers, among whom were eleven Heroes of the Soviet Union led by VVS RKKA Deputy Head *Komkor* (Corps CO) Yakov Vladimirovich Smushkevich, awaited People's Defence Commissar Kliment Voroshilov at Moscow's Frunze Central Airfield. After a short address, he asked the support staff whether enough parachutes had been provided for all passengers. The question was a little unexpected, but he received a satisfactory reply. Each of the uniformed men received his rescue equipment and, after shaking the *Narkom*'s hand and receiving an individual send-off with a wish to defeat Japanese militarism, the officers took their seats in three DC-3s. The very experienced crews were captained by Aleksandr Golovanov, Viktor Grachov and Mikhail Nyukhtikov. They had an exceptionally complex, responsible and strategically important task ahead of them.

The DC-3s were to fly from Moscow to Sverdlovsk, Omsk, Krasnoyarsk, Irkutsk and Chita,[71] over wild, featureless country and in extremely poor weather. At times the crews had to descend very low under the pouring rain and strong winds of the Asian cumulonimbus. Two days were to pass before the main wheels of the exhausted machines touched down on the dry grass of a Chita airfield, replete with factory-fresh aircraft. (Some sources claim that Smushkevich's aeroplane crash-landed, and that he suffered broken ribs and broke both his legs.)

Just three days were set aside for the group to inspect, test-fly and prepare their new mounts for the ferry to Bain-Tumen, 400km away. Intense work went on from dawn to dusk. On 4 June the main group landed successfully near the Mongolian community of several dozen yurts and shacks. Mongolian People's Republic *Marshall* Horolgiyn Choybalsan met them there.

A day later, due to rising tension along the eastern frontier, a Defence *Narkom* order brought into being the Chita Front Army Group commanded by Second Degree *Komandarm* Grigoriy Mikhailovich Shtern. This comprised the 1st and 2nd Detached Red Banner Armies, the Trans-Baykal Military Region forces, and the 57th KON (redesignated the 1st AG – *Armeyskaya Grupa*, or Army Group – on 19 June). From 1 June this Corps was to be led by *Komdiv* Georgiy Konstantinovich Zhukov, nominated by the RKKA Head of General Staff Operational Department. Zhukov took off for Mongolia on 2 June and his aeroplane landed at Tamsag-Bulak on 5 June.[72] The same day he arrived at the 57th KON Staff, requesting a briefing. Voroshilov's order of appointment was to arrive a day later.[73]

At the same time, the Far East aviation grouping was boosted by a Joint *Aviopolk* led by Spanish Civil War hero and fighter pilot Major Sergey Gritsavets. He arrived by rail, with each *eskadrily* leaving him along the route as it went to collect its aircraft.[74] After test-flying, they relocated to the conflict zone.

Soviet aviation experts pose prior to their departure for Mongolian service in June 1939.
(MoD Archives, Bulgaria)

An *eskadrilya* of fifteen gun-equipped I-16Ps led by *Palk* Timofey Kutsevalov also overflew the Mongolian border at Solovyovsk. Escorted by two I-16 tip 10s led by Hero of the Soviet Union Nikolay Gerasimov, the fighters landed at 'Leningrad', which was by now the major Soviet base in the new operational theatre.[75]

The Soviet regrouping and strengthening did not go unnoticed by Japanese intelligence. The days that it took place were calm, both sides using them to prepare for the coming storm. Air encounters were sporadic, being mainly between patrolling aircraft and recce missions monitoring force locations in depth. The Japanese were more active in the latter, having sufficient numbers of fast aircraft and experienced crews. Moreover, their air superiority assisted the effective discharge of such duties. The Japanese Command had all necessary information on Soviet equipment and troop numbers, and their locations. Covering their crews, the 24th *Sentai* and 11th *Sentai* pilots easily pre-empted any attempts by individual groups of Soviet fighters to intercept the fast Ki-15s and Ki-30s. Any short-lived dogfights followed the established trend whereby the Japanese imposed their tactics and won easily and quickly. Such encounters resulted in further defeats for 22nd IAP units, which lost another two I-16 monoplanes.[76]

The Japanese Manchuria Command reacted to these Soviet and Mongolian efforts to reinforce the air component of their Khalkhin-Gol forces. As early as 31 May, the 1st and 2nd *Chutais* from the 61st *Sentai* were ordered to relocate to a forward airfield close to the theatre of action. The aim was to place distant Soviet air bases used as equipment and field maintenance centres, such as that at Bain-Tumen, within the combat radius of the Ki-21 'heavy' bombers. The eighteen airworthy Ki-27s of the 2nd and 4th *Chutais* from the 11th *Sentai* relocated to improve air cover of distant Japanese infantry sites, and of major rear areas lying 20-25km from the conflict area. This imposed relocations of important control units. Together with a number of Air Controllers' posts, the Staff of the 2nd *Hiko Syudan* moved to Haylar.[77] Thus, a compact Japanese air component able to influence the already sizeable local conflict emerged for the first time since the start of hostilities. These were the units concerned:

> 7th *Hikodan* led by Maj Gen Hisao Hozoji:
> 1st *Sentai* with twenty-three Ki-27 fighters
> 12th *Sentai* with twelve 'heavy' Fiat BR.20 bombers
> 15th *Sentai* with six reconnaissance Ki-15-Is and eight reconnaissance Ki-36s
> 9th *Hikodan* led by Maj Gen Ikkaku Shimono:
> 61st *Sentai* with twelve 'heavy' Ki-21-I bombers
> 10th *Sentai* with six reconnaissance Ki-15-Is and six reconnaissance Ki-30s
> 12th *Hikodan* led by Maj Gen Eiji Higashi:
> 11th *Sentai* with thirty-six Ki-27 fighters
> 24th *Sentai* with nineteen Ki-27 fighters

The new formation's combat potential comprised 128 airworthy aircraft, of which seventy-eight were fighters, twenty-four 'heavy' bombers, and twenty-six recce aircraft and light bombers.[78] Its major bases were at Tsintsinhar, Haylar and Gandjur-Miao, being respectively 600km, 160km and 40km from the theatre. Ten further field airstrips were prepared to secure force operational and tactical manoeuvring.

Facing them west of the Khalkhin-Gol River at airfields built by Soviet engineer and logistics units near Tamsag-Bulak and airstrips near the river itself were the strengthened Soviet air regiments that had to cover the forthcoming action by 57th KON led by *Komdiv* Georgiy Zhukov. They comprised 318 combat-ready aircraft. The basis of the formation's air power were the 22nd, 70th and 56th IAPs. The first of these, led by Mayor Nikolay Glazykin, had twenty I-16 tip 5/tip 10s in two *eskadrily*, together with an *eskadrilya* of fifteen gun-equipped tip 17s (with twin 7.62mm ShKAS machine guns and twin wing-mounted 20mm ShVAK guns), and the 4th IAE with I-15bis led by Spanish ace *Kap* Yevgeniy Styepanov with ten confirmed victories. Chief adviser to the regiment was Major Grigoriy Kravchenko, a veteran of the China air war (six

Ki-21 bombers in action. *(MoD Archives, Bulgaria)*

victories). Major Vyacheslav Zabaluyev of the 70th IAP was to be assisted by Mayor Sergey Gritsavets[79], a famous Spanish ace with thirty victories. These were the major fighter regiments close to the river.

Major Stepan Danilov led the 56th IAP, which had to train personnel and equipment in preparation for action, and to increase force strength as necessary. Commander of the Soviet fighter forces (151 airworthy aircraft: fifty-six I-15bis and ninety-five I-16 of various types) was the VVS RKKA's most renowned ace, Mayor Ivan Lakeev[80] (twelve confirmed and twenty shared victories in the Spanish Civil War).

The operational unit's strike power mainly relied on the 116 SB-2s of the 150th SPAB and the 38th SPAB, which had relocated there in late May and early June. Of these machines, twenty-six had new M-103 engines, yet there was a shortage of combat-ready crews. The diversity of aircraft marks added to the difficulty of combat preparations. Individual Soviet and Mongolian recce and assault *eskadrily* using slow R-5 and R-5Sh biplanes were in fact unable to discharge their basic duties amid an enemy air superiority, despite their significant numbers (fifty-one aircraft, of which fifteen were Soviet[81]) and were set aside only for auxiliary duties.

The Soviet command's analysis of events pointed up the lack of combat experience and poor training of young Soviet pilots as determining factors in the negative results of the May encounters. The practiced attacks on cones were completely inadequate as methods of instilling necessary combat skills. Most

Two Soviet aces: Major Sergey
Gritsavets (in the cockpit) and
Major Grigoriy Kravchenko.
(MoD Archives, Bulgaria)

pilots had some 60 annual hours of experience in combat aircraft[82], much less
than their adversaries. The order of battle was ignored in air combat, with action
developing sporadically without any coordination. Soviet thinking was dominated
by the idea that dogfights and air battles were the major means of securing air
superiority, leading to fighter performance becoming the focus of attention. The
analysis of the experience in China and of the early the Khalkhin-Gol clashes
showed that the Soviets' basic fighters, the I-15bis and I-16, were not superior to
their most important adversary, the Ki-27. Moreover, the Japanese aeroplane was
simpler to fly and easier to convert to by less experienced pilots. Its excellent
stability at typical dogfighting speeds afforded its pilots better aiming with their
Vickers machine guns. The latter were concentrated in the aircraft's nose, above

Air force ratios in the Nomonhan area in mid-June 1939

Aircraft	USSR	Japan	Numerical ratio	Combat potential ratio
Fighters	151	78	1.93:1	1.25:1
Bombers	116	24	4.83:1	4.5:1
Reconnaissance	51	26	1.96:1	1.27:1
Overall	318	128	2.48:1/2.9:1	2.57:1

the engine, while the ShKAS machine guns were dispersed in the wings of the constantly yawing I-16 tip 5, detracting significantly from their power and speed. The analysis suggested that all hinged on the ability of individual pilots to deploy their weapons' combat potential. It also suggested that Japanese pilots were superb flyers, whose skill level exceeded that of 90 per cent of Soviet airmen (most of whose young pilots had no combat experience whatever). This was why combat planning for air superiority stressed the importance of coordination. This, in turn, was hampered by the lack of radios. In fact, the first two factory-made radio-equipped I-16 tip 17s arrived at Khalkhin-Gol, but the equipment turned out to be so heavy and of such poor performance that it was soon torn out as unnecessary ballast.[83] All that remained was to follow *eskadrilya* and *aviozveno* leader instructions implicitly as a way of attaining set objectives.

An I-15bis fighter during a low-level training flight. (*MoD Archives, Bulgaria*)

More 'ballast' was torn out of the Soviet fighters in the form of their oxygen equipment; this was actually more of a hazard due to the placing of the high-pressure bottles close to the cockpit, being apt to burst into shrapnel if hit. However, the weight saving led to altitude limitations when on patrol and to the loss of initial tactical advantage.

In terms of tactics, the Soviet aces directed their efforts towards matching fast monoplanes and manoeuvrable biplanes in ways that were effective and suited to the environment. Much attention was paid to improving young pilots' flying and combat skills. Meanwhile, several new airfields and airstrips were

An SB-2bis crew awaits the signal to start engines on a Siberian airbase. *(MoD Archives, Bulgaria) n*

prepared in the closest proximity to the front line, allowing the overflying enemy to be ambushed. Aerial reconnaissance and liaison were made more effective, and a network of VNOS (from the Russian initials for Aerial Monitoring, Warning & Liaison) spotting centres was set up.

Though ground combat was to start two days later, 17 June 1939 marked the beginning of the air action. Recce missions increased, with Soviet fighter and bomber crews being detailed to the task. Their basic objective was to reconnoitre forward airfields and the movement of enemy columns. The day witnessed the conflict's first use of 20mm wing guns. The Polikarpov fighters based directly behind the second line units not only flew recces over Manchuria, but also strafed the targets they identified. This was the first strike by gun-equipped fighters against Japanese aircraft at Gandjur-Miao airfield. Another first was the attempt by Soviet fighters to cross the border and enter 70km into enemy airspace in order to strike operational targets.[84] The use of fighters was dictated by the lack of suitably fast tactical and operational recce aircraft, able to act in a coordinated fashion and shake off Japanese fighter pursuit. Even the brand-new R-10s were ineffective. In the event the gun-equipped 'Ishaks' proved themselves very capable of achieving success against recce targets. Even Japanese tanks, which had no more than 25mm armour plating, were unable to withstand the muzzle power of the Soviet guns.

Yet the use of new Soviet technology did not bring the desired result at first. The stress from the first encounter with the enemy rendered the young and untried Soviet pilots timid and unable to cope with the influx of groups of Japanese aircraft. The continuing lack of adequate real-time control and command from the air and ground completed the negative picture.

On the other hand, Soviet bravery and daring were not in question, as noted more than once by their opponents. Especially after the arrival of experienced pilots, who injected confidence and courage into their fellows, the faith that victory in the air was attainable returned.

The biggest aerial clash since the beginning of the conflict was on 22 June. Data on force strengths and results is hard to pin down. Judging by confirmed information, after the dawn haze had cleared by 10.00am, Japanese reconnaissance aircraft began intensive flights. To deflect further combat missions involving overflying the Mongolian border, the 22nd IAP 4th IAE led by *Kap* Yevgeniy Stepanov and based near Buir-Nur was brought up to No 1 readiness.

The Japanese were first into the air, with eighteen 24th *Sentai* fighters led by Lt Col Matsumura making for the disputed territory. Their actions were diversionary at first, with the crews attempting to confuse enemy VNOS posts by the Buir-Nur Lake. Lt Gen Giga's idea was to cause an air battle after placing Soviet aviation in an invidious position, then destroy most of it in a single strike at its bases of Tamsag-Bulak, Bain-Tumen, Matad-Som, and Bain-Burdu-Nur. Without guessing the enemy's objective, St Lt Savkin's *eskadrilya* of twelve I-16s and *Kap* Stepanov's *eskadrilya* were scrambled at 15:00. The latter's I-15bis rapidly climbed to 4,000 metres and remained aloft in a patrol formation. The experienced leader had properly briefed his pilots to expect surprise attacks from above, 'from behind the sun' or the emerging cumulonimbus. His nine subordinates could not know that their experienced Japanese adversaries had already ambushed and dispersed Savkin's *eskadrilya*, wounding the leader. However, Stepanov's 'Stalin's Eagles' were to prove considerably tougher. They were ready to encounter Japanese fighters emerging from cloud. Initially, the dogfight was equal, yet numerical and technical advantage spoke, and three I-15bis, including the leader's machine, made forced landings. Diving Nakajimas continued in merciless pursuit of the landing aircraft and their fleeing pilots. The day was only saved by a squadron of 'Ishaks', which chased away the intruders.[85]

A second and more massed battle began soon after. It involved on the Japanese side aircraft sortied from Haylar, Djindjin-Sume, Depden-Sume, Gandjur-Miao, and from field airstrips near the northern shores of the Buir-Nur Lake, and near Asir-Sume and Shaten-Sume. The thirty-six Ki-27s from the 24th and 11th

Sentais formated once aloft. Soviet claims put the Japanese aircraft total in the two battles at 120 – an obvious impossibility in view of known Japanese locations and numbers. Most likely, their genuine number did not exceed sixty fighters.

'General Douglas', as *Komkor* Yakov Smushkevich had been known since Spanish days (when he had been aviation adviser to the Republicans), was determined to overturn the air superiority issue over eastern Mongolia, and decided that this was the right moment to demonstrate his formation's boosted air power. A total of forty biplane I-15bis and forty-four I-16 monoplanes managed to sortie. The air battle was exceptionally fierce – neither side wanted to cede the sky to the other.

The greatest contests took place over the Bain-Tsagan and Bain-Hoshu mountains, where twelve I-15s, twenty-five I-16s (at 4,000 metres) and nine I-16s (at 5,500 metres) were ambushed by 24th *Sentai* 1st *Chutai* fighters covered by the sun. The ambush succeeded, with the Soviet fighter group suffering a rout in the first 8 minutes. Japanese sources put the number of Soviet losses at nineteen aircraft, while Soviet sources cite ten lost I-15bis and three lost I-16s.

After that, however, the Soviets managed to impose their combat rules, not least taking advantage of the enemy's exhausted ammunition. A number of I-16s launched into pursuit of the unharmed Ki-27s. After downing an I-16 with his 7.7mm machine guns, 20-year-old M Sgt Katsuaki Kira put his mount's manoeuvrability to good use. Using brilliant flying skills at low level, he so disorientated two pursuing I-15bis that they crashed into the steppe amid a series of high-alpha and high-g manoeuvres.[86]

The encounter highlighted another Soviet design fault – insufficient fuel. This forced many a pilot to dive away from the battle and make for field airstrips with their last drops of precious petrol. After refuelling, many made it back into the air. Though this cost them the initiative, to some extent numerical superiority made up for it. Some Japanese pilots were also forced to refuel and take on extra ammunition. Supported by the 24th *Sentai* 2nd *Chutai*, their actions were much more organised and better timed.

For a long time the sky was filled with the sound of dozens of engines working at combat ratings, the dry crackle of machine guns, smoke trails, falling aircraft, and pilots baling out. The battle involved an attempt to force a Japanese pilot to land on a Soviet airfield beyond the front line. Two *aviozvena* (flights of a total of six machines) of select Soviet aces in new I-16 tip 10s intercepted M Sgt Shogo Saito of the 24th *Sentai* and directed him with machine gun fire to fly west. Left without ammunition, the Japanese appeared doomed. However, he chose a suitable moment to rev his engine to the limit, pull sharply on his control handle and chop off part of the fin of one of his interceptors. The Soviet formation fell apart in an instant, which was enough for the manoeuvrable Nakajima to escape and return to base.[87]

There was no shortage of confidence and the will to win on both sides in this first major air battle. However, all ended as if by signal some 2½ hours after it had begun. By 5.30pm the last fighters had touched down on their bases' grass strips. The petrol-fume-soaked air grew quiet and only the burning wreckage across the steppe was a reminder of the event. As usual in these circumstances, both sides counted victories and losses differently. The Soviets admitted losing thirteen I-15bis, one I-16 and eleven pilots.[88] Other sources speak of thirteen downed I-15bis and four I-16s of the total of fifty-six I-16s and forty-nine I-15bis.[89] Among the pilots lost was 22nd IAP CO Major Nikolay Glazykin, who baled out from his burning fighter, but was later found dead. The Soviets claimed thirty-one victories.[90]

Major indicators of the aerial confrontation of 22 June 1939

Indicator	USSR	Japan	Ratio
Aerial combat participants	105	54	2:1
Claimed victories	49	31	1.6:1
Admitted losses	14	7	2:1
Admitted losses as a percentage of participants	13.4%	13%	1:1
Percentage of claimed and admitted losses	28.5%	22.5%	1.27:1

The Japanese claimed forty-nine victories, admitting to seven of their own fighters being downed and four pilots dead.[91] Among the latter was 24th *Sentai* 2nd *Chutai* CO Capt Shigenobu Marimoto. One Japanese pilot who had baled out was taken prisoner and was regarded as lost for a long time. Despite the great discrepancy in figures, and the doubly large Soviet losses, it was clear to all concerned that the situation at the Khalkhin-Gol River had changed irrevocably. For the first time, Japanese crews had been forced to flee. The Japanese command was taken aback not only by the Soviet intransigence and will to win, but also by the massed arrival of great numbers of fighters in the confined airspace. It was clear that special measures were called for.

Proof of such special measures was the hurried transfer on 23 June of fifty-nine Nakajima Ki-27 fighters from the 1st *Sentai* and 11th *Sentai* at Harbin to Haylar and the forward airfield at Gandjur-Miao.[92] This was one occasion when the four wing and one fuselage tanks with their total of 332 litres permitted a considerably longer stay in the conflict area, making up for superior Soviet numbers and belligerence. Although calmer, the day did not go without a dogfight. A patrolling group of five I-16s was attacked by a pair of Nakajimas, with both sides losing one machine.

Japanese Ki-27 fighters of the 1st *Sentai* at a forward airfield. *(MoD Archives, Bulgaria)*

The Russians' activity forced Lt Gen Tetsuji Giga to intensify aerial reconnaissance over great areas at operational range into the Mongolian interior. One of his most experienced staff officers, Lt Col Yasuyuki Mayoshi, personally flew such a mission. Overflying Tamsag-Bulak, Matad-Som and Bain-Tumen, where the basic forward Soviet airfields were, he counted more than 200 combat aircraft. Immediately on his return he summarised his findings, wiring them to Kwantung Army CO Gen Kenkichi Ueda by 09.00. Clearly, the Soviet losses of 22 June had failed to affect the overall force ratio, which was to the Japanese disadvantage. The idea of a massed air strike on Soviet air forces began to gain favour in the Kwantung Army Staff. The same day saw Operational Order A-1 for an attack on the major Soviet airfields in the area. This marked the start of planning for the first massed Japanese air offensive in Mongolia. Until then, this had been taboo in Tokyo Headquarters, where it had been determined that the conflict must remain within limits. However, Japanese generals on the ground were tired of acting with one arm tied behind their backs. The liaison officer they sent to Tokyo was charged with reporting the air offensive either at short notice, or shortly after it had begun, thus leaving no time for the senior staff to cancel it.[93] Tension in the disputed area continued to grow.

The very day after relocating to a forward airfield, Japanese 11th *Sentai* pilots were scrambled in support of their 24th *Sentai* comrades who were fighting seventeen enemy fighters over the Chuchu-Urun-Obo Lake.[94] The Red Army pilots' intransigence was in evidence again, and their adversaries were finding it hard to flee from the engagement. The 'Ishaks' were significantly stronger and very quick in the dive. They could catch up with whoever they wanted, and the dense stream of 7.62mm bullets from their four ShKAS wrought certain death. Moreover, the eight Soviet fighters were led by none other than Major Ivan Lakeev, a proven Spanish hand as commander and airman. Approaching the battle area, his formation flew higher than the nine I-15bis of the 70th IAP, whose task was to engage in dogfights. They were all from the 4th IAE and were also led by a Spanish ace, *Kap* Yevgeniy Stepanov. The good combination of the manoeuvrable Bis and the fast I-16 tip 10, and the Soviet advantage in firepower, made life difficult for the Imperial pilots. Though enjoying a numerical advantage of twenty, the Japanese did not manage to capitalise on it and turned to flee when another eight I-16s arrived. Two lost aircraft with their pilots were recognised as losses for each side. Soviet archives mention seven downed Nakajima Ki-27s in the dogfight, and a total of nineteen downed enemy aircraft between Buir-Nur Lake and 'Leningrad' airbase, while the Japanese claim sixteen victories – absurd in view of the numbers involved. Two I-15bis pilots, Polevov and Grigorian, died in their cockpits; the latter was shot while trying to force-land. A Japanese pilot also died, while another was taken prisoner after baling out.[95] His fate was shared by M Sgt Shiko Miyajima, who had landed his burning Nakajima Ki-27 on enemy territory on 22 June. He had hardly managed to clear his cockpit when an overflying I-16 finished his aircraft with a series of precise hits. He then spent four exhausting days and nights without food and water in the wild Mongolian steppe, before being found by an enemy patrol and going on to experience ten no less arduous months as a prisoner of war.[96] That the first Japanese prisoners had been taken served as proof that there was change in the air above the Khalkhin-Gol River.

As related above, a second Soviet pilot (most likely Polevov) had crashed while diving in pursuit of an adversary. Similar events had occurred on 22 June, when the Japanese claimed three such cases (two I-15bis and an I-16). One was the aforementioned M Sgt Katsuaki Kira, who 'helped' his adversary hit the ground.[97] However, none of the Soviet commanders paid any attention to this or conducted any analysis into the reasons for the loss of men and machines in this sad fashion. Only when analyses were made of the action of 24 June did *Komkor* Yakov Smushkevich express concern for the levelling off in performance of his fighters. The heavier I-16 with its smaller wing area suffered considerable lag in responding to the pilot's input and could not emulate the manoeuvrable Ki-27. Gradually, such analyses became the daily routine at all VVS RKKA command levels near the Khalkhin-Gol River, and led to positive results. The mistakes and options open in all situations were subject to discussion. St Lt Viktor Rakhov's *aviozveno* assisted the process, having finally succeeded in forcing a

Japanese pilot to land on Mongolian territory. The landing was poorly executed and the aircraft had flipped onto its nose. Despite the damage, technicians soon had it repaired. While they worked on the machine, a great many pilots studied their adversary's strengths and weaknesses. After being repaired, the aeroplane was sent for testing in the USSR.[98]

Analyses apart, the air never sees a particular situation replayed in all its details. The Soviet command was the first to decide on air strikes as a way of attaining superiority. The new techniques of employing the air grouping's potential had resulted in parity, which had lasted for ten days. Naturally, this could not guarantee success for any land action, and gave rise to concern among commanders and *Komdiv* Georgiy Zhukov. This was why an idea put forward by the recently appointed 22nd IAP CO Major Grigoriy Kravchenko[99] was accepted and the contact zone was brought forward over enemy-held territory. If the Japanese pilots refused to accept the challenge, this would be followed by a strike on airfields near Gandjur-Miao. Three *eskadrily* from the 70th IAP formed the major strike groups, to be led by Major Zabaluyev and Major Gritsavets.[100] Two 22nd IAP *eskadrily* were detailed to act as reinforcements and cover.

The fighters sortied at 15.30 on 25 June. The battle order involved two echelons and comprised twenty-seven I-16s and thirteen I-15bis.[101] They were the first to clash with the seventeen Japanese interceptors from the 1st *Sentai*, led personally by CO Lt Col Toshio Kato.[102] The encounter was over Hamar-Daba Mount, but the Japanese refused the invitation and fled homeward at top speed. The Soviet pilots then abandoned the initial strike plan and launched a hot pursuit. This ended some 70km east of the Khalkhin-Gol River when they in turn encountered forty more Japanese fighters from the 1st, 11th and 24th *Sentais*. It transpired that the first Japanese group had played the role of bait; now they banked sharply and took up attack positions. A fierce battle ensued between Zabaluev's pilots and the three *sentais*. The Soviet strike plan lay in ruins, but this did not stop the pilots from demonstrating their determination. The melée of whirling machines gradually moved westward. Driven by superior enemy numbers, yet resisting in a completely organised fashion and showing great professionalism, 'Stalin's Eagles' refused to lose control of the situation, despite losing two I-16s, which fell on enemy territory, killing Lieutenants Krasnochub and Shmatko.[103] A critical moment was reached when Major Zabaluyev's 'Ishak' received more than its fair share of hits and made for the ground, trailing thin smoke. The pilot was forced to belly-land[104], and the Japanese sent a detachment of the Burgud cavalry to capture him. However, before it managed to reach the site of his landing, Major Sergey Gritsavets had alighted there and managed to rescue his commander despite all the risks and the confined cockpit of his aircraft.[105] Their departure was covered by the two young pilots Poloz and Balashev.[106] After flying for 20 minutes barely above the ground, the two landed intact at Tamsag-Bulak.[107]

Monitoring events from his Command Post on the Hamar-Daba Mount, Soviet ground controller *Palk* Aleksandr Gusev decided to scramble the 22nd IAO. The mixed group comprised twenty I-16s led by Major Ivan Lakeev and twenty-one I-15bis led by *Kap* Yevgeniy Stepanov.[108] They skilfully covered the retreat of the first group and secured its undisturbed base landing. However, Gaydobrus's fighter collided with a Japanese machine. The Soviet pilot tried to land, but damaged his machine beyond repair. Aleksandrov from the 70th IAP was luckier. He landed his damaged I-16 in Manchuria without being able to confirm his position. A Mongolian recce party found him and not only managed to rescue him, but also towed his aeroplane.[109]

The rapidly changing nature of the 1½-hour air battle is clear from the accounts written of its outcome. The Japanese concede no losses at all, yet the 1st *Sentai* alone claims twenty-eight victories.[110] Soviet claims include no fewer than ten downed and fifteen damaged Ki-27s.

This was the 150th SPAB's second day of action. The regiment had entered the conflict on 24 June when twenty-three bombers flying without cover had struck troops and war equipment from medium altitudes east of the Khalkhin-Gol River. After an *aviozveno* of three SB-2s had been intercepted by a single Nakajima Ki-27 piloted by Lt Syoichi Suzuki of the 24th *Sentai*[111] on 26 June, the denouement was rapid as a twin-engined bomber fell into the steppe. Soviet sources mention no such losses and actions. The same sources put overall 2nd *Hiko Syudan* losses between 22 and 25 June at sixty-four aircraft against losses of nineteen fighters and a single bomber.

Disturbed by the fact that the operational initiative was gradually falling into the hands of the VVS RKKA, and by its losses, the Kwantung Army Command frantically sought a way out of the emerging crisis. Over two days Japanese recce flights intensified significantly, accumulating much detail of enemy numbers and actions. The missions were flown by fast Ki-15-Is from the 10th and 15th *Sentais*.[112] Their main quarry was again Soviet airfields in Mongolia. The data they brought back was priceless and provided a complete picture of the RKKA's aircraft locations in the region. Not one Japanese recce crew was lost, due largely to the superb speed of their mounts.

The detailed information brought back allowed the Staff of the 2nd *Hiko Syudan* to complete the planning of its first air offensive, aiming to deliver a strike on enemy air strength in the region and affect its potential. Attaining the major objectives was intended to involve not just aircraft, but also reconnaissance and diversionary tactics on the ground. The routine recce on 24 June determined the number of Soviet aircraft as being 185 twin-engined bombers and single-engined aircraft. Of these, 135 were near Tamsag-Bulak, thirty-nine were south of the Buir-Nur Lake, and eleven liaison machines and duty fighters were dispersed elsewhere. Four TB-3s were reported at Tamsag-Bulak. The Soviet airfields at Matad-Som and Bain-Tumen were not reconnoitred due to worsening weather. Despite poor weather on the next day, a Japanese recce aeroplane overflew these regions at low level, discovering a further fifty aircraft east of Bain-Tumen, and another forty-four dispersed at smaller airstrips. A single TB-3 overflight was reported. The Japanese Air Command appraised the adversary as comprising a bomber brigade, four fighter squadrons and two recce squadrons.[113]

On 26 June, Japanese aerial reconnaissance did not live up to the expectations of Lt Gen Giga's Staff. Its data was contradictory and lacked the necessary detail. The leader of the 1st, 11th and 24th *Sentais*, Lt Col Matsumura, and 9th *Hikodan* CO Maj Gen Ikkaku Shimono were forced to formulate an order for a strike against 'a multitude of enemy aircraft in the vicinity of Tamsag-Bulak'. The leaders of the groups of Fiat BR.20 and Ki-21 Otsu bombers, Col Uichiro Harada and Col Kiso Mikami, did not manage to recognise any targets on the aerial photographs they were given. They were ultimately ordered to fly towards Tamsag-Bulak air base and bomb what they could find there.[114]

At 5.50am Tokyo time on 27 June, an enemy recce aircraft appeared over Bain-Burdu-Nur, base of the 70th IAP, which lay closest to the front line. A second recce machine was leaving a contrail well inside Mongolia. It was clear that strike groups would follow them. The Soviet command was expecting such a move, and the duty *aviozveno* of fighters was duly scrambled to intercept the intruders. Yet nobody could have foreseen that Japanese

Japanese Ki-15-I recce aircraft in Manchuria in the summer of 1939. *(MoD Archives, Bulgaria)*

diversionary groups would enter in depth and would cut the cables of communication lines between air units, the VVS Command Post, and the forward spotting points in the area of the forthcoming incursion.[115]

The Japanese strike group's bombers departed from their Haylar and Seinjo airfields before daybreak. The fighter pilots from Lt Col Matsumura's escort had barely begun their breakfast at their Gandjur-Miao airfield when they heard the heavy machines overhead. An immediate scramble was ordered. Despite this, the formation failed to form the desired thick battle order before crossing the front line.

By 06.00 Tokyo time, the Japanese strike formation was over Tamsag-Bulak. It comprised twenty-one 'heavy' bombers (nine Ki-21-1s from the 61st *Sentai*, and twelve Fiat BR.20s from the 12th *Sentai*), and nine light single-engined Ki-30 bombers from the 10th and 16th *Sentais*. They were covered by seventy-four Nakajima Ki-27s.[116] The group was led personally by Lt Gen Tetsuji Giga. Some Type 97 fighters and some bombers separated along the way and went to block the 22nd IAP's neighbouring Tamsag-Bulak base. Though duty fighters there were immediately scrambled under the leadership of St Lt Leonid Orlov, and though many other crews managed to depart, surprise was achieved. Some 150 aircraft participated in one of the most massive air clashes to date. The lack of organisation of the defenders' actions rendered them extremely ineffective. Nevertheless, Orlov did catch up with a recce Ki-30 Type 97, chasing and firing at it until it struck a hill 30km from the airfield.[117] While the Nakajima Ki-27s were over Buir-Nur Lake and their pilots watched the departing Soviet fighters, Col Mikami's bombers, which had arrived 10 minutes earlier, began dropping their 50kg high-explosive bombs over the emptying enemy airbase of Tamsag-Bulak from 3,000 metres. They were followed by Harada's Fiat twins at 3,700 metres. They circled while the smoke from the first strike dispersed, in order to be able to see some targets, but fierce ack-ack fire forced them to release their 600-700kg of bombs sooner than desirable. They were followed at 400 metres by Lt Col Torao Otsuka's light dive bombers; these dived at 50° to 60° until they reached 700 metres before dropping their bombs over the almost empty airfield.[118]

The first wave of the Japanese strike hastened the withdrawal of the Soviet fighters. Though the scramble signal had been given, it was late, and the explosions of falling bombs created a sense of panic. The departing aircraft were easy prey, with 1st and 11th *Sentai* pilots making use of this fact to intercept and shoot down some I-15bis and I-16s. Their actions, as well as those of other Japanese crews, were monitored and covered by Lt Col Matsumura's 24th *Sentai* fighter group. Initially they hovered at 5,500 metres and, once convinced that the enemy had been routed from the air, dived and strafed ground targets.

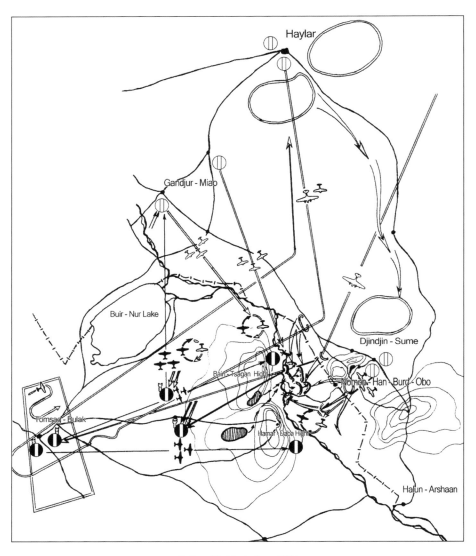

Order of battle in June 1939

Although thirty-four I-16s and thirteen I-15bis managed to enter the fight, the anti-aircraft artillery had the lion's share of the defensive action, setting light to 61st *Sentai* CO Col Mikami's bomber. The Colonel managed to belly-land close to the target airfield. Rescuing his commander, Lt Hideo Sawairi landed next to his machine and managed to lift its entire crew. Repeating the exploit of Sawairi, and having reported the downing of three I-16s and an I-15bis, M Sgt Bunji Yoshiyama landed in Soviet-controlled territory, rescued M Sgt Eisaku Suzuki, and successfully returned to base.[119] It is only fair to say that this became practically routine for Japanese pilots, with five being plucked from the Soviet forces.

Other Japanese aircraft were hit, particularly light single-engined Ki-30 bombers flying low and at very low altitude. Despite this, none was downed as a result of enemy action. The first strike against Bain-Burdu-Nur left just eighteen serviceable Soviet aircraft out of an establishment strength of sixty-three in the 70th IAP. The I-16s that had failed to get away were left burning on the ground. Ace Major Sergey Gritsavets was also forced to hide from the bombs under the broad engine of an 'Ishak'. An experienced soldier, he was well aware that any attempt to depart with the open steppe as a background meant courting almost certain death.[120] Indeed, many of the Soviet aircraft that did manage to get away from the strike were downed or had to force-land. Nine I-16s and five I-15bis were lost in dogfights. Six pilots died and five were wounded, while others made it to spare airfields. The unit lost a large amount of combat readiness.

The Japanese formation's other objective was the 22nd IAP base of Tamsag-Bulak. However, the surprise element was lost. After the successes of St Lt Orlov against enemy reconnoitring, *eskadrilya* CO *Kap* Viktor Kustov and his three I-16 wingmen caught up with the enemy reconnaissance aeroplane at 6,000 metres over Tamsag-Bulak and shot him down. Major Grigoriy Kravchenko had the regiment airborne before the arrival of the bombers and their fighter escort. The Soviets claimed two strike group aircraft attackers (a Ki-21 and a Ki-30), and three of the fighter escorts. Three I-15bis met their demise on the steppe. Pilots Grinenko and Paksyutov died, their colleague Gasenko baled out, and two others were wounded. *Aviopolk* CO Major Kravchenko pursued and downed the single-engined Ki-15. On return to base, the I-16's engine problems reoccurred, and his machine (either due to hits or poor fuel) lost power and died, forcing him to belly-land. Kravchenko made it back to base only on the evening of 1 July to report his travails to *Komkor* Yakov Smushkevich.[121]

The Japanese returned to their bases between 07.00 and 08.00 Tokyo time. Their reports exceeded the boldest expectations, yet they all knew that the Soviet air grouping retained a great many aeroplanes. Therefore, yielding to insistent calls from line officers just returned from the first strike, Lt Gen Tetsuji Giga ordered a second raid, this time 320km from the Khalkhin-Gol

River, on the Soviet airfield at Bain-Tumen. Preliminary data indicated that the major part of the Soviet bomber force and cover fighters were based there.

The Ki-21 strike group, again led by Col Kiso Mikami, appeared over the target at 13.00, strengthened by a few Ki-30s and covered by Lt Col Matsumura's supplementary tank-equipped fighters. The formation was considerably tighter this time, yet there was no sight of any enemy, either on the ground or in the air. The few visible targets on the ground were bombed, but damage was slight. Not even the AAA offered any resistance. In the circumstances, the major problem for the Japanese was fuel reserves, but all crews made it back safely to base. The overall effect of this raid was practically zero: a single I-15bis was destroyed while trying to depart (its pilot baled out), a mechanic died and nineteen airfield grades were wounded.[122]

Overall, the two massed strikes completely destroyed eight Soviet fighters and damaged many others. Airfields and their facilities were seriously damaged. Some seventeen dogfight losses were admitted by the Soviets[123], while the Japanese claimed ninety-nine dogfight victories, and forty-nine aircraft destroyed or damaged on the ground – practically the entire Soviet fighter force.[124] Total Japanese losses were set at six aircraft, remarkably two of them being recce machines.

Despite this partial success, the day had been exceptionally heavy and unpleasant for the VVS. The Japanese had managed to score a successive victory. It guaranteed operational air superiority over the coming days, and led to the CO of the 70th IAP being changed. *Komdiv* Georgiy Zhukov personally called for Smushkevich's report on the events. The airman tallied Japanese losses from 22 June to the close of the day, putting them at ninety-one aircraft for the cost of thirty-eight Soviet aircraft.[125] Despite this, the conversation was unpleasant, with the previous day's debacle hanging heavily over it. After brief but sharp exchanges, Major Vyacheslav Zabaluyev was asked to hand over command to Major Sergey Gritsavets 'temporarily', marking the sole Soviet senior air personnel change in the region.[126]

The euphoria in the 2nd *Hiko Syudan* Staff was at a peak. Apart from the great number of enemy losses, individual aces had emerged such as WO Hiromiti Shinohara and M Sgt Bunji Yoshiyama, with eleven and four victories respectively for the day. However, not everyone approved of the optimistic tallying of victories. Maj Gen Ikkaku Shimono and many other experienced officers who had taken part in the strike were aware that the Soviet command had nevertheless managed to scramble a large part of its force, and that the genuine result was a third of what was claimed – not more than twenty-six destroyed and damaged aircraft. This estimate turned out far closer to reality.[127]

One of the best inter-war fighter aces, WO Hiromiti
Shinohara. *(MoD Archives, Bulgaria)*

The Supreme Command in Tokyo took the raids against Soviet airfields as a wilful and gross infringement of prior directives that had forbidden deep incursions over Mongolia. Threatened with punishment, the Kwantung Army Command decided to rein in its air forces henceforth. The limitations did not affect the overall operational situation, however, since the weather was bad between 29 June and 2 July, with gale-force winds and strong spring showers. Both commands used the non-flying weather and the lack of reconnaissance to regroup and prepare for the large-scale clashes to come.

4

The unorthodox Zhukov

Using the partial successes scored, including those from the air, the Japanese command decided to start its planned land advance. In early July its land forces comprised 38,000 men, 310 field guns and 154 tanks. The concentration in the vicinity of the Yan-Hu Lake aimed at delivering a decisive strike and routing the Soviet-Mongolian forces.

The plan was code-named 'Nomonhan Incident Phase Two'. Its concept was identical to that of the May incursions: to create a strong strike grouping along the right flank with the aim of encircling and destroying enemy forces to the east of the Khalkhin-Gol River. Naturally, the scale of the operation planned by the staff near Djindjin-Sume was significantly larger. Under the direct command of Lt Gen Michitaro Komatsubara, the future theatre of action saw the deployment of strike units numbering 21,953 infantrymen, 2,000 cavalrymen, 124 large-calibre and anti-tank guns, eighty-seven tanks and six armoured machines.[128] The grouping could rely on 225 of the best-prepared Japanese Army Aviation units from Manchuria from within the Kwantung Army, which still had superiority in the air over the planned theatre of action.

Maj Gen Koichi Kobayashi's group, comprising the artillery-reinforced 71st and 72nd Infantry Regiments, had the objective of fording the Khalkhin-Gol River on the night of 2/3 July north of the Bain-Tsagan ridge, and to move south-south-west, thus cutting the retreat of Soviet forces. The CO of the 7th Division 26th Infantry Regiment, Col Komatsubara Sumi, had the objective of covering the side of the strike formation to prevent the arrival of Soviet reserves, as well as pursuing the enemy in case of his retreat. The regiment was accordingly equipped with the necessary vehicles. The 26th Engineers Regiment supplied support and a mobile strike group. Direct cover of mobile bridge facilities was entrusted to the 23rd Cavalry Regiment, an infantry platoon and a machine-gun company from the 64th Regiment.[129]

Together with this, the Japanese command formed a reserve detachment under Col Ika, which was to sweep behind the strike group and reinforce it as necessary. On 1-2 July a powerful holding group led by Lt Gen Masaomi Yasuoka was to use battalions from two infantry, three cavalry and two tank regiments to secure the flanking march of the strike group at its initial location. From 3 July these forces were to advance and secure the complete defeat of Soviet forces east of the river.

The timing was right because the Soviet-Mongolian forces had yet to make good their losses from recent fighting, having a little over 12,000 men, 109 guns, 189 tanks and 266 armoured vehicles spread across eastern Mongolia.[130] The 57th KON Command had information on the enemy concentration at Djindjin-Sume and Yan-Hu Lake and expected the advance, but was unclear about where the main thrust of the strike was planned. The decision was for forces to be directed at the assumed action sites, and to arrive there by 3 July. Suffering from a lack of roads and constant rainfall, *Komdiv* Zhukov ordered the 11th TBR, 7th MBBR and 24th MSP (*Motostrelkovoy Polk*, Motorised Infantry Regiment) on a 120km march from Tamsag-Bulak to a line 20km west of the Bain-Tsagan ridge to parry a possible enemy river crossing and strike. Despite these measures, by the start of the action Zhukov had just 3,200 active men and 1,000 Mongolian cavalrymen covering the left flank of his forces. He could also call on thirty-six field guns with calibres over 76mm and sixty-two armoured vehicles. Tanks remained one of his aces, but they were engaged on a transit.

Lt Gen Michitaro Kamatsubara issued his famous Order 105 at 15.00 on 30 June 1939. Its instructions included the fording of the Khalkhin-Gol River, the rout of the enemy, and his pursuit to complete destruction. The day before the advance was quiet; Japanese aviation did not undertake any flying over the main strike area. This did not deceive the Soviet forward forces, and in fact made their commanders to take additional measures to raise combat readiness. These measures were prudent, for at 21.00 on 2 July, when the day's heat fell to tolerable levels, units from the 7th and 23rd Japanese Divisions, supported by artillery and engineers and commanded by Maj Gen Koichi Kobayashi, advanced towards the Khalkhin-Gol and delivered a strike on Soviet and Mongolian forces. The mobilised deployed Soviet infantry regiment defending the river's west bank and bridge crossing was dispersed and turned in disorderly retreat. Japanese tanks from Lt Gen Yasuoka's holding group advanced south with headlamps lit, marking the way for the infantry and cavalry advance and ensuring the continuity of the attack throughout the night. Using boats, pontoons and other means, the Japanese advance guard forded the Khalkhin-Gol River.

Daybreak on 3 July saw Maj Gen Kobayasi's forces overcome fierce resistance by the 15th Mongolian Cavalry Regiment, and by 08.00 they embarked on fording the river and making their way to the heights that gave their name to one of the bloodiest clashes in this conflict – Bain-Tsagan. The Soviet and Mongolian forces that had remained east of the river were threatened with encirclement and rout. Fierce fighting ensued, with the Japanese initially successful, advancing with the support of by 3rd and 4th Tank Regiments (with eighty-seven tanks). The Soviets were relieved by the armoured battalion of the 6th Cavalry Division, which counter-attacked, stopped the Japanese tank advance, and took up defensive positions covering the Soviet bridge crossing.[131]

Aviation again played an active role in the daylight fighting. The June clashes had not affected the potential of the air groupings that faced each other in the conflict. The Soviets admitted the loss of seventeen I-16s, twenty-nine I-15bis and one SB-2, with two I-16s, two I-15s and the SB-2 being non-combat-rated. Available numbers comprised ninety-three I-16s, forty-five I-15bis, 132 SB-2s and some thirty-five R-5/5Sh (ten of the latter being Soviet and the rest Mongolian). The Japanese admitted the loss of eleven Ki-27s, one Ki-21 and one Ki-30, with several more battle-damaged non-airworthy machines.[132] If we believe these figures, there were 120 airworthy Nakajimas (and thus a relative parity in fighters), with an approximately three-to-one Soviet strike aircraft numerical superiority.

As early as 2 July, Japanese aviation offered close air support to its advancing forces. Concurrently, Soviet twin-engined SB-2s began to bomb the advancing enemy and his rear to a tactical depth, taking advantage of weak Japanese anti-air defences and the none-too-coordinated Japanese fighter cover. Both sides employed the stepped method, avoiding deep penetrations over enemy-held ground.

The next day was decisive for the land battle and saw an escalation of air action. The *Kantogun* decided to boost the role of the air component in supporting the advance and in covering the land forces from constantly patrolling Soviet SB-2 and R-5Sh assault aircraft. Units of the 70th and 22nd IAP assumed the latter task; I-15bis biplanes supported by gun-equipped I-16Ps from the 22nd IAP 5th IAE strafed and bombed enemy anti-aircraft defences at Bain-Tsagan and the bridge area.

A Ki-30 light bomber after a close air support mission over the Khalkhin-Gol River.
(MoD Archives, Bulgaria)

Komkor Yakov Smushkevich tried to make use of his Spanish experience. Over Guadalajara he had employed what he termed the 'air conveyor', a stepped use of air potential that ensured that the enemy was constantly covered by squadrons of fighters and bombers offering direct air support to the land forces. The air conveyor had been successful in Spain while the Republican air force had enjoyed air superiority, but such superiority had not been won over the Mongolian steppes. Moreover, enemy aviation had taken the initiative, with 10th, 16th, and 61st *Sentai* bombers successfully attacking and dispersing the Mongolian 6th Cavalry Division in the early hours of 3 July. The Japanese followed this up with further close air support group sorties.

The groups of Soviet bombers and fighters numbering a total of some seventy SB-2s, ten R-5s and 120 I-15bis and I-16s enjoyed a short-lived tactical operations window, being shortly interdicted by the total strengths of the 11th and 24th *Sentais*. Subsequently, an air battle was joined by more than 300 combat aircraft from both sides. It developed from engagements by Capt Yevgeniy Stepanov's strike group. He sortied with eight I-15bis covered by ten I-16s.[133] Low morning cloud kept them at low level, then over their targets the weather improved. They attacked from the south so as to keep the sun behind them during aiming and strafing, yet it was precisely from there that Japanese fighters appeared. Yet again they had the advantage of height, but failed to impose their characteristic combat tactics due to the skills of the Soviet escort group. The indecisive clash led to force escalations on both sides. The gun-equipped I-16Ps led by Lt Trubachenko also became involved[134], delivering a strike on the bridge crossing from a height of 2,000 metres, and dispersing the Burgud cavalry and infantry close to the bridgehead. On their third approach, they were engaged by newly appeared Japanese fighters, which seriously challenged the heavier and slower I-16Ps. It had already became clear that this mark of the famous Soviet fighter stood no chance in a direct contest with a Ki-27. Now they were saved by the 22nd IAP's I-16 tip 10s patrolling at some height. In view of the enemy's great activity, on his second sortie Major Kravchenko scrambled his entire regiment for a strike against an enemy forward field airstrip. His force numbered five *eskadrily*, each with between fifteen and eighteen aircraft; one of them was detailed to cover the actions of the remaining four. They attacked the duty fighter stands as soon as they arrived above them, successfully parrying scramble attempts by the pair of duty machines. They went on to complete three strike runs over the aprons and the furiously firing anti-aircraft emplacements. After returning to base, the regiment went on to two further fights, again acquitting itself as the region's elite VVS RKKA unit. The first clash resulted from an attempt by the 2nd IAE led by St Lt Viktor Chestyakov to reconnoitre the results of the strike on the forward airfield. He was attacked by eight Ki-27s, which put his unit in an exceptionally grave situation. Two more *eskadrily* led by Major Kravchenko sortied to help their colleagues, but ended up merely pursuing the enemy. Nevertheless, the recce task was completed, with seven destroyed aircraft being counted on the ground (two while taxiing out for departure).[135]

This active use of aviation by the Soviet command was not incidental. Short of manpower, *Komdiv* Zhukov tried to control events by recourse to the numerical superiority of the Soviet and Mongolian forces in terms of tanks, armed vehicles and aircraft. Apart from engaging in air superiority contests, Soviet airmen offered close air support to their fellow gunners (themselves enjoying a numerical superiority over the enemy), managing to destroy some thirty tanks. Despite the resistance, the Japanese command skilfully exploited its early success and managed to transfer a great quantity of men and battlefield machines over the bridge crossing. Reconnaissance reported to *Komdiv* Zhukov that some 10,000 enemy troops with some 100 anti-tank weapons had managed to take up two defensive positions at the Bain-Tsagan Mount. The energetic soldier grew convinced that he must on no account lose the initiative, making the fullest use of resources at his disposal to that end, regardless of any losses. He therefore resolved to deploy his anti-tank units throughout the theatre with no delay. First to report in Zhukov's staff was the 11th TBR CO *Kombrig* (Brigade CO) Mikhail Yakovlev. After a briefing, at 09.15 he was ordered to attack the heights with his 132 serviceable tanks but with no infantry or artillery support. The order set a precedent in military history and remains without parallel today. The powerfully armed yet thinly armoured Soviet BT-5/7 tanks had to attack from three directions across bare and open country entirely exposed to the enemy's artillery. The attack was to take place at high speed, best suited to the tanks' performance and fire characteristics. A tank battalion was detailed to organise a diversionary attack from the south jointly with the armoured battalion of the Mongolian 8th Cavalry Division and the 185th Heavy Artillery Battalion.[136]

The epic attack began at 10.45 with support from some forty I-15bis armed with small bombs. In the event, the latter could not complete the task, being intercepted by a large group of Ki-27s. The I-16s patrolling at great height entered the fray, with the clutch of dogfighting aircraft, the roar of engines and the crackle of machine guns providing a mere background to the land action. A wedge formation of seventy-three SB-2s from the 150th and 38th SPABs appeared overhead flying in inner formations of nines. Some of them emptied their 100kg warloads from 3,000 metres over Hill 744 (Bain-Tsagan Mount). Others made for the Khalastin-Gol River and the Yan-Hu Lake, bombing enemy tactical reserves. Accelerating, the tanks entered the direct vision of the anti-tank weapons on the Bain-Tsagan heights. The steel avalanche began to shed a number of burning machines, some in turn rapidly shedding their surviving crews. On one of the lines of attack, thirty-four tanks were left from at total of fifty initial attackers. The overall rate of loss in the suicidal attack by the 11th TBR amounted to eighty-two BTs, or 62 per cent of its strength. Despite the losses, the armoured avalanche crossed the enemy lines and returned after inflicting considerable losses on the infantry and artillery on the hillsides. At 13:30 the tank brigade received reinforcements from Major Ivan Fedyuninskiy's 24th MSP, which attacked the sector south of the Hunhu-Usu-Nur. By 14.00 the fifty-nine armoured vehicles of the 7th MBBR, under *Kombrig* Aleksey Lesovoy, also arrived.

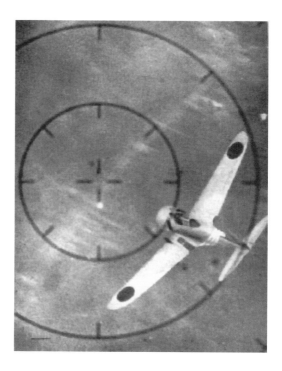

Sighting a Ki-27 during dogfight training.
(MoD Archives, Bulgaria)

Concurrently, the east bank of the Khalkhin-Gol River was seeing intense tank battles with great Japanese losses. The fire of eight Soviet tanks and twenty armoured vehicles destroyed forty-one Japanese tanks.

Attempts by single-engined Japanese bombers to counter the armoured enemy forces also failed to bring the desired result. They caused a second massed air battle involving mainly *eskadrily* from Major Kravchenko's *aviopolk*. The battle took place above the VVS Command Post at Hamar-Daba Mount, and the Japanese scored the initial successes. Using their fighters' manoeuvrability advantage and exploiting the lack of experience of their opponents (the younger of the regiment's pilots), they brought down an I-16. Another I-16 left the battle, force-landing with sixty-two hits on its fuselage and wings. Two rounds had hit the pilot's seat, with the armour yet again proving its worth and saving the airman. After this, Soviet air battle aces Major Kravchenko and St Lt Rakhov took the initiative and began fighting with rapid level changes. This disadvantaged the Japanese with their structurally weaker aircraft, yet they refused to flee, hating to lose face. Soon the battle progressed to a series of dogfights between the leaders, with the Soviet airmen scoring victories. The two Japanese pilots baled out and were captured.[137] The victory cleared the sky for the crews of the 150th SPAB, who delivered another strike on enemy reserves, this time at the disputed Nomon-Han-Burd-Obo. Despite some delay, the departing Soviet bomber squadrons were intercepted by a lone Nakajima; Sgt Jiro Okuda pursued the formation for 12 minutes, shooting down one aircraft.[138]

The VVS RKKA had again won air superiority. At the close of the day, *Komkor* Smushkevich received reports of thirty-two downed Japanese aircraft for the total loss of a single I-16[139], whose pilot had died in the wreckage. The SB twins alone had delivered more than 6,000 100kg and 250kg bombs. This seems to have been the first operational Soviet air victory in the region. Japanese pilots claimed eleven downed Soviet aircraft (four SB-2s, six I-16s and one R-Z). What was striking about these reports, however, was that, despite their great partiality, they contained the frank admission of seven totally lost Ki-27 fighters.[140]

Battles at the Japanese bridgehead on the western bank of the Khalkhin-Gol River continued unabated on 4 July 1939. Crews from the 2nd *Hiko Syudan* were more active in the air, as Japanese bombers attempted to pre-empt the Soviet counter-offensive against Bain-Tsagan and secure their infantry's defensive actions. The light bombers and twin-engined Fiat BR.20s delivered 36 tonnes of bombs along the front line.[141] Their escorts also saw action, with pilots from the 1st, 11th and 24th *Sentais* demonstrating their customary doggedness in attempting to avenge the previous day's reversals. Their main targets were initially I-15bis biplanes acting with a height advantage. Thereafter followed dogfights with covering I-16s, which in turn gave way to Major Mikhail Burmistrov's bombers from the 150th SPAB. His groups arrived in waves over the relatively narrow theatre that was their objective. The *aviozvenas'* formations usually endured only the initial minutes of action, soon yielding to individual contests. The roar of engines never ceased over the Bain-Tsagan Mount, enveloped as they were in the smoke and dust of battle. The sky was torn by the fiery traces of burning aircraft, which rendered the white parachutes of their crews all the brighter. Some of the aircraft that were hit landed on the steppe. One of them was piloted by 3rd *Chutai* CO Capt Takeo Fukuda. His wingman, M Sgt Tomio Hanada, watched the proceedings from nearby, guarding against further Soviet fighter attacks. Others from the 11th *Sentai Chutai* also offered cover. On seeing his commander land safely on enemy-held ground, Hanada decided to rescue him. He landed next to the leader's damaged machine and, using the limited space left and his Ki-27's excellent take-off performance, fulfilled his mission.

There were numerous cases where the aerial fight resumed on the ground, with downed pilots resorting to the use of side arms and even hand-to-hand fighting. Overall, Japanese crews claimed ten downed twin-engined bombers, thirty-five I-16 and I-15bis fighters[142] and a sole R-5. This data remains unconfirmed, yet the overall picture suggests that the 2nd *Hiko Syudan* did indeed have the upper hand in the air.

However, the success in the air was not shared by the Japanese land contingent, which was forced to repel a third massed attack on Bain-Tsagan by Soviet and Mongolian forces. The battles continued without respite throughout the night and the following day. Although much inflated, the previous day's Soviet air losses were felt and led to a reduction in sorties on 5 July.[143] At the day's start, some sixty twin-engined bombers from the 38th SPAB, accompanied by fifty I-16s, attempted to strike the retreating Japanese land forces and the bridgehead itself. They were intercepted and attacked by the two *chutais* of the 1st *Sentai*, led by unit CO Lt Col Toshio Kato. Yet again, the *sentai* pilots reported victories: five SBs and seven I-16s destroyed for no loss. Soviet sources admit only the loss of the bombers, whose crews also perished. Despite weak air support, by 15.00 the heights had been cleared of Japanese troops, who were now pursued as they fled towards the bridgehead. This was blown up before many of them managed to flee to the east bank of the Khalkhin-Gol River, so many died there or were taken prisoner. At the same time, eighteen SB-2 bombers from the 38th SPAB struck Halun-Arshaan railway station. The crews acted without fighter cover and were attacked twice by Japanese fighters. Two bombers and four Nakajimas fell in the fierce dogfight.[144]

An official communiqué by the Soviet forces in the People's Republic of Mongolia announced the military victory over the aggressor and his final expulsion from the west bank of the Khalkhin-Gol River. As regards aviation, it spoke of forty-five enemy losses, of which twenty were claimed to be single-engined bombers. According to the same source, the price paid was the loss of nine combat aircraft, including two SB-2s.[145] According to the Japanese, the figures were entirely different: sixty-eight totally written-off red-starred machines were supposed to have fallen victim to the *sentais*.

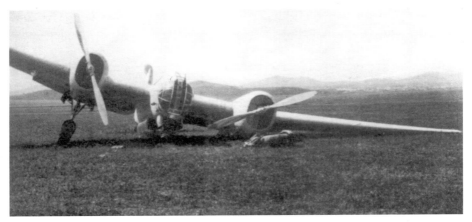

Heavy landing: a battle-damaged SB-2 returns to its base. *(MoD Archives, Bulgaria)*

On 6 July the air action continued, albeit at a lesser intensity, regardless of the almost complete silence on the ground. Precise fire from the manoeuvrable Nakajimas of the 1st and 24th *Sentais* claimed another four SB-2s and twenty-two I-16s (if one is to believe the Japanese statistics, the Soviet air grouping would by now have suffered total attrition). The name of WO Shinohara was again mentioned, having added six victories to his combat total since the start of the conflict. The Soviets admitted the loss of just one bomber. Pilot Krasihin was supposed to have made a navigational error, taking him over the front line to the side of the safe route and falling victim to friendly anti-aircraft fire. The gunners were instructed to fire at everything outside the designated safety zone, and had not even tried to identify the SB, flying at a mere 200 metres. One engine was shot through and set alight, and Krasihin was forced to belly-land. His aeroplane burned out completely, but the crew were unharmed. The relatively calm situation during the day did not stop the three fighter *sentais* from claiming ninety-four victories for the period 2-6 July. AAA claimed another five victories, and the Japanese admitted just four losses. WO Mamoru Hanada and M Sgt Kitayama force-landed, but returned safely to base the next morning.[146] Genuine Soviet losses for the period amounted to sixteen machines, while Soviet fighters claimed thirty-two victories for the period.[147]

An SB-2bis after a belly-landing. *(MoD Archives, Bulgaria)*

Another important event on 6 July was that the CO of the Front Group, Second Degree *Komandarm* Grigoriy Mikhailovich Shtern, lent part of his air resource (of the 4th Heavy Bomber Air Regiment from the Trans-Baykal Military District), initially in the form of a squadron, and later as a group of heavy TB-3 heavy bombers, for the purpose of reinforcing the air grouping in eastern Mongolia. The formation was commanded by Major Egorov and was based on the Mongolian airfield of Obo-Somon. In fact, the overall number of serviceable machines did not exceed twenty-three. The older marks were essentially intended to fly transport duties, whereas the modernised versions began to deliver strikes on enemy positions from the night of 8 July. The lumbering and heavy four-engined machines usually departed in groups of three to nine at intervals that allowed them to bomb from a height of 500 to 2,000 metres. Their warload comprised eight 250kg bombs. The result of the raids was to deliver more of a psychological harassment than genuine damage to the enemy, who was simply not allowed to sleep in peace.[148]

Perhaps this was the reason for frequent Japanese attacks during the same period. They had limited aims and committed small groups of men, but among the more effective ones took place on the night of 8 July. Its objective was positions held by 149th SP (*Strelkovay Polk*, Infantry Regiment). The raid marked an escalation of tension along the entire front, and the culmination was the inclusion of the 11th TBR in the battle for the Major Remizov heights. The tank crews again achieved their objective, succeeding in repelling the attempted enemy advance, yet losing (on 12 July) their renowned CO *Kombrig* Yakovlev.

Subsequent attempts by Japanese forces to organise less ambitious advances were accompanied by renewed air action by both sides. On 8 July fifty-one Soviet I-16 and I-15bis fighters fought some thirty Ki-27s. The Soviets claimed twenty-one Japanese aircraft for the loss of three 'Ishaks' and

Major Egorov's TB-3 heavy bomber group at a front-line airfield. *(MoD Archives, Bulgaria)*

three pilots.[149] The next more ambitious fight came on 10 July when the number of participants was twice as great: forty I-16s and twenty-six I-15bis of the 22nd IAP and forty Ki-27s, strengthened by reinforcements from both sides comprising thirty-seven I-16s from the 70th IAP and twenty Ki-27s. The contest mainly took place at some 3,000 metres and went on for some 20 minutes. The Japanese saw it as a successive occasion for a victorious statement (sixty-four enemy losses for the loss of a single fighter). WO Mamoru Hanada (seventeen victories) was hit, but managed to land his Ki-27, which had only been slightly damaged, among friendly forces. He was at once removed to hospital where his leg was amputated, but he died on the morning of 12 July. He was the first Japanese ace to die over Mongolia.[150] The Soviet side declared eleven victories and three lost I-16s; two pilots were declared dead and another four wounded. The Deputy CO of the 22nd IAP, *Kap* Balashev, managed to land with a head wound, later dying in hospital. He was posthumously proclaimed a Hero of the Soviet Union on 29 August.[151]

The calm after the intense conflict that had lasted for some days was a good time for replacement of losses, and for analysis. Only the *Kantogun* issued official statistics. For the period between 3 and 10 July, Ki-30 and Ki-36 light bombers of the 10th and 15th *Sentais*, assisted by 'heavy' Ki-21s and Fiat BR.20s, had delivered 174 tonnes of 15kg, 50kg and 100kg bombs. The high effectiveness of the Ki-30 light fast bomber set against Russian anti-aircraft defences was noted, as was the ineffectiveness of the twin-engined bombers, which were forced to flee AAA by striking from above 4,500 metres, rather too high for any precision. Japanese raids were officially admitted to have cost the loss of five aircraft (a Ki-30, two Ki-21s and two Ki-15s), all on 3 July. Meanwhile, since the start of the conflict the 2nd *Hiko Syudan* claimed to have scored 398 victories (twenty-one of them twin-engined aircraft), with no fewer than 174 between 3 and 11 July. Another thirty-five Soviet aircraft were said to have probably been downed. Since the start of the campaign, just forty-seven Japanese aircraft were supposed to have been lost.[152]

The remains of one of the few crashed Ki-21 heavy bombers. *(MoD Archives, Bulgaria)*

Statistics compiled and published later by Soviet military historians note Japanese losses between the start of hostilities and the end of the Bain-Tsagan battle at 161 combat aircraft, of which 157 were fighters. Japan's own losses were set at 103 aircraft, of which eighty-nine met their end in combat (thirty-three I-16s, forty-three I-15bis, twelve SBs and one R-5).

**Loss indicators in aerial combat from
the beginning of the conflict until mid-June 1939**

Indicator	USSR	Japan	Ratio
Claimed inflicted losses	398	161	2.47:1
Claimed inflicted losses of fighters	367	157	2.34:1
Admitted combat losses	89	47	1.89:1
Admitted losses as a percentage of claimed losses	22.4	29	1:1.3

The absurd manner of determining and announcing victories and losses by both sides in the conflict was yet again shown by the 12 July battle between not more than forty aircraft from the 1st *Sentai* and thirty-nine I-16s from the 22nd IAP. (Reinforcements included six I-16s and fifteen I-15bis from the 70th IAP.) The Japanese approached the Khalkhin-Gol in three waves at different levels. The initial Soviet objective was the lowest wave, which yet again gave the higher-positioned Japanese waves the tactical advantage. However, the Soviet pilots demonstrated skills they had acquired in combat with the result that neither side gained the advantage in the 45-minute clash. Thereafter both sides tried to make up for the lack of genuine success by waging a propaganda battle. The Japanese claimed eleven downed adversaries for the cost of three of their own aircraft failing to return. Major Grigoriy Kravchenko also reported eleven enemy losses, this time without losing any of his own.[153] In reality, one Soviet fighter was brought down (its pilot baling out and surviving), plus three Japanese Ki-27s. The same battle saw the aircraft of 1st *Sentai* CO Lt Col Toshio Kato set alight. He left his torched machine, landing behind enemy lines. Sgt Toshio Matsu-ura landed in the nearby steppe, rescuing his commander, but the latter's serious burns kept him off active duty until 1941.

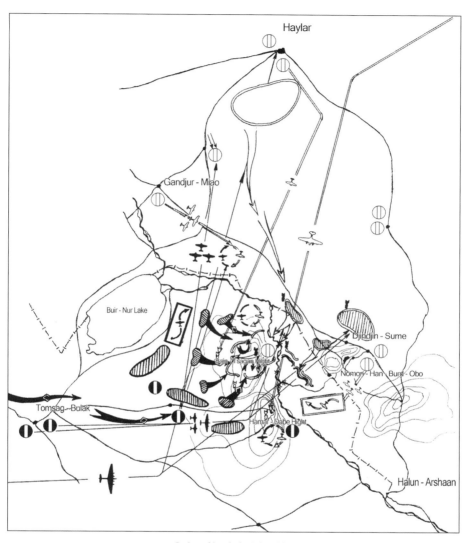

Order of battle in July 1939

5

Fighting for air superiority

Komdiv Georgiy Zhukov did not exploit the Japanese land retreat immediately. Lack of reserves forced him to be satisfied with the construction of a solid bridgehead fortification on the eastern bank of the Khalkhin-Gol River. In the air as on the ground, both sides needed an operational interlude, and this temporary calm gave the opportunity for force regrouping, strengthening and reorganisation. An order by the Soviet *Narkom* of Defence arrived in Mongolia on 15 July, decreeing the creation of the 1st AG (Army

Group) from the forces deployed along the Khalkhin-Gol front. The group was to be commanded by *Komdiv* Georgiy Konstantinovich Zhukov, who was shortly later promoted to *Komkor*. *Palk* Aleksandr Gusev was appointed the new Group's CO VVS, and *Komkor* Yakov Smushkevich was to head planning and operations. Coordination and synergy between the active and reserve forces, and with the Mongolian forces, was to be the responsibility of the Front Army Group commanded by Second Degree *Komandarm* Grigoriy Mikhailivich Shtern.[154]

New aircraft began to arrive to enhance the air component in mid-July. The RKKA Command demanded and received some 200 aircraft of all types, the majority being I-16 tip 10 fighters and gun-equipped I-16 tip 17s. The delivery also marked the first time newly produced I-153 'Chaykas' had arrived in a war zone. They were slated to undergo their field-testing over the Mongolian steppe in order to prove their fitness for purpose. Twenty were brought to the Army delivery station and inspected by Smushkevich, who was pleased by the look of one of the few biplane fighters with a retractable undercarriage. He noted the upper wing with its clear I-15 ancestry, a feature that many pilots regarded ambivalently in view of the limitations to forward visibility it imposed, something particularly important for precise aiming prior to firing. The new aircraft first armed a 70th IAP *eskadrilya*. Major Sergey Gritsavets was appointed its CO, his deputy being another Spanish-experienced pilot, Major Boris Smirnov. It was the later that, together with a group of selected fighter pilots, they went to test-fly and accept the new type. Another five aircraft of this type went to the 22nd IAP.[155]

Soviet expert flyers: (l-r) Gritsavets, Prachik, Kravchenko, Korobov and Smirnov. *(MoD Archives, Bulgaria)*

Soviet fighter units in the theatre continued to receive highly skilled personnel from Baltic and Black Sea naval air units. These pilots were transferred without redesignation in order to acquire experience; many were commanding officers or senior ranks, yet flew as ordinary pilots. The changing circumstances dictated the relocation of the 70th IAP, which departed to the Ihe-Tashigay-Nur system of airfields, some 90km from Tamsag-Bulak. Personnel also arrived to strengthen the 56th IAP, initially commanded by Major Stepan Danilov, and later by *Palk* Timofey Kutsevalov. The unit ceased to be a base for the preparation and onward distribution of newly arrived pilots and fighters, taking on genuine combat reinforcement duties in air superiority contests and in operational area defence.

The same period was used by Soviet air commanders to analyse the results of combat. Many of them reached the conclusion that the I-16, including the later marks, was insufficiently fast and had poor performance at high altitudes. The chief operations engineer in Mongolia, Ivan Prachik, proposed a field test of production I-16s with the new and more powerful M-62 engine. Two days after the request, a transport aeroplane brought several examples of the power plant to the 'Leningrad' base.[156] The engine mounts were the same as for the standard M-25, and Prachik's group needed just three days to fit the first aeroplane. Although a significant performance improvement was noted, the basic modification of this mark was also subject to a number of engine-related restrictions. However, despite the safety measures taken, the modification led to a number of failures in combat, some leading to personnel losses. Yet despite a still limited engine life, it did lead to new marks of the I-16 and I-153, whose production began the very same year.

The 'Chayka' first arrived at 'Leningrad' for conversion flying and mock dogfights. Though significantly better than its I-15bis predecessor, the machine turned out to be underdeveloped in many respects. Its planned VISh auto-feathering propeller was still unavailable, further cutting the biplane's speed and altitude performance, and particularly hampering its take-off. Everyone remarked on the great field length the new machine needed before it unstuck (significantly more than the I-16 and unusually so for a biplane) and on its sluggish climb, though these were balanced by good controllability.[157] Speed performance was best at above 4,000 metres. A great benefit noted by the new aeroplane's pilots after their first firings was the excellent focus of its fire. The four rapid-firing ShKAS machine guns in its nose could literally cut though a non-armour-plated opponent.

Meanwhile the Soviet logistic and engineer services recognised the vulnerability of the few airfields in the operational area and began to prepare many new airstrips where Soviet *eskadrily* could disperse. Apart from that, forward and dummy airstrips were also set up, featuring a great number of dummy aircraft. Deliveries of the latter included seventy-five models of the I-16. To check the deception, *Komkor* Yakov Smushkevich sent one of his most experienced pilots, *eskadrilya* CO *Kap* Yevgeniy Stepanov, together with two wingmen, on a flight over a supposed new airfield for fighter redeployment. The *aviozveno* duly spotted and reported the airfield, only to discover the deception afterwards.

The fate of the remaining airworthy I-15bis hung in the balance. Eventually they were deployed mainly for close air support and as night-fighters covering the Command Post and forces to the rear. They were relocated to new airfields, and some of the pilots released from them, including Yevgeniy Stepanov, went on to receive new I-16Ps. The newly formed squadron of gun-equipped fighters was also detailed to cover the Command Post at Hamar-Daba and Tamsag-Bulak, but only in daylight.[158] Japanese strike and recce aircrews had long assigned a premium to these two points. The heavy 20mm gun rounds were rather effective against bombers and, once in position, the gun-armed 'Ishaks' proved effective interceptors.

Before departing in a DC-3 to take charge of the new equipment in the Trans-Baykal region, a great many Soviet pilots went through Tamsag-Bulak to examine the captured Japanese war equipment assembled there from the Bain-Tsagan battle. Their pride and delight in contemplating at close quarters what they had until recently only viewed in their gun-sights could hardly be concealed.[159]

The 2nd *Hiko Syudan* also used the calm to review combat preparedness and readiness. Staff considered that the 12th *Sentai* with its Italian Fiat BR.20s had not lived up to expectations due to incomplete crew training and the aeroplane's demonstrably low combat potential. The type was relocated away

A Soviet pilot near his camouflaged I-15bis: these aircraft were deployed on close air support duties only by the close of the Nomonhan conflict. *(MoD Archives, Bulgaria)*

The disappointing Fiat BR.20 bomber failed to live up to expectations in the Nomonhan conflict.
(MoD Archives, Bulgaria)

from the front and replaced by the 16th *Sentai*'s 3rd *Chutai*, armed with Ki-30 Type 97 light bombers. The 1st *Sentai* fighters were pulled back to complement the 12th *Hikodan*. Recce aircraft of the disbanded 7th *Hikodan* were immediately detailed to the 15th *Sentai*, transferring to the 2nd *Hiko Syudan*.

This reorganisation regrouped and restructured the Japanese Army Air Forces in the region significantly better, with Lt Gen Giga's operational grouping, opposing the Manchurian forces, comprising a Staff under whose direct command was the 15th Reconnaissance *Sentai* (four Ki-4s, six Ki-15-Is and ten Ki-36s); Maj Gen Ikkaku Shimono's 9th *Hikodan*, which was detailed mainly support and strike duties with its 10th *Sentai* (five Ki-36s and nine Ki-30s), 16th *Sentai* (twenty Ki-30s) and 61st *Sentai* (nine Ki-21-Is); leaving Maj Gen Eiji Higashi's 12th *Hikodan* with its 1st *Sentai* (twenty-three Ki-27s), 11th *Sentai* (forty-two Ki-27s) and 24th *Sentai* (twenty-six Ki-27s) to air superiority duties.[160] Thus the grouping retained its air superiority capability, yet had insufficient strike power to cover surface forces. In structure and composition, it was limited to waging solely defensive operations.

Although by the close of July the two sides in the Nomonhan Conflict had yet to complete the augmentation of their squadrons with aircraft and personnel, and were yet to be ready for large-scale combat, the sky over Mongolia grew restive again. The number of recce overflights, inevitably with fighter escort, increased, frequently leading to engagements. On 20 July such

One method of sending
reconnaissance data
gathered by Ki-36 crews.
(MoD Archives, Bulgaria)

a clash involved the conflict's first ramming, carried out by a Soviet pilot
–from a head-on position! It took place during a 22nd IAP 2nd IAE mission.
Eskadrilya CO St Lt Vitaliy Skobarihin saw that Lt Vasiliy Vuss was being
attacked by twin Japanese fighters. One of them was assuming a firing
position, so a quick reaction was called for to pre-empt the attacker's further
actions. Skobarihin entered a head-on attack, the two aircraft closing at almost
900kmph. The Japanese fighter deviated at the last moment, but too late – the
propeller of the 'Ishak' tore through parts of his tail and fuselage, its wing
tearing off an undercarriage leg. The Type 97 fell away to earth. The collision
was so powerful that it tore off Skobarihin's seat belts. He struck the
instrument panel and blacked out. Coming to, he recovered a spin and
managed to make it to base, landing on even ground to the side of the main
runway strip so as not to hinder the landing of others. The other Soviet pilots
in the fight reported downing another two Japanese fighters.[161]

St Lt Vitaliy Skobarihin moments after the ramming…

…and posing by his I-16 tip 10.
(MoD Archives, Bulgaria)

This incident ended almost two weeks of tranquillity in the air. It still obtained on the ground, while advances were planned and forces were resupplied, for the two sides' air staffs had a standing objective of winning and retaining air superiority, and they pursued it thoroughly. A single spark could start the fire. On 21 July limited Japanese bomber forces struck enemy communications, while manoeuvrable Nakajima Ki-27s took to wholesale harrying of the enemy in the air. Preventing the Soviets' two fighter waves from departing were the pilots of the 1st and 24th *Sentais*, who attacked some ninety-five I-16s and sixty-two I-15bis of the 22nd and 70th IAPs. The engagement began at 09:45 over Bain-Hoshu Mount, gradually turning into a major battle lasting some 90 minutes and covering a wide area over both sides of the front line. Not one participant felt able to leave the battle even after his munitions were exhausted, an indicator of improved tactical discipline. In one dogfight, M Sgt Shogo Saito again showed bravery verging on madness by attempting (as he had done a month earlier) to ram an I-16 after having run out of ammunition. This time his adversary was well skilled and managed to escape. Regardless, Saito was nicknamed the 'Ram King'.

The adversaries' air units tended to meet above the disputed territory east of the river. The Japanese claimed victories against thirty-nine Soviet fighters for the loss of three machines[162], whose pilots baled out; two were reported as having returned to base, while the third (Capt Keisike Yamada) killed himself to prevent his capture. Soviet statistics recognise the loss of five I-15bis and all the pilots, and the wounding of another three pilots.[163]

Regardless of the inflated Japanese propaganda, the worsening situation in the air forced Soviet commanders to review their tactics. Young and inexperienced pilots arriving at the fighter units were unable to offer proper escort to bombers. This necessitated the 9 July order to remain in force, raising the twin-engined SBs' bomb-dropping altitudes from 6,500 to 7,500 metres to evade enemy fighter interception. Raids on 9, 13, 14 and 15 July proved ineffective, but at dawn on 22 July fifteen SB-2s escorted by thirty fighters easily evaded the pursuit of scrambled 1st and 11th *Sentai* Ki-27s thanks to their superior altitude. Yet, while losses were prevented, the raid was again imprecise, with bombs being scattered too widely.[164] The Soviet bombers' bombsights were insufficiently precise, and the aircraft themselves were structurally limited to bombing from level flight or shallow dives. *Komkor* Yakov Smushkevich carefully analysed the results of the raid, determining that the only way to achieve acceptable bombing precision was to deploy his strike component in greater numbers and tighter formations. Under the circumstances, modern military science would support this conclusion. This makes the Khalkhin-Gol conflict the first where aircraft were massed over a relatively narrow stretch of front and against individual targets as a way of attaining decisive objectives. World military experts, who monitored events ever more closely, reached the same conclusions as Smushkevich, inevitably applying them in the world war that followed, as well as subsequently. Though rejected, Douhet's doctrine had attained its practical application. The Battle for Mongolia reached a scale hitherto unknown, despite being part of a local military conflict remote from the major theatre where its participants would later pit themselves.

The closing days of July demonstrated another rule pertinent to the new environment: regardless of losses, victory belonged to the side with greater strategic reserves. Prior to a new day of activity on 23 July, the 2nd *Hiko Syudan* managed to assemble barely three-quarters of its personnel. Moreover, even available Japanese fighter pilots were tired after almost three months of countering a numerically superior adversary whose forces and potential continued to grow with ever more new arrivals. The massed actions of Soviet fighters grew apace, with the Japanese having to make up for their lack of numbers with more sorties – individual pilots made up to five or even seven sorties a day.

Returning to 23 July, eight raids by Soviet twin-engined bombers over Manchuria involved more than 140 sorties, strengthened by some 150 sorties by escorting Polikarpov fighters. The three *sentais* of the 12th *Hikodan* often fought valiantly, engaging in almost continuous fierce combat over the front line and the Buir-Nur Lake. The fighting was exceptional in its extent, which was unknown in combat practice to date. Despite their small number, Japanese bombers were also most active in the fight for air supremacy. Using thick cloud, groups of Ki-21-Is and Ki-30s covered by Ki-27s made 128 sorties aimed at major Soviet Command Posts, and at the supply airfield where new machines were arriving (including the aforementioned I-153 'Chaykas').[165]

In fact, three newly arriving 'Chaykas' piloted by *Kaps* Smirnov, Korobkov and Gerasimov also entered the fray. This was the new and still top-secret fighters' first taste of blood. They were at a disadvantage, and their pilots – though experienced – were not yet completely at home in their cockpits. The day was saved by Soviet duty fighters on patrol. *Kap* Viktor Kustov's *eskadrilya* intercepted the diving Japanese raiders, and gun-equipped 'Ishaks' also joined in. *Kap* Yevgeniy Stepanov's lead *aviozveno* managed to shoot up the Japanese leader badly. Nevertheless, the raiders managed to drop their 48 tonnes of bombs and retired in full combat formation. Stepanov himself was fired upon by the escorts and barely glided back to base with his engine out of action, having shot down a Ki-27.

As soon as he landed, Stepanov was detailed not to rest, but to take charge of another eight I-16 tip 10s. They would bring his *eskadrilya* up to strength for its task of covering command sites and supporting bombers overflying the front line. The unit was to be based on a duty landing strip at a special site known as Point 91.[166] Once there, however, the heavy I-16Ps yet again proved to be unable to defend themselves from Japanese fighters and discharge their duties effectively. They were slower and less manoeuvrable than their opponents, and lacked the refinement of command and controllability needed to match their great power. The remaining gun-equipped fighters were sent to Mayor Grigoriy Kravchenko's regiment where they were to be used exclusively for ground-attack duties.

Yet again, Japanese boasts were excessive: at the cost of a single Ki-30 and four Ki-27s (one from the 1st *Sentai*, in the cockpit of which acting 1st *Shutai* CO 1st Lt Shozo Koizumi was killed, and three from the 11th *Sentai*) lost in dogfights, and of three Ki-15-Is of the 15th *Sentai* destroyed on the ground by a group of I-16s (which also damaged Col Katsumi Abe's Ki-36 as it took off), the claim was that the enemy had lost forty-five I-16s and three SB-2s in the air, plus seven I-16s and eight SB-2s due to AAA action.[167] The actual Soviet losses comprised four downed I-16s, with no bomber losses mentioned.[168]

The air war continued with the same level of ferocity over the two following days. On 24 July the Japanese reported the downing of thirty-six single-engined aircraft and four twins at the cost of four Ki-27s with their pilots. The day had been genuinely difficult for the Soviet bombers. Various SB-2 versions flew in formations that imposed a speed of 280-300kmph and constant altitude when

A Ki-21-1 heavy bomber deployed at a main airbase. *(MoD Archives, Bulgaria)*

manoeuvring. This made them vulnerable both to enemy fighters and AAA.[169] Misfortunes began in the morning with the collision of two 38th SPAB bombers over the target; their crews baled out over enemy territory, being lost from sight thereafter. On their return, a large Japanese fighter group attacked the formation. The thirty-five I-16 escorts from the 56th IAP succumbed to the attack from above and failed in their objective, allowing another three SB-2s to be lost from the formation flying slowly at 5,000 metres with the loss of the crews. Another two bombers trailed smoke and eventually force-landed, being written off. The fighter escort acted in an uncoordinated fashion, returning to base having lost four machines. They claimed six downed Ki-27s, in addition to the eleven claimed by the Soviet bombers' gunners. The Japanese admitted just two Nakajima losses. M Sgt Shogo Saito had brought down an SB but had been wounded by the bomber's rear gunner.

The so-called 'Vyaznikov Group', or the 38th SPAB 2nd BAE, had no better luck. It flew its mission without fighter escort, and was also subject to lengthy attacks by enemy fighters, losing two crews over the target. The elite 22nd IAP took the sole revenge for this lack of Soviet success by intercepting a group of Japanese Ki-30s and downing two of them over the Mongolian steppe for no loss.[170] The 12th *Hikodan* pilots, who were the major Japanese participants in this day of contest for air superiority, were attributed another fifty-nine victories at the cost of seven Ki-27s[171], and acting 1st *Sentai* 2nd *Chutai* CO 1st Lt Shatoshi Ito was killed in one of them.

The early morning of 25 July began with the downing of a Japanese dragon balloon by a wing of I-16s from the 70th IAP. In return for this daring Soviet act, some fifty 1st and 11th *Sentai* aircraft met a classic Soviet fighter formation of forty I-16s and five I-15bis, again from the 70th IAP. Both sides rapidly escalated their efforts in what had become a feature of the conflict. Some thirty-two I-16s from the 22nd IAP and forty-six I-16s of the 56th IAP arrived from the west.[172] The Japanese could not realistically garner more than thirty fresh Ki-27s. It all culminated in a terrific air battle involving practically the entire fighter force in the region. In the course of an hour, more than 200 single-engined machines circled over Hamar-Daba Mount. Soviet pilots claimed sixteen victories, and the Japanese reports were equally impressive. M Sgt Tomio Hanada reported five successive victories. His colleague and friend WO Hiromiti Shinohara managed to down four I-15bis before being hit and forced to land on the steppe. Noticing the smoke trail left by his Nakajima, M Sgt Yutaka Aoyagi glided down to rescue him and landed within 70 metres of his downed comrade. However, before they could take off again Aoyagi was wounded by fire from approaching Russian tanks. Luckily, another participant, M Sgt Kooiti Iwasse was even more daring. Despite the danger posed by a nearby Soviet tank column, he landed, took both of his comrades into his narrow aft cockpit compartment and departed unhurried, passing a few metres above the BT-5 tanks that were making for his erstwhile base. The other pilots of the unit strafed Aoyagi's Ki-27 to prevent it from falling into enemy hands.[173]

M Sgt Sintaro Kadzima also had to force-land in Mongolian territory, ShKAS rounds having pierced his petrol pipe and fuel tank. In skilled hands, the otherwise sound aeroplane landed well. Another sergeant from the same 11th *Sentai*, M Sgt Bunji Yoshiyama, landed nearby and plucked his comrade. However, a valuable trophy had fallen into Soviet hands, Kadzima's aircraft being sent to a Moscow test centre as early as 27 July on Smushkevich's orders.[174]

In fact, 25 July was not the Japanese success Tokyo propaganda claimed. One reason was that the VVS RKKA had parried increased enemy activity by launching the new Polikarpov I-153 'Chayka' into combat. The Soviet operational air command had done much for its battle christening, mostly due to subjective factors. Mayor Gritsavets had decided that it was time for the *eskadrilya* equipped with the new machine to taste fire. Almost all *eskadrilya* pilots had Kapitan or Major rank, but flew as ordinary pilots. With the enormous importance of ensuring a successful launch in mind, the experienced soldier selected eight of his best pilots. After the group had departed, they headed for the front line and climbed to 3,000 metres. It was a matter of moments before they were spotted by an enemy patrol from the 24th *Sentai*. The opposing numbers were evenly matched. The Japanese identified the enemy as being old I-15bis (easy prey for the significantly faster Nakajimas), failing to note the lack of undercarriage. As if to reinforce the deception, Gritsavets turned west in apparent flight from battle. The deceptive manoeuvre succeeded. As the distance between the adversaries reduced sufficiently, the leader signalled for his 'Chaykas' to turn through 180 degrees and launch into the attack. The surprise was complete. Using the powerful fire of almost 100 shots a second, and the good horizontal manoeuvrability of the 'Chayka', the group downed two Japanese aircraft and forced the rest away.[175] The story that the 'Chaykas' had initially intentionally dropped their landing gear is a myth, for in such a configuration their engines would have overheated. Still, the victory was a fact confirmed by the Japanese, who described the new machine as the 'I-17'. In fact, the day's fighting saw formal recognition of only those two aircraft losses, while the Soviets officially confirmed the non-return of four I-16s to base.

Despite the good result from the first use of the new retractable-undercarriage biplane, it would be an exaggeration to say that the Japanese had been astonished. In fact, they rather considered the new type archaic due to its obsolescent configuration. Although they did not yet have precise data on the new Soviet weapon, they were clear on the fact that it could neither fly faster, nor higher, than Japanese fighters, and before long they had developed methods of effectively countering it. Thereafter the ban on Soviet I-153 pilots overflying the Mongolian border was lifted.

In fact, the ban was lifted for all Soviet aircrews that had hitherto been confined to Mongolian airspace. If anything, their regiments were oversupplied with men and machines, and this level of oversupply was actively maintained by logistics and by the operation's commanders. For the first time since the conflict's start, commanders actually faced the problem of being unable to utilise fully the potential of their aerial units due to the sheer narrowness of the front line and the limited tactical tasks they were undertaking. At the same time this fact played into the hands of Lt Gen Tetsuji Giga and the 2nd *Hiko Syudan* Staff. They could counter the numerically greater enemy with modest outlays of forces and money, and greater intensity of use. The analyses of the use of Soviet aviation since the start of hostilities led to a change in the operational aspect of its employment that made itself apparent within the next few days.

A great, though almost embarrassingly trivial, Soviet/Mongolian problem was the mosquito. The billions of incredibly large and aggressive insects were a true scourge that additionally depleted the threadbare nerves of pilots, technicians and staff officers alike. They were particularly irritating to active combatants who were barely able to rebuild their strength after flying missions. In order to ensure at least a couple of hours of proper sleep without the attentions of the mosquitoes, Soviet airfields began to literally blow them away by using the engines of stationary liaison Po-2s, with personnel meanwhile taking a blissful snooze.[176]

The operational change in the deployment of Soviet airmen came into effect on 27 July. For several days following this date, poor weather precluded large-scale air battles. However, the Soviet command had realised that it could hardly expect to win superiority in such set-piece combat. Yet again, Spanish Civil War experience came to the rescue. Spain had been the first theatre to see large numbers of fighters strike operational targets, mostly enemy airfields. Pairs and *aviozvenas* of fighters, mainly fast monoplanes, were accordingly sent to reconnoitre the locations and numbers of Japanese aircraft. The pilots successfully delivered the necessary information, proving the effectiveness of the new approach as regards recce. Then nine I-16s covered by ten similar machines sortied to storm Uhtin-Obo airfield, some 15km south-west of Gandjur-Miao[177], which was home to a Japanese *sentai* of some twenty fighters. As the strike began, the *sentai*'s machines were on the ground, facing the runway, and clearly not expecting any attack. The strike group of 'Ishaks' began a dive from some 1,000 metres, aiming not only at the lined-up silvery Nakajimas, but also at the fuel tanks behind them. After two approaches by each *aviozveno* and the expenditure of some 10,000 rounds, all aircraft returned to base unharmed. Reports mention four or five Ki-27s being left to burn on the ground.

The next day was calm, but overnight, the air was filled only with the roar of heavily laden TB-3s flying at 1,000 to 1,500 metres, whose crews were continuing the war of attrition. As a rule, they would depart from Obo-Somon airfield at between 17.00 and 18.00 in order to cross the front line as darkness fell. The selection of targets was such as to allow area bombing using munitions not larger then the FAB-100 (*Fugassnaya Aviobomba*). As noted above, these raids had more of a nuisance value than anything, yet the occasional direct hit did destroy some major enemy administrative targets at operational depth. At the same time, despite the fact that Japanese AAA crews proved disorganised and lacked coordination with searchlight commands, some bombers sustained hits. In order to provide for an emergency landing site, a searchlight-equipped airfield was set up between Tamsag-Bulak and Hamar-Daba Mount. In the event it remained unused, crews preferring to use the old airstrip at Obo-Somon that they could easily reach with an engine out. On 28 July the simultaneous failure of two engines brought down a TB-3. The *Komisar* of the 100th SABR, Kirillov, who had flown in the navigator's station, died, but all other ranks walked away.

On 29 July at dawn, the first to start up their engines were Major Grigoriy Kravchenko's 22nd IAP fighters. At 07.15 they struck the Japanese airfield of Alay, some 8km north of the Uzur-Nur Lake and 12km beyond the border.[178] The airfield was the main base of the 24th *Sentai* 1st *Chutai*, and aerial reconnaissance had showed nine fighters and five bombers based there. The strike involved three *eskadrily*, one of which comprised gun-equipped fighters, plus the command *aviozveno*, a total of twenty-seven I-16s of various marks.[179] The group approached at an extremely low altitude of 100-150 metres to avoid discovery, and the early hour added to the surprise. Meanwhile, Japanese crews at a nearby airfield hosting the 11th *Sentai* 1st *Chutai* were warming up their engines and were unable to assist. The two *eskadrily* and the command *aviozveno* climbed to 2,000 metres and struck from the direction of the sun, covered by eight I-16s that were also monitoring developments on the ground from 3,500 metres. After the first approach, a Ki-27 hit by gunfire blew up and began to burn fiercely. Three more approaches later, the Soviets decamped, only to return at 09.40, precisely as three Japanese machines were taxiing out while two more were running up to depart. The I-16P *eskadrilya* led by Mayor Kravchenko again approached at minimum height and again managed to surprise the Japanese[180], who hardly expected a follow-up raid. On the ground there was chaos, with fires being put out and efforts being made to restore order. This time the ten gun-equipped 'Ishaks' made six approaches. The gun rounds again showed great effectiveness and power, with overall enemy losses for the two raids amounting to ten aircraft burned on the ground, while the two approaching Ki-27s were downed. Despite their efforts to fight back, *Chutai* CO Capt Saiji Kani (nine victories)[181] and 2nd Lt Syoichi Suzuki (seventeen victories)[182] were killed. The 1st *Chutai* had had its potential cut in half.[183]

After the fighters, a group of twin-engined SB-2s departed for Nomon-Han-Burd-Obo, their target some army stores. Unharried by anyone, the bombers delivered their 100kg bombs, returning with no losses.

In the afternoon almost sixty pilots from the 1st and 11th *Sentais* tried to avenge the defeat suffered by the 24th *Sentai*. They conducted a fierce battle over the Khalkhin-Gol River, involving on the Soviet side 120 I-16s, I-15bis and I-153s. Several Japanese pilots pretended to be preparing to ram Soviet machines as a way of countering their numerical superiority, diving almost vertically through the ranks of Russian fighters. These daring manoeuvres managed to destroy the formation and coordination between the various Soviet units and flights, and events began to turn in favour of the Japanese. Cpl Jiro Higashi's shot down one enemy aircraft, cut the cords of the pilot's parachute with the wingtip of his aircraft as the latter baled out, then pursued and shot down another aircraft.[184]

A dramatic moment involved a dogfight between 1st *Sentai* leader Major Fumio Harada and St Lt Viktor Rakhov. The latter was a test pilot with no combat experience, who had nevertheless scored seven victories with the 22nd IAP, where he was appointed Deputy CO to Mayor Kravchenko. Soviet literature names Rakhov's opponent as 'Colonel Takeo' and injects a great dose of myth into the encounter. Both pilots demonstrated excellent handling and took their machines to the limit. 'Takeo's' aeroplane was hit and he baled out over Soviet/Mongolian-held territory; his attempt to kill himself was pre-empted by Red Army troops. Under interrogation, Harada asked VVS CO *Palk* Aleksandr Gusev if he could meet his opponent, and bowed to him as a sign of respect. A story by returning Japanese PoWs stated that Harada was shot dead for attempting to disarm his convoy in 1940. He was the third Japanese pilot to fail to return after the battle. Following Harada, Maj Tadashi Yoshida took command of the 1st *Sentai*. Japanese statistics claimed fifty-one (!) I-16 monoplanes for the loss of two Ki-27s. Another five Type 97s were badly hit and sent for repair.[185] The genuine number of downed Soviet aircraft was three, and Soviet dead included I-15bis pilot Lt Kralin, while I-16 pilots baling out included Suslov and Pavliuk.

The 'hot' month ended with an attempt by 9th *Hikodan* bombers to perform forty sorties on 30 July in revenge for the Soviet raids, hitting the Soviets' major Command Posts and forward airfields. Not facing any real opposition, the fighter *sentais* of Maj Gen Higashi's 12th *Hikodan* scored six victories for no loss. The following day, Soviet patrol activity was greater, and Soviet actions were mainly directed against Japanese fighter and reconnaissance aviation. Three brief dogfights brought four reported Soviet victories for no loss. Making up for this, Japanese AAA downed an SB-2 and forced two more to land with engine hits. This brought Japanese statistics to 386 destroyed Soviet aircraft over the brief period between 22 and 31 July. Confirmed Japanese losses came to forty-one aircraft, or three times more than in the previous month. Actual Soviet losses had also doubled, totalling seventy-nine aircraft in combat (thirty-nine I-16s, fifteen I-15bis, one I-153, and twenty-four SB-2s) plus nine non-combatants (two I-16s, four SB-2s, an I-15bis, an I-153 and a TB-3).[186]

Awaiting the green take-off flare: St Lt Viktor Rakhov in his I-16 tip 10. *(MoD Archives, Bulgaria)*

This Ki-27 fell victim to Viktor Rakhov. *(MoD Archives, Bulgaria)*

The July battles were mainly aimed at securing air superiority. Both sides understood that without it, their planned advance operations were doomed. Battles took place practically daily and called for dynamic air staff deployment. Commanders not only had to monitor the results of combat, but also to map any changes in the situation on the ground and in the air. For the latter task they could rely less and less on their old, all-wood R-5s. These were relegated to largely flying over their own territory, special tasks involving artillery direction, liaison and monitoring, and were banned from overflying the front line. Newly arrived (for field testing) R-10 reconnaissance monoplanes were almost 100kmph slower than Japanese fighters; crossing the border was also a great challenge for them and could lead to unnecessary losses. As well as not being sufficiently strong, they were also not fast enough.

Therefore, after a series of successful tests, Soviet aerial reconnaissance in Mongolia began to use specially trained SB-2 and I-16 tip 10 crews. On 1 August the latter type armed a specially formed reconnaissance *eskadrilya* led by *Kap* Borziak, who was assigned an area extending 200km over the front line, and 100km deep. This new recce initiative came under the microscope of the VVS Command Post at Hamar-Daba Mount. It was decided that the new unit would relocate to an airfield between the Command Point and the covering squadron led by St Lt Arseniy Vorozheykin, and within artillery range of forward Japanese positions.[187] The recce unit's main targets were to be the enemy's tactical and operational reserves, as well as the locations of their air grouping.

The latter was showing some concerted movement involving the relocation of thirty-three Ki-27s from the two *chutais* of the elite 64th *Sentai* from Canton to Haylar. The unit's pilots and their CO, Major Yatsuo Yokoyama, had a wealth of Chinese combat experience. In order for Lt Gen Tetsuji Giga to practically double his unit's clearly insufficient strike power, he also assumed command of the 31st and 16th *Sentais* with their twenty-nine Ki-30s.[188] Thus, the number of serviceable aircraft at the 2nd *Hiko Syudan* reached more than 200. However, Soviet aerial reconnaissance more than doubled this number in its reports. Zhukov's Staff officers were working with data showing 252 fighters plus 144 single-engined, and fifty-four twin-engined bombers.[189]

The Japanese also reconnoitred the situation actively. Their Ki-15 recce machines were practically uncatchable by Soviet fighters, being very fast. Their main enemy remained AAA and skilled ack-ack crews. Soviet patrols over set areas or close to the front line also failed to yield results. Lacking oxygen equipment (removed to save weight), they could not gather sufficient height to be able to catch the Japanese recce crews over Mongolia. This forced the Soviet command to keep relocating their false airfields and aircraft models.

Things were entirely different with regard to the Ki-36 tactical aerial reconnaissance aircraft. Even though very manoeuvrable, its performance

A 1st *Chutai* 64th *Sentai* Ki-27 on a patrol flight. *(MoD Archives, Bulgaria)*

was similar to that of the I-15bis, and it was usually supported by large groups of Japanese fighters. Lacking such escort, the type was usually a sitting duck, as shown below.

At 07.25 on 2 August, the Japanese base of the 15th *Sentai*, some 18km north-west of Djindjin-Sume, was the target of an air raid flown by the 70th IAP led by CO Major Vyacheslav Zabaluev. The strike group comprised twenty-three I-16s covered by nineteen other 'Ishaks'. Their approach remained unnoticed by the enemy, Zabaluev having gone around the target and come back at it from the south over Eris-Ulayn-Ubo Mount.[190] He then turned sharply north and went into the attack. The airfield, aircraft, personnel

A Ki-36 before a tactical recce mission. *(MoD Archives, Bulgaria)*

encampment and maintenance facility came under fire. The Japanese aircraft
were not dispersed, despite the more frequent Soviet raids, and from the air
they looked as if they were in a great circle, in the middle of which were the
accommodation tents and yurts. A tactical recce Ki-36 managed to scramble
into the air, piloted by CO Col Katsumi Abe, one of Japan's most experienced
aces. Despite his efforts and furious manoeuvres, and the diligence of his
gunner, the group of stumpy fighters easily shot down the lone adversary
before tackling its grounded brethren. Staff cars, crates, munitions and barrels
of fuel were easy prey. Each pilot began his attack individually, managing
some four or five strikes at various targets per pass. Individual pilots managed
to make up to eight dives, using more than 18,000 rounds. Reports claimed
twelve burning aircraft on the ground, of which four were brought down in
the act of scrambling, as well as cars and stores.[191] The strike groups were
protected from possible ambushes over the front line by *Kap* Yevgeniy
Stepanov's *eskadrilya*, which confirmed the claimed enemy losses.

    Attacks such as this claimed a great many Japanese victims – fighter pilots,
bomber crew members and ground personnel. Yet this did not prevent a single
Ki-21-Ia of the 61st *Sentai* raiding a forward I-16 Soviet airfield located close
to the front line that very afternoon. This hasty act did not bring the desired
result, nor did a raid by a small group of Ki-30s the following day. They tried
to raid build-ups of Soviet/Mongolian forces, but were intercepted and one
was downed by a patrolling pair of I-16s.

Soviet statistics show 3 August as the day of the next aerial ramming, this time by 56th IAP *eskadrilya* CO *Kap* Viktor Kustov. He attacked some twenty enemy aircraft, assumed to have been Fiat BR.20s (in fact, they cannot have been more than twelve, and were most likely Ki-21-Ias, being the sole twin-engined Japanese bombers under Lt Gen Giga's command). His quarries were escorted by a large number of Ki-27 fighters. The fight was exceptionally fierce. Furious fire by the bombers' gunners repelled Kustov's first attack and those of the handful of Soviet pilots who had managed to steal through the Japanese fighter escort. Kustov's I-16 then began behaving erratically, suggesting beyond doubt that he was wounded. The Spanish air ace's second attack was on the leader's Fiat (or Ki-21-Ia). Then his guns and machine guns stopped firing and his wingmen realised that he was out of ammunition. Viktor went on to sweep his wing through the bomb-laden Japanese machine's tail. The bomber went into a dive and crashed into the swampy banks of the river that marked the front line. *Kap* Kustov himself also perished.[192]

Soviet raids over the days to come were less successful. Regardless of the deceptive manoeuvres they employed, they invariably found Japanese airfields empty, their fighters airborne and ready to attack. On the early morning of 4 August, the 2nd *Hiko Syudan* successfully fled a raid, going on to bomb enemy positions along the front line, while Ki-27 escorts intercepted returning Soviet groups and claimed seven victories. A successive clash over Hamar-Daba Mount was initiated by an I-16 *eskadrilya* from the 22nd IAP.[193] Regardless of losses by both sides (Soviet pilots' claims include eight downed Japanese machines), the engagement grew fiercer. WO Muneyoshi Motojima (sixteen victories) was shot down and killed.[194] Lt Col Kojiro Matsumura was hit and his aircraft set on fire; he force-landed in hostile territory, seriously burned. M Sgt Goro Nishihara immediately landed alongside the blazing debris of his CO's Ki-27, pulled the unconscious pilot out of the cockpit and transferred him to his own aircraft, flying him safely back to base.[195]

Lt Aleksandr Moshin used up all his ammunition to down an enemy fighter. Yet, instead of leaving the engagement, he launched into a pursuit of a Ki-27. 11th *Sentai* 2nd *Chutai* pilot M Sgt Tokuyasu Ishizuka simulated a fall to flee, but his pursuer was tenacious. The two fighters flew at minimum heights and top speeds; the I-16 now had the upper hand. Having settled on a ramming, Moshin merely revved his engine and sliced off part of his adversary's tailplane and rudder with his prop. The uncontrollable Ki-27 crashed and burned, while Moshin managed to land nearby. The mechanics needed just 2 hours to change his damaged propeller and return his aeroplane to service. M Sgt Ishizuka, thrown out of the cockpit by the impact, managed to open his parachute just before reaching the ground, landing on the west bank of the Khalkhin-Gol River. He was found unconscious on the east bank by a Japanese patrol on the morning of the 9th. After a few days' rest he returned to his unit.[196] The Japanese fighter was the Soviet's 116th aerial victory since 23 July.[197]

This did not close this exceptional chapter in Soviet military history. Together with the fighters, the 150th SPAB saw some action, its fast bombers raiding enemy reserves and ammunition depots in the rear close to Halin-Arshaan. Having delivered the strike and while turning back, group leader *Komisar* Mikhail Yuyukin was hit by two ack-ack rounds. His fuel tanks exploded, together with an engine. Attempting to extinguish the flames, Yuyukin slip-dived unsuccessfully. He then ordered the crew to bale out, but only the navigator managed to do so. The *Komisar* aimed his doomed machine into an ammunition dump and perished in the explosion, together with his gunner. This was one of history's first 'fire ram raids'.[198]

On 5 August the VVS again tried to surprise Japanese units at their forward airfields, leading to new large-scale battles. A long time before dawn, the 1st and 11th *Sentais* managed to scramble and meet the nearly sixty approaching I-16s. As usual, the combat formation fell apart into a number of individual dogfights, which allowed the Japanese to claim their usual large number of victories (twenty-seven this time) for jus two Ki-27s lost. The 24th *Sentai* fighters organised a high-altitude patrol and engaged another formation of ten SB-2s escorted by fifteen I-153s.[199] The 'Chaykas' were flown by Major Sergey Gritsavets's aces, led by himself, and they managed to repel the Japanese attack. The Soviets claimed five downed enemy aircraft. An I-153 that the enemy misrecognised as an I-15bis also fled the fight in a dive, leaving a thin silvery trail. The downed 'Chayka' was flown by St Lt Viktor Rulin on his first combat sortie. He landed on friendly territory with a broken petrol pipe and, after a field repair, his machine returned to the ranks. The sole Japanese victory admitted by the Soviets in these two dogfights was a single I-16, while the Japanese confirmed losing two fighters, one of them piloted by ace WO Taro Kobayashi (ten victories).

The same period in early August saw a meeting at the office of Second Degree *Komandarm* Grigoriy Shtern at which *Kap* Nikolay Zvonarev, CO of a special assignments group, was present. After a short discussion, the meeting resolved that on 5 August five I-16 pilots would ferry five fighters, fitted not only with machine guns but also six 82mm missiles, from Chita to a 22nd IAP airfield and report for duty to the airfield Command Post.[200] A number of 'Chaykas' led by *Palk* Kuznetsov would also ferry to the same airfield on the same day. There were arguments among the flying ranks as to which machine was the more manoeuvrable. The two COs – Kuznetsov and Kravchenko – decided to demonstrate their mounts in mock dogfights. The new retractable-undercarriage biplane lacked the aforementioned automatically feathering propeller and could not withstand significant g-load for long, thus 'stretching out' its manoeuvres. Kravchenko came out top in both mock dogfights, being in firing position after two or three turns and proving that the new aeroplane was not yet fully developed.[201] Despite this, the relatively new 'Chaykas' were entrusted with providing reliable cover for the missile *aviozveno*. The crews of both were forbidden upon pain of death to cross the front line or pursue adversaries beyond it. Thus, for the first time since the Great War, which saw unguided missiles used on the Western Front, it was the Khalkhin-Gol River that saw the return of missiles. The weapons themselves were designed by Korolev, who was subsequently to attain world fame as a spacecraft designer. It was now due for its field trials.

A sharp worsening of weather over the Nomonhan Plateau on 6 August forced the adversaries to limit their aerial activity. A day later, Soviet fighter regiments again tried to surprise the 2nd *Hiko Syudan* on the ground, again by flying in at low level. Initially luck was on their side, with cloud failing to obscure all landmarks. The sixty I-16s were aiming for military targets in and around the major Japanese base in Manchuria, the city of Haylar. Ultimately, the surprise was lost due to the appearance of 11th *Sentai* fighters, led by Capt Taniguchi. The group of 'Ishaks' abandoned its initial intentions and attempted to decamp, but M Sgt Daisuke Kanbara nevertheless managed to catch and shoot a lagging I-16. Seeing his victim descend and land on friendly territory, he did the same, jumped clear of his cockpit, caught the Russian pilot and cut him dead with a blow of his samurai sword. He then hastened to depart and claim his ninth victory (plus three probables).[202] M Sgt Saburo Kimura shot down one enemy fighter, but was hit in the left thigh. Initially he lost consciousness, but recovered sufficiently to staunch the bleeding and fly back to base.[203]

In revenge for the previous day's attempted raid, on 8 August, despite poor weather, Ki-30s flew twenty-three sorties against enemy positions. On 12 August twenty-two bombers from the same units supported an attack by a Japanese infantry regiment, reinforced with artillery and light tanks, on a Mongolian cavalry unit. This put an end to the lull in the air.[204] The successful supporting raid failed to change the overall trend towards a worsening of the Japanese position in the air. To confirm this, an air battle ensued between 137 Soviet I-16s from all three air regiments. The encounter featured the serial inclusion of groups of ten to twenty Japanese fighters, whose numbers rose to sixty-odd, but was insufficient to ensure success for the tactical task of taking the battle east, over Japanese-held territory, and defeating the enemy there. Instead, the contest took place largely over the VVS Command Post at Hamar-Daba Mount. It resulted, according to Soviet data, in the loss of eleven Ki-27s and two I-16s. Japanese sources claim no losses, but death certificates show the demise of Imperial aces WO Masao Ashida (thirteen victories) and Sgt Jiro Okuda, who had claimed fourteen victories in happier days.[205]

The close of July and early August saw a considerable reduction in the effectiveness of Japanese aerial activity at Nomon-Han-Burd-Obo, an indicator that mostly affected fighter *sentais*. Not only did the number of victories in aerial combat fall, but their own losses grew, and many of the best pilots fell in combat or were wounded. Two *sentai* and two *chutai* COs were among the lists of dead or missing in action, while the COs of a further three *sentais* and two *chutais* COs were wounded and retired from action. The survivors were physically and psychologically fatigued and were ever less combat-ready amid conditions that called for intensive flying and challenging tasks. Their mounts were also much fatigued, and the percentage of airworthy aircraft fell with each passing day. In the first week of August the number of Ki-27s available to the Japanese allowed less than 5 hours' daylight flying. Overall Japanese losses between 21 July and 8 August totalled 173 aircraft, of which 161 were fighters, and a static balloon. For the same period the Soviets admitted fifty-three combat losses plus eight aircraft lost outside combat. Though Japanese losses are certainly greatly inflated, it was a fact that they were heavy and enforced a serious limitation on sorties. The activity of Japanese aviation was limited to striking the Soviets' main bridge crossing, artillery positions, and their tactical reserves.

A major reason for this situation was the continuing and systematic Soviet raids on forward Japanese airfields. These strikes brought additional and unexpected tension to the daily lives of the Japanese *sentais*. There was practically no relaxation time for flyers and ground personnel; nobody could be certain when and where the enemy would appear. Meanwhile, Soviet air strikes became ever more massive, gun-armed I-16Ps being particularly effective. Nothing could stand in their way. Their sudden and surprising appearance at low level, combined with adequate manoeuvrability and great firing power, paralysed Japanese fighter cover. Even if covering fighters managed to get airborne, they were easy targets for the attackers. Japanese anti-aircraft gunnery on the approaches to airfields countered the raids using different firing patterns, but its effect was minimal, for the I-16 was a tiny, rapidly moving target.

Another major reason was the considerable tension of aerial combat, which had continued for much longer than Japanese planners had planned for. The 2nd *Hiko Syudan*, as well as all other Japanese air units, suffered from a chronic shortage of trained pilots who could be rotated for personnel in action. At the very outset of the Mongolian campaign, the Japanese numerical inferiority in the air had caused some stress among crews, and this further increased fatigue. Also, pressed by the China war, the *Kantogun* was forced to reject instructions from above to conduct routine personnel rotation, the only way in which the 2nd *Hiko Syudan* could have replenished its physical strength. The sole exception was the 61st *Sentai*, which was detailed for rest and recuperation to Chinchinhar on 5 August. The departure of its 'heavy' bombers did not affect the situation at the front during the calm that preceded future decisive advances. Such action continued to be planned in the staffs on both sides of the front line.

For their part, Soviet commanders also learned the necessary lessons from the initial months of hostilities and continued to study combat experience. They paid particular attention to discipline in maintaining formation order, inasmuch as it was possible to maintain it in fast-moving air combat. The Soviet fighter presence at high altitude became visibly greater, with new fighters coming on strength with their oxygen equipment intact. Having mastered rapid firing at high speed in their I-16 monoplanes and their new I-153 biplanes, 'hit and run' became a favourite tactic, bringing success and guarding against repeats of the senseless losses of May and June. Bomber crews also changed basic tactics. This was helped by the formation on 13 August of the 100th SBABR (*Skorostnaya Bombardirovachnaya Aviobrigada*, or Fast Bomber Air Brigade).[206] The SB-2s now flew in large formations at heights of more than 6,000 metres. This often allowed them to deliver their bomb loads unchallenged and return unpunished before any Ki-27 could climb to their level. The sole Japanese method of countering the Soviet bomber threat was to maintain constant fighter patrols at high altitudes. However, this was rather too challenging for their fatigued pilots and insufficient number of suitable fighters. Moreover, the latest types of the I-16 were significantly more dangerous to the Ki-27 – their improved performance, 9mm seat armour and protected fuel tanks rendered them safe against the Japanese 7.7mm rounds. Their pilots were also more skilled, meaning that significantly greater Japanese effort and expenditure had to go into each successive victory against an enemy machine.

The middle of August was exceptionally unfavourable for flying. It rained heavily for days on end. Each interlude between downpours was marked by evaporation that cut visibility greatly. This continued for almost a week, with the sky remaining silent. The silence was deceptive, however, as both sides pondered the coming offensives. At this juncture, far from the remote and godforsaken corner that was the theatre of war, the Governments of the USSR and Japan attempted to find a negotiated end to the conflict, with Shigenori Togo meeting Soviet Foreign Minister Vyacheslav Molotov in Moscow.

Despite these efforts, the *Kantogun* Staff had no intention of dropping their search for a rapid victory. The concept developed by Japanese Sixth Army CO Lt Gen Ogisu Rippei was for a general advance to be prepared by 24 August with a view to encircling and routing the Soviet/Mongolian forces in the swampy valley of the Khalastin-Gol River. Without coordinating this in advance with Tokyo, by mid-August the Japanese command began to concentrate fresh forces for the new land advance. Slated for the battle were 500 heavy guns, 180 armoured machines and 75,000 troops.[207] Japanese aviation was brought to readiness, replenished, and concentrated on ten major airfields. The lull in fighting offered a chance for recreation and planning. As early as 7 August, Lt Gen Giga was discussing with his subordinates a massed raid on Soviet operational airfields on the model of the 27 June strike. The plan entered the detail stage as the rains began, and 18 August saw an order being sent to *sentai* COs to bring their units up to readiness for 'Operation S'. A little later, its commencement was announced for 21 August. On hand were eight *sentais* with 145 combat aircraft, comprising eighty-eight fighters, twenty-four light bombers, twelve heavy bombers, and twenty-one reconnaissance aircraft. The latter's crews used the slightest improvements in the weather to reconnoitre the locations and numbers of Soviet aircraft.

The Joint VVS and Land Forces Command Post at Hamar-Daba Mount was witnessing similar events. *Kap* Yevgeniy Stepanov's *eskadrilya* spent five days and nights on No 1 Alert beneath the Command Post of Point 91 (the codename of an ambush airfield). His pilots did not scramble only because of the awful weather. The same airfield hosted an *aviozveno* of recce I-16s subordinated by the VVS reconnaissance *eskadrilya*. However, photographic recce for operational planning was mainly the province of the SB-2.[208] Soviet command, relying mainly on aerial photography to determine enemy locations and numbers.

Amid this tense atmosphere, the Mongolian People's Hural awarded orders to a large number of Soviet airmen.[209] They were decorated personally by Marshal Horolgiyn Choybalsan on 18 August in honour of the USSR Aerial Fleet Day. The ceremony was held at the 22nd IAP base airfield and ended with an air parade involving eighty-five I-16s and I-153s, which also went on to cross the front line so as to demonstrate their might to an enemy who could expect to feel it within a few days. Moreover, the I-153 group led by Mayor Aleksandr Nikolaev performed aerobatics, with the astounded Japanese watching in disbelief and not daring to challenge this daring show of strength.[210]

The evening before the celebration, the regimental COs and *Komisars* were summoned to the VVS Staff Command Post at Tamsag-Bulak, housed in three deep and well-equipped trenches. The wall was hung with charts showing the all-too-familiar pattern of the front for the day. What was new were the red arrows indicating the planned strikes by Soviet land and air forces.[211] Their targets were also clearly highlighted. Second Degree *Komandarm* Grigoriy Shtern began with a situation report, then announced the coming Soviet offensive, planned for 20 August. Its aim was to deliver a pre-emptive blow to the Japanese Sixth Army on Mongolian soil, in advance of the planned Japanese offensive on 24 August. Komandarm Shtern's announcement made it clear that aviation was to strike first; thereafter it would support the three Army groupings commanded by *Komkor* Georgiy Zhukov. The newly formed 1st AG had already put its 57,000 troops, 438 tanks, 385 armoured cars and 542 guns in place. Their numbers were superior to those of the enemy by 1.5:1 in infantry, 1.7:1 in machine guns, 2:1 in guns, 4:1 in tanks, and 3.6:1 in aircraft. Particular attention was paid to the need to ensure close cooperation between the different services.[212]

The latest data on the situation in the air and on enemy air strength was reported by 1st AG Aviation CO *Palk* Aleksandr Gusev. The tasks before the airmen were set out by *Komkor* Yakov Smushkevich, the man directly responsible for the air offensive. Also read was Moscow's Order No 0068 of 17 August 1939[213], which instructed the VVS grouping to deliver, before the end of the artillery's 'softening up' process, strikes along the enemy's main defensive axis and on his tactical reserves. On the basis of these tasks, a thorough plan detailed the sequence of force deployment for attaining the set objectives. Participants in the meeting were expressly forbidden from entering any information on their maps, and were instead asked to memorise everything. Any notes taken were to be of a general character. To ensure secrecy, it was decided that squadron leaders would be advised of their objectives only 3 hours prior to going into action.[214]

VVS personnel numbers in early August grew apace alongside the more than 200 newly delivered aircraft. The force comprised three fighter air regiments (the 22nd, 56th and 70th), an airfield cover element of 244 I-16s, sixty-two I-15bis and seventy I-153s, and a fast bomber brigade with 181 SB-2 medium bombers of various marks.[215] Alongside them were twenty-three heavy TB-3 bombers. Soviet and Mongolian special aviation forces comprised forty-three light bombers, and recce and liaison U-2s, R-5s, R-5Shs and R-10s.[216] The grand total of 623 aircraft (of which 580 were combat types) was dispersed between the sixty-three base, forward, reserve, ambush and dummy airfields built by Soviet engineer forces. These fields also hosted the 8th and 32nd IAP units that retained their reserve status until the conflict's end, not taking part in combat and not being included in Soviet command force reckonings.

As the air grouping grew, so did the challenges of its logistics back-up. Some 650-700km of unmetalled roads witnessed day and night supplies of fuel, lubricants and ammunition. Against an establishment of 4,900 vehicles, the 1st AG initially had a mere 2,636 serviceable vehicles. After 14 August they were joined by another 1,250 vehicles and 375 tanker trucks, which delivered more than 6,500 tonnes of ammunition, 7,500 tonnes of aviation fuel and 4,000 tonnes of food supplies to stores. The 1st AG VVS had reckoned on ten sets of ammunition and fifteen refuellings per aeroplane.

All these Soviet measures were undertaken amid strict secrecy.[217] The purpose was for the enemy not to become aware of anything unusual or that suggested preparations for an offensive. Every movement involved in the regrouping and concentration of the twenty Soviet and Mongolian units took place under cover of darkness, in full blackout, radio silence, smokescreens, the roar of TB-3s, or sound effects propagated by loudspeakers.[218]

On the eve of 'VVS Day' and under cover of secrecy, few noted the 16 August relocation of *Kap* Zvonarev's missile *aviozveno* of five aircraft to a forward airfield. In order for it to be covered, the best-prepared 'Chayka' *eskadrilya*, led by ace Major Aleksandr Nikolaev, also relocated to the same airfield. The latter was ordered not to let a single missile fighter fall; they were to stay away from dogfights, and flee the area immediately after firing their unguided missiles. An early recognition feature of the missile machines was the broad unpainted stripe along their fuselages. (Later, the Japanese used this to good effect and pursued them doggedly in the air. Zvonarev barely limped away from a dogfight with

Air force ratios in the Nomonhan area on 20 August 1939

Aircraft	USSR	Japan	Aircraft ratio	Combat potential ratio
Fighters	376	88	4.27:1	2.69:1
Bombers	204	36	5.66:1	6.12:1
Reconnaissance	43	21	2:1	1.36:1
Overall	623	145	4.29:1/3.98:1	3.39:1

forty hits. The recognition band was accordingly introduced on other types, while the missile carriers gained a second number on their rudders.[219])

It was only on the afternoon of 19 August, as if to reinforce the palpable tension, that twenty-five I-16s from the 22nd IAP used the improved weather to overfly the front line at low heights and deliver a surprise strike against the base of the 64th *Sentai*, leaving two Ki-27s burning. On the same day, SB-2s bombed Halun-Arshaan railway station, which marshalled the majority of Japanese logistics supplies. One bomber crew failed to return to base.[220]

The 1st Army Group's Air Component Command in a tent at Hamar-Daba. *(MoD Archives, Bulgaria)*

For its part, the Kwantung Army also tried to increase its air component in advance of its planned 24 August offensive.[221] Japanese deployment lagged behind that of the Soviets, yet 15 August saw air units moved to forward airfields close to the Mongolian/Manchurian border. Two days later their crews flew over the future combat areas. Overall, the VVS RKKA forces in the region continued to enjoy an almost threefold numerical superiority over the Japanese air grouping. This was particularly evident as regards strike aircraft, indicating the significantly more ambitious aims that *Komkor* Zhukov's Staff had set itself.[222] Even though in July and the first ten days of August, Japanese statistics claimed 515 Soviet aircraft destroyed for the loss of just sixty-four of its own[223], things were now moving towards a new operational plane, with differing potentials. Naturally, Soviet losses were greatly inflated by the Japanese and the claims had more of a propaganda nature (for instance, as regards July, actual Soviet losses were eighty-eight against the Japanese claims of 481, or a five-fold inflation). Moreover, the Soviets were not only able to make up for their losses, but also to boost the air grouping in the theatre to new highs. The same could not be said of the Japanese. The loss of fighters over China and in the Nomonhan conflict had exceeded the abilities of the Imperial aircraft industry. Also, whereas the hardware shortage could be made up given a lull, trained personnel shortages continued to be a serious problem for the Japanese armed forces. Between the start of aerial combat over eastern Mongolia and early August, some forty-four pilots had perished, with seventeen more wounded. That month's first days saw eight more deaths and seven pilots invalided out. Seven out of every ten of these airmen had more than 1,000 flying hours' experience, with many of them having more than 2,000 hours in the air, the result of not less than three or four years in genuine combat. The period saw more than 80 per cent of *chutai* leaders leave the ranks, thus threatening the very fabric of military air command. The average daily combat-hour age of each Japanese pilot was some 6.5 hours, with the lack of rotation bringing with it a series of health complaints – back pains, disturbed sleep, watery eyes, and breathing difficulties for reconnaissance pilots forced to fly at great heights. The physical and psychological exhaustion also told on senior commanders. Col Katsumi Abe was killed on 2 August and 24th *Sentai* CO Lt Col Kojiro Matsumura, an enigmatic personality who had led Japanese fighter action in the region since the very start of hostilities[224], was badly wounded in combat with Soviet Spanish aces. These losses marked the beginning of a change in the air situation, as well as in the conflict as a whole. Henceforth, the Spanish Civil War maxim that whoever controlled the sky would also control the world come to exert a strengthening grip on events.

6

The closing battles

On 20 August most forward Soviet airfields were covered in thick fog, yet the war machine set to work. The crews had their readiness instructions. If they departed with the weather unchanged, the first wave to strike main or secondary targets would navigate by reference to the Hamar-Daba Command Post. The area above the point was codenamed '*Kvadrat 623-B*.[225]'. To the relief of Soviet commanders, however, as the sun rose it evaporated the dew enveloping the ground. The first wave of Soviet strike aircraft made for the enemy's defences on the eastern bank of the Khalkhin-Gol River, its task to knock out the enemy's anti-aircraft defences. Nine fast bombers neared the front line at medium height. Japanese ack-ack batteries fired up furiously, giving away their positions without realising they had been set up. The three SB *aviozvena* (nine aircraft) approached from various directions at 2,200 metres, released their bombs and banked gently left and back, leaving the sky to forty-six I-16s of the 22nd and 70th IAPs. The latter unit's nine fighters flew the highest, being the escort group. Eleven 'Ishaks' were also armed with small bombs. Together with the twenty-six gun-equipped monoplanes, they comprised the basis of the strike groups flying at low level.[226] Having sighted the firing Japanese AAA, the Soviet pilots began their methodical extermination.

The offensive's beginning saw layer upon layer of Soviet aircraft massing from the west for the great air raid that largely underpinned the operation. As the 150 SBs from the three fast bomber regiments, led by Heroes of the Soviet Union *Palk* Vladimir Shevchenko and *Palk* Ivan Dushkin, neared the Khalkhin-Gol River at between 4,000 and 5,000 metres, the Soviet heavy artillery opened up. This was the signal for the pilots of the 22nd IAP to end their strike and decamp to a covered zone. Thus the entire airspace was under the control of the 144 fighters of the 22nd, 56th and 70th IAPs. At 05.45 the strike upon major Japanese defensive targets began at tactical depth, along the southern and northern banks of the Khalastin-Gol River, near the Uzur-Nur Lake and Djindjin-Sume. Fire was directed by signal flares, yellows allowing artillery officers to fire, greens prompting action from the air, and reds stopping fire. The softening-up continued for 2 hours without any Japanese air support being noted. Close coordination between artillery and air crews improved precision significantly and wrought heavy damage on the Sixth Army defences. All Soviet aircraft returned to base.[227] After filing sortie reports, the crews breakfasted, then preparing for the next massed strike.

The Soviet air armada reappeared over the Khalastin-Gol River at 08.45. It comprised fifty-two fast bombers and 167 escort fighters from the 22nd and 70th IAPs.[228] Artillery fire intensified again, stopping dead seconds before 09.00, the time set for the attack. Advancing under the strains of the *Internationale*, Soviet and Mongolian infantry units were covered and advised by the coordinated action of strike and reconnaissance aircraft. Hamar-Daba Mount marked the basic air patrol zone, as well as providing a navigational fix for overflying aircraft. Artillery and air fire was also directed from there by means of terrain models. The lack of radio forced the VVS Command Post to direct its fighters using massive 20-metre-long arrows made of white cloth. Thought primitive, this helped amid the emerging aerial confrontation. This had begun at 08.20, 4,000 metres over Bain-Tsagan Mount, where sixty-four I-16 and twelve I-153 fighters encountered a number of Ki-27s, downing two of them. At 09.10, at 3,500 metres over the Dungur-Obo region, twenty-three Soviet and thirty Japanese monoplane fighters also fought, with the same result. However, this time several Japanese machines made it through to the second Soviet bomber wave and attacked it straight in, constantly pursued by a significantly stronger adversary. Three SBs were damaged; one took 500 hits and returned to base with an engine emitting thick smoke.[229] Another's main undercarriage was hit, giving way upon landing. Yet no strike force crews were lost. The battle was also joined by six pilots from *Kap* Borziak's recce *eskadrilya*, the unit then resuming the use of its 'Ishaks' for their intended task of tactical aerial reconnaissance. Some missions betrayed pilot ignorance of their own and the enemy's machines. Soviet commanders had acknowledged this widespread weakness for some time. This time it led to the downing of an SB-2 that an I-16 patrol had mistaken for a Ki-21.[230]

The Japanese also tried to deliver an air strike. At 09.30 a small group of Ki-30s penetrated to a tactical depth and bombed a forward airfield. They released thirty-six 50kg bombs, destroying (according to their crews' claims) twelve of the seventeen aircraft on the airfield. The claim has not been substantiated, but what is beyond doubt is that the I-16s that responded rapidly cooled the raiders' enthusiasm, chasing them away.[231]

The Soviet fighters' success in countering enemy action allowed the strike air unit to cover the land force advance by bombing Japanese regiments in their trenches, their artillery emplacements, and their rail echelons. Thus at 11.30 three groups, each of nine SB-2s, delivered their deadly loads near the Uzur-Nur Lake, while at 12.30 two groups of nine bombers each bombed Halun-Arshaan railway station. Further raids followed at 14.45, 15.45 and 17.20 near Nomon-Han-Burd-Obo.[232]

The lack of an active opposition in the air allowed the use of fighters for ground strikes. Between 11.00 and 13.00 Djindjin-Sume and Halun-Arshaan saw waves of thirty-two I-16s strafe Japanese/Manchurian forces. At 16.20 fifteen I-16s, covered by another five Soviet monoplanes, attacked the airfield near Djindjin-Sume, which hosted thirty-seven 64th *Sentai* fighters and a Douglas transport. The half-hour raid resulted in the reported destruction of six Ki-27s on the ground, together with the lone twin and another six fighters that were left burning. The two duty Ki-27s were downed while attempting to scramble. After the raid, the Japanese unit had to relocate to an airfield further away from the front line.[233]

Nakajima Ki-27 fighters from the 64th *Sentai* at a forward airfield. *(MoD Archives, Bulgaria)*

At 16.30 a group of Japanese aircraft numbering some forty Ki-27s from the 11th *Sentai* and ten escorting Ki-21-Ias from the newly returned 61st *Sentai* were sighted. Their objective was immediately clear, for they were heading long and straight for the Hamar-Daba Command Post. They were intercepted by twenty-three I-16s and eleven I-153 'Chaykas' led by Major Aleksandr Nikolaev, all from the 22nd IAP. The group also had within it the first RS-82 missile-armed I-16 tip 10s, which were undergoing Army trials.[234] Their test pilots had fired the first missiles at their Moscow base barely a month earlier, and were now faced with the task of firing their 82mm unguided ordnance from rail pylons beneath both wings. This was their third combat sortie, and the first with the new ordnance fitted. The air battle began at 5,000 metres, gradually dropping to 2,000 metres. The latter level also saw the first missile attack: from a range of about a kilometre, all the missiles were fired at the Japanese with the aircraft in combat formation. According to pilots' reports, two Ki-27s were hit by the missiles, falling apart in mid-air. The gruesome spectacle forced the other Hinomaru-emblazoned fighters to flee towards Halun-Arshaan and Djindjin-Sume. Their pursuit saw Soviet pilots claim three more victories – neither corroborated nor denied by Japanese archives. Incidentally, it is worth mentioning that over the entire length of its service, the missile unit fought fourteen battles and downed thirteen enemy aircraft (ten Ki-27s, two Ki-21s and a Ki-4) for no loss. The effectiveness of the new weapon was deemed sufficient to put it into production. Reports noted that aerial combat simply ended once the fiery arrows scored a hit. However, logic dictated that this happened rarely due to the great course divergence (10 metres for every 100 metres travelled) and the difficulty of judging range, a critical judgement in view of the requirement to set the detonator to go off at a set time after launch.

Moreover, with shrapnel danger limited to within a 6-7-metre radius of the explosion, scoring a victory was a matter of chance. Thus, the effect of the new ordnance was more psychological than physical.[235]

The 'heavy' bombers made use of the fighters' absence to drop seventy-seven 100kg bombs on a forward Soviet airfield, land forces and combat equipment near the main bridge across the Khalkhin-Gol River. They flew amid strong anti-aircraft fire by forty 76mm guns, which were particularly precise at heights of 7,000 or 8,000 metres. Soviet fighters took over outside their fire cover. A bomber was damaged, while the gunners of other machines claimed to have downed thirty-two Soviet fighters.[236] This fantastical claim remains unconfirmed.

By escalating their effort, the *sentais* continued to counter the Soviet aerial offensive until the day's close, reporting thirty-five victories (two SB-2s and thirty-three fighters) for no loss. M Sgt Bunji Yoshiyama again showed initiative in a dogfight. After damaging an I-16 with his machine guns, he launched into a pursuit of it, only to run out of ammunition. He then landed alongside the Soviet plane, shot its pilot dead with his side arm, took his TT pistol and watch, and successfully returned to base.[237]

Japanese air strikes became more intensive in the second half of the day. Single-engined Ki-30s dropped a total of 183 50kg bombs, mostly against enemy Command Posts and airfields. Their reliable escort precluded any encounters with I-16s or 'Chaykas'.

Soviet data on the results of the day's aerial combat differ significantly from Japanese ones. Sorties numbered 1,094 – 350 by bombers and 744 by fighters. The latter, for five losses, scored sixteen victories on the ground and in the air (fifteen of these being Ki-27s). Ten victories were scored by the elite 22nd IAP.[238] Regardless of the great differences in the two sides' statistics, two major conclusions emerge: that the intensity of the confrontation in the air reached levels beyond the Japanese abilities, and that as a result of this Japan lost the operational initiative. This much is admitted in his memoirs by the then new CO of the 24th *Sentai*, Major Hidemi Yuzuhara. These results were obtained by significantly better coordination and massing by the Soviets. They also influenced events on the ground.

The start of the land offensive found the Japanese forces along the Khalkhin-Gol River not operationally ready to oppose the large-scale action dictated by *Komkor* Georgiy Zhukov. They had not completed their regrouping and force concentration in advance of their planned 24 August offensive. Crushed by artillery fire and an avalanche of tanks and armoured cars not yet encountered in military history, their defences began to give. Acting as planned, the much more mobile and mechanised Mongolian and Soviet forces went around the Japanese flanks to the north and south, gradually encircling the 80km front.

Covering the advance of its armies, Soviet aviation continued to hold on to its air superiority in the days to come, regardless of efforts by Lt Gen Tetsuji Giga and his Staff to change the course of events. The Japanese again relied on sudden air strikes against major Soviet air bases and control points. The air operation had been planned in early August and was cleared by a special Tokyo message on 7 August. The objective called for the involvement of some 70 per cent of airworthy aircraft, and for the best crews.[239] The rest were placed on operational standby.

At 02.30 on 21 August, the 16th *Sentai* was placed on a higher state of alert. Two hours later the first six Ki-30s departed, setting off to escort some forty fighters to the central area of the front and crossing the front line at 05.00. The pilots attempted to find their targets, but the dawn light was insufficient for target identification, and the strike group dropped its bombs on what it presumed were runways close to the VVS Command Post at Hamar-Daba. Time did not allow scope for any more action, for fifty-four I-16s and ten I-153 'Chaykas' had intercepted them. The battle went on for about an hour at heights of between 3,000 and 3,500 metres. Two Ki-30 Type 97 bombers were shot down.[240]

As the Soviet fighters returned to base, the second Japanese strike wave arrived – six Ki-30s from the 10th *Sentai*. This time visibility had improved, allowing them to identify ten twin-engined SBs at an airfield near Tamsag-Bulak. They dived over six of their targets, setting two alight.[241] Their escort did not encounter enemy aircraft, the raid being harried solely by ground fire. On their retreat, the bomber crews passed several recce Ki-36s that were going

Members of a Ki-30 crew before a mission. *(MoD Archives, Bulgaria)*

to reconnoitre the state of major enemy targets prior to the decisive effort by the main Japanese air force. The recce machines were in action by 07.00, and spotted a significant number of Soviet aircraft at forward airfields. This moment saw the start of constantly escalating aerial confrontation, against a backdrop of fierce fighting on the ground, where the 6th TBR had entered the fray in pursuit of its objective of encircling the Japanese forces.

At 08.30 fifty-two I-16s and some forty Ki-27s clashed 2,000 metres over Dungur-Obo, both groupings having been sent to clear the airspace. The fighting lasted about an hour, after which the remains of three Japanese fighters were left burning on the ground.[242] However, the peak of this action was yet to come, in the form of a proper air battle. The Japanese raid had found the Soviet observation and reporting system in a state of incomplete readiness. The twenty-four Ki-30s from the 10th *Sentai*, twelve Ki-21-Ias from the 61st *Sentai*, and fifteen Ki-36s from the 15th *Sentai*, covered by 12th *Hikodan* fighters (eighty-eight Ki-27s from the 1st, 11th and 64th *Sentais*)[243], approached the front line at 4,500 to 5,000 metres. Thereafter they cut their engines to idle and glided to reach their targets near Tamsag-Bulak at 3,500 metres. The mission had two objectives: to counter VVS action, and to support the Japanese land forces. Several targets were designated, including operational airfields near Tamsag-Bulak, army columns and artillery emplacements. Groups of between six and eight bombers were assigned to each target. This fragmented the attention of AAA and that of the 123 I-16s, fifty-one I-153s and thirty I-15bis that were already airborne. At 10.00 local time, six light bombers from the 10th *Sentai* arrived over a field airstrip north of Tamsag-Bulak, finding only a few light aircraft there; clearly, the Soviet command had managed to scramble the local machines away from the strike. The *sentai* leader then made for the secondary target, a column of some fifty vehicles. The attack was unsuccessful, with just one vehicle set alight. Yet the 16th *Sentai* arrived precisely over an airfield south of Tamsag-Bulak, identifying eight SBs on the ground and managing to destroy five of them. However, this was the last success obtained, for the numerical superiority of Soviet fighters began to tell, coupled with their tactically beneficial positions. They did not allow the enemy to continue his attacks, forcing him to defend himself and thus taking the initiative away from him. After an hour, Soviet sources claim that thirteen Ki-27s and two Ki-30s had been downed.[244] The loss of three I-16s was admitted, as well as a similar number of I-153s, and a single SB-2, which sustained a direct hit from a Japanese bomb. The 'Chayka' pilots baled out, but those of the 'Ishaks' had no such luck. Bomb shrapnel flying from a hit I-16 on ground duty killed another four men. As could be expected, the Japanese version of events was entirely different. It claimed seven Polikarpov fighters destroyed on the ground, together with eighteen SB-2s. Bomber gunners claimed another fourteen Soviet fighters.[245]

These two events were followed by a short lull, with a new escalation coming in the early afternoon. At 14.40 eleven 'Chaykas' and fifty-eight I-16s dispersed a group of five Japanese bombers and thirty fighters at between 2,000 and 5,000 metres above Yan-Hu Lake. In three-quarters of an hour three of the bombers and seven Ki-27s were shot down. The pursuit that followed occupied the airspace between the Yan-Hu and Uzur-Nur lakes and saw ten Ki-27s fight with fifty-two I-16s at 15.10. This unequal battle ended with the downing of two Japanese monoplanes. A short while after the sky had emptied of aircraft, at 17.30, above the fierce land battle and the banks of the Khalastin-Gol River, some fifty-two I-16s, eight I-153s and sixty Ki-27s met at between 3,000 and 5,000 metres. Their pilots fought until their fuel allowed just enough range to return to base or a reserve airfield. Both sides demonstrated their combat experience. Mayor Gritsavets's 'Chaykas' used the concentrated power of their machine guns, scoring two victories. One I-16 was also lost. The 64th *Sentai* 1st *Chutai* pilot 2nd Lt Katsumi Anma claimed this victory, but received eleven hits, and when he reached base his aircraft was considered to have been half destroyed.[246] This battle ended the action for the Soviets. During the day they had made 893 sorties and downed twenty-seven enemy fighters and seven of his bombers.[247] Seven Russian fighters had been lost in action[248] and one had burned on the ground during the raid on Tamsag-Bulak airfield. As regards the pilots of the 12th *Hikodan*, they reckoned to have scored forty-five victories (forty-four Polikarpov fighters and an SB-2). These results were rather optimistic, especially against admitted 2nd *Hiko Syudan* losses of just six aircraft (a Ki-36 from the 15th *Sentai*, a Ki-30 of the 16th *Sentai*, a Ki-27 of the 1st *Sentai*, and three Ki-27s of the 64th *Sentai*).[249]

Soviet bombers continued to raid enemy fortifications and their rear. Between 07.30 and 17.50, groups of between nine and twenty-seven SB-2s flew 212 sorties. Another fourteen sorties were performed for reconnaissance purposes. This total was increased by Mayor Egorov's group's nineteen TB-3 sorties to raid Japanese Army concentrations in the hours of darkness. An SB was downed in combat, another failed to return for reasons unknown, two fell to anti-aircraft fire, and one was destroyed by a bomb at its base airfield. Most bombers were lost while descending to drop their warloads. In order to improve precision, heights for this had been set at between 1,500 and 2,000 metres, a level all too vulnerable to any anti-aircraft ordnance with a calibre of more than 20mm. Another reason concerned the failure to include in the formations groups for knocking out AAA emplacements, the need for which had been known since the first day of the Soviet advance. This brought Soviet losses to a total of thirteen aircraft from 1,138 sorties. The day set a record as regards air activity for the conflict as a whole, and was an example of the worth of massed action for the attainment of decisive operational objectives.

On 22 August tension in the air was palpably lower. In view of the difficult position of the Kwantung Army, the 2nd *Hiko Syudan* was ordered to concentrate on the enemy's mechanised and tank units, which were gradually closing the circle around the Japanese forces in Mongolia. Japanese airmen tried using small groups of between three and five bombers from the 9th *Hikodan* (plus fighter escort) to influence the outcome of the ground fighting. To relieve the ground regiments, they attacked Soviet artillery positions. The odd dogfight did result, though with less ardour and scale then on the previous day. At 08.00 Soviet fighter pilots intercepted the first mixed group over the Herimt-Nur Lake, and claimed seven victories, five Ki-27s and two Ki-30s.[250] The remaining Japanese bombers failed to engage in precision bombing and hurried back to base. As witnessed by 9th *Hikodan* CO Major General Ikkaku Shimono, this haste was helped by effective fire from Soviet anti-air defences, which forced commanders to discuss raising the bomb drop levels to more than 3,000 metres.

The second group battle was at 16.45. Nine I-16s and eight I-153s patrolling over Yan-Hu Lake were directed against twelve twin-engined Ki-21s escorted by twice that number of Ki-27s. Despite their numerical superiority, the Japanese crews did not rise to the challenge. The bombers dropped their bomb loads ahead of their target and tried to flee the pursuit that had commenced. For one of them, the outcome was fatal. This, as well as the lack of action by the Japanese fighters, demonstrated the Japanese psychological and physical exhaustion. In analysing the day's flying, Col Kiso Mikami, CO of the 61st *Sentai*, noted just 145 Japanese combat sorties, something that underscores the improved effectiveness of Soviet air patrols. It was they who claimed two bombers (a Ki-21-Ia of the 61st *Sentai* and a Ki-15 of the 10th *Sentai*) plus two fighters (a Ki-27 from each of the 1st and 11th *Sentais*). One of the latter losses claimed the life of another Japanese ace, 11th *Sentai* 2nd *Chutai* CO Capt Koji Motomura, with fourteen confirmed kills. The Japanese claimed nine downed I-16s plus three SB-2s for the day.[251]

Soviet fighters remained the most active of all aircraft types, notching up 528 sorties and downing three Ki-27s for the loss of just one aircraft. The lack of any active challenge in the air allowed the commander of the 22nd IAP to arrange ground attacks, their main targets being near Djindjin-Sume, Obod-Sume, and the Uzur-Nur and Yan-Hu lakes. A total of seventy-five sorties were devoted to the task. The SB bombers also completed fifty-three other sorties, losing one of their number to a Japanese fighter. Six TB-3s bombed Japanese positions at twilight.[252] Over the first three days of the great Soviet land offensive (20-22 August), the VVS Staff reported a total of fifty-three Japanese aircraft destroyed in aerial combat. The 2nd *Hiko Syudan* archives mention just fourteen aircraft losses in combat conditions; this could be yet another illustration of wishes being mistaken for facts. In reality, Japanese losses were rather heavy. While equipment could be replaced, the loss of seventeen dead and seven invalided-out pilots in a matter of days impacted most gravely on the potential of the 2nd *Hiko Syudan*.[253]

In reply to the order received the previous day, on 23 August the crews of sixty-eight Japanese single-engined bombers and seventeen twin-engined Ki-21-Ias made four sorties each, while their 12th *Hikodan* escorting fighters made up to five sorties per serviceable aeroplane. However, this did not stop the Soviet tanks: the new dawn saw the complete encirclement of the Japanese ground forces. Their aviation tried to remain active in attempting to forestall the coming rout, but could not stop the twin-engined SB-2s (with fifty-three combat sorties on 23 August alone), or their fighters. For the two days of 23 and 24 August Ki-27 pilots made seventy-five combat sorties for the benefit of the front-line forces. Despite the two 64th *Sentai* victories, and a single 1st *Sentai* victory against groups of respectively twenty and fifty I-16s, one Japanese aircraft fell to 'Stalin's Eagles', with three others seriously damaged. Acting 1st *Sentai* 2nd *Chutai* CO Capt Ivao Masuda was killed. The Soviets, incidentally, did not admit any fighter losses. One crew that did not return from its mission was Major Semenov's, from the 150th SPAB; a Japanese AAA unit claimed to have shot down an SB-2 bomber.

Preparing Ki-21-la heavy bombers for a mission. *(MoD Archives, Bulgaria)*

The bombing successes of the 2nd *Hiko Syudan* on 25 and 26 August were again modest and failed to influence the overall operational situation. However, they were real enough, and reflected the recent training conducted among 9th *Hikodan Chutais* in preparation of the Kwantung Army's planned 24 August offensive. The aerial confrontation escalated once more. On the one hand were the samurai spirit and technical superiority, on the other were numerical superiority, firepower, and the will not to lose grasp of a victory that had come palpably close.

The first clash was at 09.55 on 25 August over Yan-Hu Lake, which saw seventy-six I-16s and thirty-two 'Chaykas' from the 22nd and 70th IAPs clash with more than eighty Ki-27s from all fighter *sentais*. The battle went on for an hour, spreading to reach the skies over Uzur-Nur. Soviet pilots reported fifteen victories without mentioning any losses.[254] After them, forty-seven I-16s from the 56th IAP encountered almost the same number of Nakajimas above Hamar-Daba Mount and Kargan-Sume. Both sides tried to clear the airspace and lay it open to planned bomber raids, but Soviet pilots affirmed their control of the air, notching up ten more victories for no loss.

Bombers joined the fray in the afternoon. First to try and hit their targets were the Ki-30 crews from the 16th *Sentai*. Using all of their twenty airworthy machines, and covered by some thirty Ki-27s, they flew at 3,000 metres attempting to avoid a mighty Soviet patrol of seventy-three I-16s and nineteen I-153s. Thanks to their mounts' performance, the pilots and gunners were successful in repelling most Soviet attacks. A single bomber crashed onto Mongolian soil, and its fellows were forced to drop their bombs ad hoc. Instead of being directed at aiming, the crews' attention had been drawn into the fierce battle that went on from 14.20 and 15.25. The Japanese fighters were not so lucky; Soviet statistics claim that twelve remained for ever on the field of battle. Nevertheless, they offered reliable defence to their 'charges'. Yet at about 17.35, and without much reason, the bombers shed their escort and tried to cross the Soviet duty loiter zone. This mindless move by the nine Ki-30s cost them five machines (unconfirmed by Japanese sources).

So keen were 'Stalin's Eagles' to keep tasting blood that they next attacked a group of their own SB bombers. Returning from the successful mission, they spotted the twins at a range where their silhouettes resembled those of Ki-21s. *Kap* Nikolay Zvonarev led his missile-armed machines into the attack. As the range closed, he could see the insignia along his quarries' fuselages and wings; realising his error, he pulled away from the attack. However, the lack of radio hampered communication with the other aircraft, and most of them repeated their leader's manoeuvre. However, perhaps because the 'targets' were now at firing range, Lt Fedorov was busy fixing them in his sights and ignored his leader's and fellows' action, instead launching two RS-82s. One exploded close to the bombers' leader; initially it maintained its heading and height, but thereafter entered a sudden dive to its destruction; only the navigator managed to bale out and survive. The gunner and the renowned 150th SPAB CO, Major Mikhail Burmistrov, who had led his unit into twenty-two daring raids, perished. Investigations ascribed the loss to Japanese anti-aircraft fire, but tellingly Fedorov did not receive the Order of the Red Banner that was 'standard issue' to all other missile pilots, being awarded the lesser Valour Medal.[255]

The closing sounds of that tense day were provided by another fighter action. At 18:25 eleven I-16s and thirteen I-153s from the 22nd IAP led a 35-minute defensive battle against a numerically superior enemy, something ever rarer over the past couple of months. The Soviets demonstrated their increased combat skill, reporting five victories after returning to base with no losses. WO Eisaku Suzuki was 'bounced' by an I-153 and shot down 4km south-east of Djindjin-Sume airfield.[256] This brought the overall tally for the day to forty-four Ki-27s and eight bombers brought down.[257]

The situation in the air was getting ever worse for the Japanese. For all their doggedness in defence, their airmen were failing to offer close support to their land forces – they had their hands full with ensuring their own survival. Bomber gunners contributed four confirmed and two probable victories[258], yet the main burden of the battle for air superiority bore down on the fighter units. The pilots of the nearly eighty Ki-27s from the four *sentais* of the 12th *Hikodan* claimed eighteen victories, five losses, and six damaged Ki-27s. Deaths included that of 1st *Sentai* Matsuzo 2nd *Chutai* leader 1st Lt Yoshihiko Tanijima (sixteen victories), 2nd Lt Matsudzo Kasai, and WO Eisaku Suzuki (eleven victories). Renowned aerobatic masters 64th *Sentai* CO Major Hachio Yokoyama and Captain Seizo Okuyama had been forced to bale out. The former was found badly injured by Burgud cavalrymen and was invalided out of the service after having both his arms amputated, while the latter spent two days wandering on the steppe before contacting friendly forces and returning to his unit.

Major Yokoyama's luck was not shared by renowned Soviet fighter pilot St Lt Viktor Rakhov (eight personal and six shared victories). Wounded in the stomach, he managed to force-land on the steppe and was rapidly evacuated to a field hospital at Tamsag-Bulak, thereafter being repatriated to Chita military hospital. Despite all efforts, he died on 29 August, the day that saw the decree awarding many Soviet pilots Hero of the Soviet Union status. His name featured on that Decree.

Overall, between 20 and 25 August the elite 22nd IAP took part in eleven massed air battles and delivered twelve ground strikes. Its pilots had fifty-one victories recognised for the same period.[259] On 24 and 25 August Soviet air units claimed to have downed seventy Japanese aircraft.[260] Mongolian R-5s were most active during the period. Col Dembril, CO of Mongolia's sole Air

Regiment, became the first ever Hero of the Mongolian People's Republic. The efforts of the lumbering wooden biplanes with their strange insignia were supported by the three fast bomber regiments that were methodically destroying the encircled enemy's support points. Over the two days, the number of combat sorties to deliver strikes reached 218, with 96 tonnes of bombs delivered.[261]

Mongolian presence: local R-5 pilots took an active part in the closing August battles, though they were covered by Soviet fighters. *(MoD Archives, Bulgaria)*

Though Soviet data on Japanese losses are inflated, the actual position of the Japanese air arm was becoming critical, though not as critical as that of its fellow ground forces. The by now week-long effort had seen individual pilots fly up to seven sorties a day, and had driven 2nd *Hiko Syudan* personnel to the limit of their endurance. Fatigue caused the loss of otherwise excellent crews, with great experience and many victories behind them. Yet there was no let-up in the pressure exerted by a numerically superior and well-supplied adversary.

In order to strengthen its air grouping at least partially and make up for the great losses, the Japanese Command relocated forward its 33rd *Sentai*, equipped with Ki-10 biplanes. Initially, the Kwantung Army Command had not intended to deploy this unit and its obsolescent equipment, but attrition dictated otherwise. After touring the theatre of action, 33rd *Sentai* pilots prepared to commence their missions.

The major Japanese biplane aircraft: a 33rd *Sentai* machine at a Manchurian airfield in the early spring of 1939. *(MoD Archives, Bulgaria)*

Efforts were also directed at supplementing fighter squadrons that covered the encircled but still resisting battalions of the 26th, 28th and 71st Japanese Infantry Regiments. In order to boost these, whose fate was growing ever less hopeful, on 26 August 31st *Sentai* bombers went into action escorted by twenty fighters from the 24th *Sentai*. A short time after they arrived above the encircled troops, they were joined by the complete force of the 22nd IAP. The *eskadrilya* of I-153s found itself closest to the silvery light bombers, and the fifteen biplanes were tasked with disarming the escort, and succeeded instantly. This enabled Major Grigoriy Kravchenko and his wingmen to shoot down a bomber on their first pass. Thereafter, the fight continued only between the fighter components, the bombers having dropped their bombs and fled. This in turn undermined the morale of the escorts, who also fled. On returning to base, the Soviet fighter pilots reported six more victories for no own losses. The Japanese air effort had proved wanting, and contributed to the failure of a breakout attempt on the ground. Tasting ultimate victory, on 26 August alone Soviet fighter pilots made 790 combat sorties and took part in seven air battles and some twenty dogfights. Soviet propaganda reported the downing of forty-one Japanese fighters and seven bombers for no loss. The eighty-one strike sorties[262] by SB-2 bombers mainly targeted the encircled enemy land force. Soviet aircraft constantly 'hovered' over them, preventing any attempt at air support and using opportunities to deliver strikes.

On 27 August the elite 9th *Hikodan* was again over the front line. The crews faced an exceptionally tricky situation, with the sky full of enemy fighters. Onboard guns overheated from firing at the blunt-nosed silhouettes of I-16s and I-153s. Some of the latter left the battle trailing smoke; others, however, pulled upward and dived again. One of the attacks ended with a Ki-30 entering an increasingly steep bank ending in a corkscrew, and eventually crashing near a burning 'Ishak'. The Soviets then rose to the challenge of newly arriving 11th *Sentai* fighters. Some forty Ki-27s clashed with the fifty-five I-16s on the scene. The six victories scored by the coordinated Japanese bomber formation that was now disappearing over the horizon were now boosted by three more.[263] All were scored by WO Shinohara. Yet the Japanese paid a heavy toll, losing three Ki-27s and two pilots, among whom was Shinohara himself. The death of this ace of fifty-eight victories (according to Japanese propaganda), who had been declared leader of all fighter pilots, had an extremely negative effect on 12th *Hikodan* morale. His unit's records are very telling. On 27 May WO Shinohara was Capt Kenji Shimada's wingman and brought down four I-15bis over Yan-Hu Lake. The following day he shot down an R-Z. Another five I-15bis followed. On 27 June he scored eleven victories against Soviet biplanes in a raid over Tamsag-Bulak. His victories numbered forty-eight by 7 August, and fifty-five by 21 August. Eyewitnesses of his death report an I-16 colliding into his Ki-27, causing him to lose control. At the moment of his death, the 26-year-old was one of the world's top aces, and was posthumously promoted to the rank of Lieutenant for his services to the Empire of the Rising Sun. Naturally, his victory tally was absurdly inflated. If it were true, he would have been responsible for the destruction of practically all airworthy I-15bis in the area since the start of the conflict. Yet Soviet figures claiming that 164 Japanese aircraft (123 fighters, thirty-six bombers, and five staff aircraft) had been downed for the loss of just sixteen aircraft between 20 and 27 August were no less absurd. The official TASS report claims forty-eight Japanese losses for 27 August alone.[264]

In the days to come, the intensity of land and air combat gradually declined. The Japanese air grouping made forty-six sorties in the early hours of 28 August, with all aircraft claimed to have returned to base. A bomber was nevertheless hit and burned on a forward strip that had been prepared for the planned Japanese offensive, having been attacked by a squadron of I-16s and nine SB-2s. The lack of encounters between Soviet aircraft and Ki-27s did not stop the former claiming eleven victories against the Japanese for no loss.

On 29 August the Japanese made 137 sorties against enemy positions, and claimed to have downed forty-seven Russian machines. Yet the reality continued to be most unhappy. Large numbers of Polikarpov fighters flew over Japanese-controlled territory, strafing it. Seven I-16s were shot down or damaged by fire from anti-aircraft positions on the hills below or by gunners aboard the 10th *Sentai* bombers who were overflying the narrow strip of contested territory. Bombers from the 9th *Hikodan* made two raids, both times

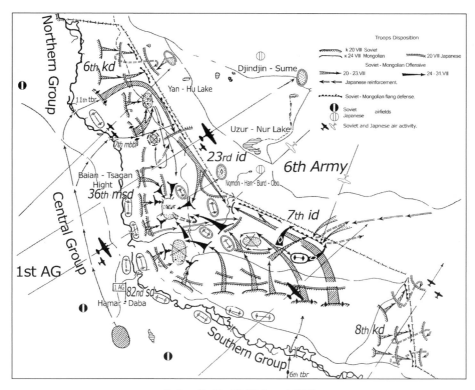

Order of battle, 20-30 August 1939

battling with some forty I-16s. Sporadic encounters by 1st and 24th *Sentai* pilots, who were acting as escorts to the raiding parties, led to eight more victories for no loss.[265] The Soviet side stated that the battles involved seventy I-16s and twenty-five I-153s, who downed four Japanese fighters and one bomber; they confirmed a single I-16 loss[266] (other claims are that eight Japanese aircraft were lost)[267].

The most significant event in this otherwise routine day at war was the publication of an order creating thirty-one men Heroes of the Soviet Union, ten of whom were airmen. As a curious aside, tank crew members outnumbered airmen for the first time in the Soviet state's short history.

Perhaps it was the TASS announcement of the awards that drove the Japanese airmen to try to demonstrate their resolve to continue fighting regardless of events on the ground. They still felt masters of the sky, and with some reason. With an approximate numerical ratio of 1:4 in favour of the enemy, they were not only continuing to resist the Soviet military machine, but also draw blood from it. The next day was marked by active 9th *Hikodan* action against twenty-nine artillery regiment forward positions. The bombers set fourteen vehicles ablaze, yet the forty-odd escorting Ki-27s from the 1st, 11th, 24th and 64th *Sentais* failed to withstand the pressure of the numerous enemy patrols (eighty-eight I-16s and twenty-five I-153s) and, though claiming twenty-four victories, in reality lost the initiative and allowed two 31st *Sentai* Ki-30s to fall. Bomber gunners claimed another seven confirmed victories and one probable. Only a single crashed I-16 was confirmed lost by the Soviets after becoming involved in a dogfight, of which the Japanese continued to be masters until the end of the conflict. 'Stalin's Eagles' claimed to have shot down nineteen Ki-27s instead of the two the Japanese admitted had failed to return to base.[268]

On 31 August Mongolian territory was cleared of Japanese units. The last land battles saw twenty-seven Japanese bombers and seventy fighters from the 1st, 11th and 64th *Sentais* enter battle with 126 I-16s. This was the month's last air battle. The Japanese claimed to have brought down twenty Soviet fighters for the loss of three aircraft and four pilots. The Soviet side claimed to have lost a single I-16 and scored twenty-two victories, one against a single-engined bomber.[269] These figures were not confirmed (except the death of 31st *Sentai* 1st *Chutai* CO Capt Jiro Inoue, and the crash-landing of Capt Saito, 2nd *Chutai* CO from the same unit); yet it is a fact that, from this day onwards, Soviet aircraft were confined to their side of the border. The I-16 reconnaissance *eskadrilya* sortied three times, flying only within the border.[270]

Measures to improve camouflage began, including applying deception patterns to Soviet aircraft, which were mostly finished in bare metal. The aircraft were painted green on top, with blue bellies. Initial attempts were not too successful, appearing to accentuate rather than hide the aircraft, especially in flight. More colours were gradually added to match the surroundings and their natural hues. This led to the 22nd IAP 'Chaykas' becoming most variegated.[271] Some of them (numbering not more than the establishment of an air regiment, some sixty or seventy machines) ferried across to the two forward operational airfields that *Komkor* Georgiy Zhukov had ordered to be built on land cleared of the Japanese to the east of the Khalkhin-Gol River. This was the closing Soviet aviation manoeuvre in the theatre. After a testing month that had cost fifty-four combat and twenty-three non-combat losses (of which just twenty combat and two non-combat had involved SB bombers and the rest fighters), the Soviet air arm had successfully won and held onto air superiority. Its significantly improved coordination had brought lower and lower losses, with the final advance claiming just twenty combat losses. The overall tally included Soviet claims of 208 victories between 20 and 31 August (146 fighters, thirty-five bombers, twenty-two reconnaissance aircraft, and five staff machines). For the entirety of the campaign – from 15 May to 30 August – the Soviets claimed 575 Japanese aircraft and a snake static balloon destroyed.[272]

Proof that these figures were greatly inflated comes from the gradual rather than sudden reduction in Japanese air activity, and from the maintenance of some combat tension in the air until the very close of the conflict.

Japanese commanders carefully monitored the actions and state of their air arm at the Mongolian/Manchurian border. Since the start of the Soviet offensive on 20 August, they had admitted losing forty-three aircraft, or 25 per cent of their genuine technical potential. Pilots killed or seriously wounded numbered twenty-nine. Of these losses, twenty-nine aircraft and twenty pilots were accounted for in the closing week of fighting. The wounded numbered thirty-two, most of them invalided out and failing to return to active service before the conflict's end.

If we are to compare these numbers with actual 1st AG VVS losses, we will see that non-combat losses doubled the figures (Soviet combat losses amounted to twenty aircraft, but the number of I-16s damaged for other reasons was equally great); this number represented just 6 per cent of establishment strength, not taking into account the enormous reserves.

The limitations imposed by the Tokyo Headquarters, especially after the start of the Ribbentrop/Molotov talks, led to a search for local solutions to optimise Japanese potential. This was especially valid as regards strike aircraft, where enemy numbers were crushingly superior. Despite the constantly reducing numbers of the 10th, 16th, 31st and 61st *Sentais*, between 23 August and 1 September Japanese bomber crews constantly tried to halt the advance guard of the Soviet/Mongolian forces. Their actions involved dropping seventy-five 100kg bombs, 706 15kg bombs, and 4,362 50kg bombs.[273] Thanks to their fearless fighter escorts, bomber losses were not too heavy. Despite this, after ten days of tenacious fighting, men and machines were on the edge of total exhaustion. First to retreat from the front, albeit unwillingly, were the 61st *Sentai* crews, who departed from Haylar in the early morning of 1 September.

During the same period, 12th *Hikodan* fighters tried to maintain sufficient activity to cover their remaining bombers. Their tasks were reduced mainly to airspace clearing and to escorting the raiding formations. In discharging them, their main adversaries were again the Soviet fighter units. Their plentiful numbers, alongside their changed tactics, rendered the fight rather torturous for the Japanese. The Soviets' basic objectives were the bombers and, in attempting to prevent precision bombing, they tried to avoid the escorting Ki-27s. With their high speed, the now-camouflaged variegated green fighters would pierce the Japanese fighter formations and open fire on the heavy, lumbering bombers before climbing away. The dogfights that had been entered into so readily during the conflict's two earlier months, and that had brought so much loss to the VVS RKKA, seemed to have passed into history. It was speed, the power of the rapid-firing ShKAS guns, and the 'hit and run' tactics that brought success to the Soviets in early September.

The new Soviet tactics committed the entire potential of their Japanese counterparts, allowing groups of SB-2s and scattered recce machines to act mostly unpunished. Nevertheless, in the ten days of fierce fighting during late August, the 12th *Hikodan* notched up 112 victories at the price of seventeen Ki-27s (three from the 1st *Sentai*, five from the 11th, one from the 24th, and eight from the 64th). Bearing in mind that this type was being produced at the rate of one a day, the loss was not too significant in absolute terms. Yet, taking it alongside losses on the China front, the problem assumes different dimensions.

Nevertheless, the Kwantung Army air grouping did have reserves, and did try to make up for the shortage of machines. What was worse was the fact that capable airmen were dropping out of the ranks, some of them for ever. Apart from Shinohara, they included a *sentai* CO, three *chutai* COs, and a number of leading aces. Personnel matters became so critical that the 2nd *Hiko Syudan* Staff was forced to turn to Headquarters for help.

The help thus secured began to arrive in this distant theatre after 26 August. After the 33rd *Sentai*, which joined the Japanese air grouping on the Nomonhan Plateau with its thirty old Ki-10 Type 95 biplane fighters, reinforcements arrived at the 24th *Sentai* (in the form of one *chutai* of twelve Ki-27s) and the 1st *Sentai* (a *chutai* of six aircraft originally intended to serve with the 11th *Sentai* before it received its dozen new machines).[274]

Though the major Japanese land force was now routed and forward Soviet and Mongolian units were becoming entrenched along the border, the ground was still seeing clashes and attempts to provoke new hostilities. These clashes largely arose at battalion level, but the provocations ended after 4 September. Soviet reconnaissance aircraft were particularly active in this period. The SB-2 bombers made very frequent inroads of up to 150km into Manchurian airspace, their crews closely monitoring enemy force locations and movements.

The growth in the Japanese air grouping as a result of reinforcements from the rear bothered the Soviet command. The new arrivals declared their intention of not ceding the sky as early as 1 September. Above the Khalastin-Gol River, 188 Soviet fighters (145 I-16s and forty-three I-153s) from the three air regiments fought some 120 Ki-27s and Ki-30s in mixed groups pursuing diverse tactical objectives. The fight took place at between 3,500 and 5,000 metres and featured the stepped arrival of most participants. They fought for more than an hour, with the spinning ball of fighters attracting reinforcements and shedding burning machines or those whose fuel had become critical.

The two sides gave entirely different accounts of the results of the successive massed air battle. The 12th and 9th *Hikodan sentais* claimed thirty-three victories, with losses put at five Ki-27s (one of which claimed 64th *Sentai* 2nd *Chutai* leader Capt Shuichi Anzai, while the 1st *Chutai* CO from the same *sentai*, Capt Fumio Maruta, was wounded). Two other aces also perished: M Sgt Takayori Kodama (eleven victories) and M Sgt Tokuya Sudo (ten victories). Another Japanese pilot baled out, landed within Mongolia, and shot himself shortly before being taken prisoner. The new 2nd *Chutai* CO was the subsequently famous Second World War ace Iori Sakai, who ended his Mongolian career with eight victories. According to his memoirs, the first month of hostilities had cut personnel in his squadron by two-thirds. On one occasion, he landed with fifty hits.

'Stalin's Eagles' listed nineteen Ki-27s and a Ki-30 in their battle journals.[275] Three I-16s failed to return, together with their pilots. Two of them died in the wreckage of their aircraft, with the third baling out and falling prisoner, subsequently being exchanged for a Japanese counterpart. Deputy *eskadrilya* CO St Lt Fedor Cheremukhin was forced to land with a holed petrol tank on the steppe not far from Tamsag-Bilak. Both he and his machine were rapidly taken back to base, being declared heroes the following day. Lt Aleksandr Moshin was wounded and sent to Chita military hospital.

The Japanese biplanes made their debut over the border on 2 September, clearly seeking to pick a fight. Over Buir-Nur Lake, three Type 95 fighters from the 33rd *Sentai*'s 2nd *Chutai* led by 1st Lt Soichi Okamoto were met by a 22nd IAP *eskadrilya* led by the aforementioned St Lt Fedor Cheremukhin. The experienced leader rightly reasoned that the I-16 tip 10 had significantly greater speed and firepower, though less manoeuvrability, and initiated the correct tactic for the fight: shooting from further away and avoiding close level manoeuvres. After the skirmish, two downed Kawasaki Ki-10s were reported for no loss. Okamoto claimed the unit's first four victories of the Incident. M Sgt Shozo Saito tried in vain to ram one, but was obliged instead to force-land.[276]

The encounter again escalated into an air battle. Excellent visibility allowed a great area to be observed, and each engagement was as visible as a flare by pilots on the ground; they immediately scrambled and flew across to assist their comrades. First to arrive were the 1st *Sentai* monoplanes. More Soviet fighters followed them. The previous day's events repeated themselves. The fight developed over Hamar-Daba Mount and the Humurgin-Gol River, at the same levels that offered optimum performance to both sides – 3,500 to 5,000 metres. After 45 minutes that witnessed more than 250 machines fighting (175 of them Soviet), the sky grew quiet. The Japanese admitted losing one fighter and suffering damage to four, and claimed three more victories, of which the Soviets admitted only one, claiming in their turn eight victories – six against Ki-27s.[277]

With the slow deterioration in the weather, 3 September saw a tactical winding down of the aerial confrontation. The lull was, however, short-lived, for the next day's weather improvement was used by both sides, with another clash south-east of Shirin-Obo and over the Humurgin-Gol River. There were sixty-eight Soviet and some forty Japanese fighter sorties. Initially, eleven I-153s and thirty-nine I-16s of the 22nd IAP fought with and pursued twenty Ki-27s, then eleven I-16s and seven 'Chaykas' from the 70th IAP did the same

with a similar number of Japanese biplane fighters led by Capt Takeo Kawada.
Kawada had been forbidden to engage personally, but 2nd Lt Tadashi Harada
and M Sgt Akira Ishikawa charged in, followed by the rest of the formation.
Nine confirmed and three probable victories were claimed, including three by
Ishikawa personally, although he force-landed after suffering severe wounds,
from which he died the next day. 2nd Lt Harada and M Sgt Hiraki also failed
to return. On the same day the 33rd *Sentai*'s 3rd *Chutai* was also engaged,
claiming thirteen victories.[278] Soviet reports claimed the loss of nine Ki-27s, a
Ki-10, two I-16 tip 10s, and a 'Chayka'.[279]

An I-16 tip 10 from the 22nd IAP after a belly-landing in Mongolia in September 1939.
(MoD Archives, Bulgaria)

On 5 September, while escorting recce Ki-36s and Ki-15-Is over the
Humurgin-Gol River, twenty Ki-10s and five Ki-27s clashed with sixty-two
Soviet fighters. The recce machines got away, but the VVS claimed to have
downed seven Ki-10s and a Ki-27.[280] In reality, two Ki-10s fell on the
Mongolian side of the border; the pilot of one baled out and managed to get
away. An I-16 failed to return, while another was shot down by enemy anti-
aircraft fire, having been an easy target below cloud at up to 2,000 metres.
Patrolling between 2 and 5 September, 33rd *Sentai* pilots claimed forty-one
confirmed and eight possible victories at the cost of three of their own aircraft.
On 4 and 5 September, the fighter *sentai* wrote off just five aircraft for various
reasons, yet despite these low losses the Imperial air group now had just 141
combat aircraft.[281] Before the downpours that began on 6 September, the
Soviets had reinforced the 22nd IAP with fifteen I-16 tip 10s from *Kap*
Gorlov's *eskadrilya* and, despite the departure of the heavy TB-3s, the 1st AG
VVS retained its four-fold numerical superiority.

7

The final rush

Far from the Mongolian steppes, Tokyo Headquarters assessed the position and concluded that the Kwantung Army units at the disposal of the *Kantogun* were insufficiently prepared in terms of quality and quantity to undertake the Khalkhin-Gol offensive. This meant that the conquered ground was lost permanently. Another important factor that forced an end to hostilities was the early arrival of winter on the high ground. Unlike the Red Army, Japanese troops in the area had no equipment whatever for waging warfare in such conditions. The Kwantung Army Staff concurred with the conclusions, and accordingly accepted a 5 September Tokyo order banning any further offensive action. The underlying reason for this was that Germany had pressed Japan for an end to the aggression.

In these conditions, it fell to the Japanese air grouping to act as a means of winning time and securing better armistice conditions. In this sense, it helped that no Japanese air commander had any sense of having been defeated in the same way that his ground-based fellows had. Quite the reverse! Bearing in mind the results, the Japanese airmen had every reason to feel that they were their nation's sole representatives to have emerged from the confrontation with honour, having denied absolute mastery of the air to the VVS RKKA to the very last moment. Superiority, yes – but for just a month, and at a high price in destroyed aircraft and experienced pilots killed.

Yet, the state of the 2nd *Hiko Syudan* was clearly such that it could not generate sufficient air power to enable its use as a political lever. Thus, as from 7 September the 9th and 12th *Hikodan* were reinforced, and the 2nd *Hikodan* left Changchung for Haylar and its network of airfields. From 9 September the Japanese could again rise to the Soviet VVS with 295 aircraft. Moreover, 2nd *Hiko Syudan* CO Lt Gen Tetsuji Giga and the unit's staff were made subordinate to Eijiro Ebashi, a man equal in rank but more senior in the staff hierarchy. Tokyo relied on him to save the situation and complete the difficult mission ahead.

Since August 1936 Lt Gen Ebashi had headed the *Koku-Heydan*, or Joint Air Command, set up to control overall air matters both at home and in Taiwan, Manchuria, and Korea. The *Koku-Heydan* Staff was initially based in Japan, being moved to China in July 1937 to be closer to the air and army elements in the war area. As early as May 1939 Tokyo Headquarters had wanted the *Koku-Heydan* to fix its entire attention to the Nomonhan situation. Though impressive in its air potential, the Japanese operational grouping was dispersed over a huge area and could not devote all its efforts to future offensive actions. Politics also militated against an escalation of the conflict. The new government of Abe Noboyuki intensely sought a way out of the crisis, being determined, however, to trade terms for the armistice. The sole trump card in the political bargaining was the power of Lt Gen Ebashi's air establishment.

On 11 September the weather worsened still further, with snow falling on high ground for the first time. This led both sides to bring forward their winter preparations. Lt Gen Matsuzo Ebashi used the lull to regroup his units, dividing them into four *Hikodan*s. The 2nd *Hikodan* comprised the *chutais* of the 9th, 16th, 29th and 65th *Sentais* (thirty Ki-10s, eighteen Ki-30s, six Ki-15-Is and sixteen Ki-32s). The 9th *Hikodan* comprised five *sentais* – the 10th (six Ki-30s and six recce Ki-15-Is), the 31st (twenty-eight Ki-30s), the 33rd (twenty-seven Ki-10s), the 45th (twenty-eight Ki-32s) and the 61st (thirteen Ki-21-Is). The 12th *Hikodan* was to have the 1st, 59th and 64th Fighter *Sentais* with sixty-five Ki-27s, and the *Yokoseku-Hikodan*, or special group, retained the 15th Reconnaissance *Sentai*, together with the 11th and 24th Fighter *Sentais* with their forty-six Ki-27s.[282]

This force concentration was too late, for the outcome both of the war and of the coming peace talks was already clear. The Soviet Command drew a line under the Soviet air mission and as early as 12 September ferried twenty of them via Ulan-Bator to Moscow in two transport aircraft. This date saw the official start of peace negotiations between the USSR and Japan.

The talks did not stop Japanese reconnaissance aircraft continuing to fly. Their crews reported finding sixteen twin-engined and sixty-eight single-

One of the Ki-32 missions that represented the last effort of the Japanese air component in the Nomonhan conflict. *(MoD Archives, Bulgaria)*

Air force ratios in the Nomonhan area on 11 September 1939

Aircraft	USSR	Japan	Aircraft ratio	Combat potential ratio
Fighters	362	158	2.29:1	1.57:1
Bombers	166	79	2.1:1	2.48:1
Reconnaissance	54	18	3:1	1.95:1
Overall	582	255	2.28:1/2.46:1	2:1

engined aircraft near Tamsag-Bulak and the Buir-Nur Lake. This added to artillery recce reports that had fixed the positions of Soviet ambush airfields east of the Khalkhin-Gol River.[283]

Making use of the corroborated and analysed recce reports, on 13 September Lt Gen Ebashi ordered a massed air raid on the enemy's major bases at a tactical depth as soon as the weather allowed it. The objective was clear: to strengthen the hand of Japanese diplomacy at the negotiating table. The plan called for the single-engined bombers to relocate to forward airfields. The crews of all 255 airworthy machines (158 fighters, sixty-six bombers, thirteen 'heavy' bombers and eighteen reconnaissance machines) were brought up to operational readiness. The recce machines kept flying, and apart from confirming artillery reports of active Soviet ambush airstrips, made a census of an airfield network near the Buir-Nur Lake, setting its population at thirty-three single-engined and fifteen twin-engined aircraft.[284]

While land forces contemplated each other peacefully across the snow on both sides of the border, the Japanese now intended that the sky would see the final battles. In view of the complex situation along Russia's western border, where final preparations were in hand for an imminent incursion into Poland, Stalin had given orders for any provocation to be countered solely defensively. Therefore, the *Koku-Heydan* raid, although not entirely expected, failed to achieve surprise.

In the early afternoon of 14 September (at 14.20), ten Ki-30s of the 10th *Sentai* raided Soviet airfields about 20km south of the Buir-Nur Lake from medium heights. The eighteen Ki-27s from the 1st *Sentai*[285] that escorted them were led personally by the unit's CO, Maj Tadashi Yoshida. They successfully countered the attack by seventy-five I-16s and fifteen I-153s. Despite this, the huge numerical disparity allowed individual Soviet fighters to pierce the escort and claim victory against a bomber. The Japanese fighter pilots declared three confirmed and six probable victories. Soviet figures show the Japanese losing four aircraft, for no losses of their own.

The fact was that neither side sustained any loss. The Soviets remained at a high degree of readiness, yet their command received a negative reply from Moscow to its request for a retaliatory raid. This confirmed the ban on infringing enemy airspace. Only reconnaissance aircraft were excepted from this, but the exception was only temporarily as regards some tactical recce types. Their reports showed that the enemy's air potential was in a state of readiness.[286] The sole change these reports brought was an order for fighter pilots to standby on duty sitting and strapped in their cockpits.

The 14 September actions of Japanese air commanders turned out to be just the prelude to the next day. Soviet pilots were indeed sitting in their Polikarpovs' cockpits, yet nobody could have expected the scale of what was coming; after all, peace negotiations were nearing their end. Even the routine enemy reconnaissance at 09.30 was ignored. It had been known for a long time that ground duty crews could not scramble and catch the Ki-15. With its top speed of 481kmph, it was the fastest in the conflict. The growing roar of dozens of engines an hour later was the first inkling Soviet observers had of what was coming.

In due course, some thirty 16th and 31st *Sentai* bombers appeared in the air in perfect combat formation. Their targets this time were the airfields some 45km south-west of Hamar-Daba Mount, home of the main strength of the 22nd IAP. Soviet duty forces, comprising nine I-16s, scrambled. The giant white arrow on the ground indicated the intercept heading for the enemy, and the white rectangle next to it meant that the enemy was flying at one level. This was not high – barely 2,000 metres for the strike formation – yet some of the twenty-five direct cover fighters from the 1st *Sentai* were far higher. Using this advantage to stall the approach of the enemy, they lunged into immediate attack. The lack of serious defence assisted the Ki-30 crews in dropping their bombs at 11.00. Even so, the threat of enemy attack made their actions hasty. Though they claimed to have

A rare chance to play between sorties: Mongolia, late September 1939. *(MoD Archives, Bulgaria)*

destroyed three SB-2s on the ground (in fact, the type was absent from the raided airfields), and their gunners claimed to have shot down an I-16, overall the raid was ineffective. The number of Soviet fighters in the air grew gradually, with duty crews arriving from the 56th and 70th IAPs and changing the numerical ratio. The Japanese then began a retreat across the border. On their way, several Ki-30s dived over a remote ambush airstrip where they had spotted several I-16s, setting one of them alight by strafing. As for the 1st *Sentai* pilots, they claimed to have seen another four I-16s fall in flames during the battle.[287]

The next raid was at lunchtime. Apart from the single-engined Ki-32, it involved two squadrons of 'heavy' bombers from the 61st *Sentai*. Their actions were covered by twenty-one Ki-27s (twelve from the 11th *Sentai* and nine from the 64th). Targets included the 56th IAP base 35km west of Hamar-Daba Command Post. The regiment had a great number of I-153s, whose silvery shapes were clearly visible on the ground, highlighting the unit's position. Apart from the great number of new aircraft, the regiment also had many new and inexperienced pilots. Though three squadrons of I-16s scrambled from nearby airfields, the Japanese got there first. The 'Chayka' crews scrambled haphazardly from beneath the raid, fleeing the bombs only to face a battle from a position of extreme disadvantage. One biplane was soon ablaze, followed by another, which broke up under the g-forces to which its pilot subjected it. The buzzing enemy prevented the hapless pilot from baling out, and he perished in his crashed machine. Another 'Chayka' started burning, its pilot managing to bale out. The flames then stopped and the uncontrolled aeroplane began a descent that ended with its crashing. Other I-153s – the main targets of the Japanese air attack – were also in trouble.

They were only relieved as I-16s reached the battle. Their pilots were 22nd IAP aces, together with aces from *Kap* Zvonarev's group.[288] The battle now raged anywhere from ground level to 7,000 metres. While attempting a forced landing on the steppe, a 64th *Sentai* aircraft was blown up. Another two Ki-27s from the 11th *Sentai* fell in flames. One was piloted by 1st *Chutai* CO Capt Kenji Shimada, an ace with twenty-seven victories to his credit, and who had been in the area since the conflict's outset. Another ace to die was M Sgt Bunji Yoshiyama, with twenty victories on the Mongolian front since May.

This I-153 'Chayka' was one of the last victims of Japanese aces. *(MoD Archives, Bulgaria)*

Japanese fighters from the 1st *Chutai* 11th *Sentai* earlier in the conflict, after a bloody fight. On the extreme left is Capt Kenji Shimada and on the extreme right is WO Hiromiti Shinohara. *(MoD Archives, Bulgaria)*

These unexpected raids angered the Soviet Command, which organised a 'free hunt' with four I-16 *eskadrily*. Keeping within the border, they undertook the closing engagement of the conflict. They encountered eighteen Ki-27s from the two *shutais* of the 59th *Sentai* led by its CO, Lt Col Isaku Imagava[289], who were new to the area. After a half-hour battle, the *sentai* notched up eleven victories, but at the cost of six aircraft and five pilots, including 1st *Chutai* CO Capt Mitsugu Yamamoto.

Soviet statistics for the day show 212 fighter sorties and 180 enemy overflights, of which twenty were brought down. The loss of six aircraft, of which five were 'Chaykas', was acknowledged. The battle brought successive proof that the new type was far from perfect, and unfit for modern aerial warfare.

The Japanese raids were deemed a success, leading to the claimed destruction of thirty-nine Soviet aircraft in air battles, with another four to eight probable losses, nine aircraft damaged, and four or five destroyed on the ground. Yet they were in reality the final failure, leading to the loss of nine fighters, a bomber and eight pilots (of whom two were squadron leaders). This was a senseless loss, far more hurtful to the Japanese than any loss they had inflicted on the Soviets.

Overall, September had seen twenty-four Japanese aircraft brought down and 121 victories claimed. Soviet figures show 1,953 fighter sorties and fifty-seven SB-2 sorties, resulting in seventy-one Japanese aircraft losses – sixty-eight fighters, two recce aircraft and a sole bomber – at a cost of fourteen

Soviet losses. Several hours after the last shots were fired over Nomon-Han-Burd-Obo, a peace settlement was signed in Moscow between the USSR and the Mongolian People's Republic on the one hand, and Japan on the other. It came into force at 13.00 on 15 September.

The ceasefire order arrived the same evening and was immediately put into effect by both sides. The last encounter between the adversaries was on the following morning. On 16 September a *chutai* of 64th *Sentai* Ki-27s patrolling along the border noted fifteen I-16s doing the same over the main stream of the Khalkhin-Gol River.[290] Each formation was careful not to cross the border, and the two monitored each other for several minutes, flying in parallel. This was the end of the air war over Mongolia – a war often cited as an example, yet so far not completely understood.

8

In search of the victors and the vanquished

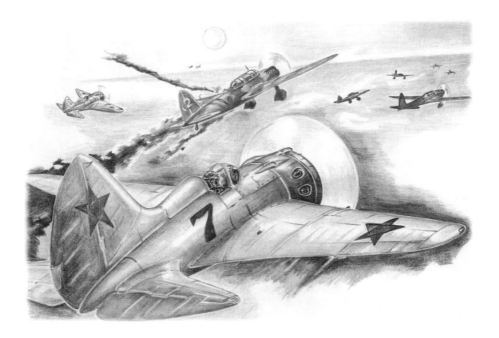

Whereas the modern Japanese Army, created 70 years before the events described here, undoubtedly suffered its first serious defeat at the operational level, the answer to the question as to who lost and who won in the air war over the Nomon-Han-Burd-Obo remains debatable. What is beyond debate is that, amid exceptionally difficult conditions, the 2nd *Hiko Syudan's sentais* did for an extended period enjoy superiority over their enemy, despite the latter's numerical superiority. Even with the benefit of hindsight, this remains a remarkable success for Japan's airmen.

However, despite their ability to some degree to reduce the combat effectiveness of the Soviet strike air element, and to counter the Soviet fighter force, the skilled use of reserves, the rapid learning of lessons from existing experience and that gained in the initial two months of hostilities, and the exploitation of opportunities both as regards men and technology, did allow the VVS RKKA to secure success for the land operations planned by *Komkor* Georgiy Zhukov and his Staff, and for the attainment of the Soviets' preferred final outcome. This has to be the reason why so many Japanese pilots felt they had failed in their duty and mission. Indeed, three senior officers of the 2nd *Hiko Syudan* and several others besides could not live with the thought of defeat and of having been taken prisoner, and ended up taking their own lives by committing ritual suicide.

If we were to assess the scale of air combat during the Nomonhan conflict, we would be forced to note the lack of any operational analogy until the second half of 1940, when the Battle of Britain entered its decisive phase. Bearing in mind the narrowness of the front line, which did not exceed 80km, and the fact that on occasion more than 300 aircraft were in simultaneous dogfights over it, one could even claim that no analogies exist in the entire history of military aviation. The rates of increase of air groupings shown in Diagram 1 would set the numbers of combat aircraft on both sides of the front line at the closing stages of the conflict at some 840 machines, while the density of air groupings was some 15 aircraft per kilometre of front line; over 60 per cent of these were Soviet.

The rates of increase in aircraft numbers shown in Figure 2 and of the monthly losses demonstrate the development of the aerial conflict and had a great influence on the evolution of the overall operational situation. The period in which the Japanese had superiority over the Khalkhin-Gol coincided with the Japanese ground offensive and the establishment of a bridgehead on the river's eastern bank. Once air superiority passed to the Soviet side, *Komdiv* Zhukov and his staff acquired the ability to advance on the ground and attain their ultimate objective.

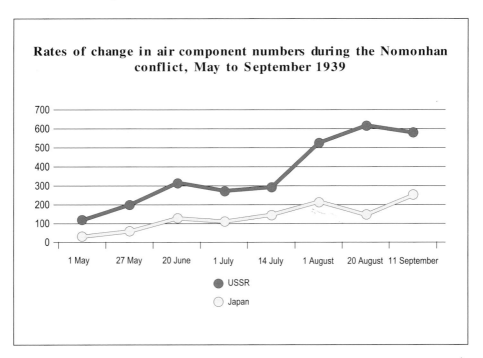

Rates of change in air component numbers during the Nomonhan conflict, May to September 1939

Ratios of aircraft losses in the Nomonhan conflict

Indicator	USSR	Japan	Ratio
Flying personnel fatalities	159	152	1.05:1
Pilot injuries	102	66	1.54:1
Recognised aircraft losses	207	162	1.28:1
Recognised aircraft losses in combat	145	88	1.65:1
Recognised aircraft losses on ground from enemy action	62	74	1:1.19
Recognised fighter losses in combat	130	63	2.06:1
Enemy claims of aircraft losses	1,260	646	1.95:1
Percentage of recognised to claimed losses	16.4%	25%	1:1.52
Damaged aircraft subsequently returned to action	436	220	1.98:1
Damaged fighters subsequently returned to action	385	157	2.45:1

The main reason for Zhukov's operational success was the change in air superiority. In turn, the main factor for this change was the availability of sufficient reserves of aircraft and personnel. An additional condition was the ability to direct these reserves in a timely fashion to such a remote and limiting operational theatre. The Soviet command was significantly more hampered in juggling forces and means, yet more flexible and decisive in its reaction to operational circumstances.

Another important factor was the consensus at various Soviet leadership levels as to the importance of attaining victory and its importance for subsequent events at the strategic level. Until the close of the conflict, the Japanese leadership system failed to achieve a uniform standpoint on the significance of the events in the Nomonhan area.

The difference in attitudes comes across in the manner in which the numbers of Japanese aircraft changed, as shown in Figure 2. After the increase in hostilities in late July and August had been reported to the outside world, Japanese political and military leaders seemed unable to comprehend how important the handful of brave but exhausted samurai were to the Empire's international standing, fighting as they were over a patch of godforsaken Asian land. The efforts of September turned out to be belated and were paid for by the blood of additional airmen.

Other than this, the human losses suffered by Japanese airmen cannot be called great for a military conflict of this scale. The 2nd *Hiko Syudan* archives and, later, those of the *Koku-Heydan* mention 152 dead and missing in action, and sixty-six wounded. This total includes sixty pilots, sixty-four strike aircraft crew members, and twenty-eight reconnaissance crew members (other sets of numbers show the deaths of ninety-five fighter pilots, forty bomber crew members, and twenty-eight reconnaissance crew members).[291] Other figures put the overall losses of Kwantung Army air personnel during the conflict at 116 killed, sixty-five missing in action, and nineteen wounded. Yet others state that 141 were killed, and eighty-nine were wounded.[292] Though none too clear, all this information points to Japanese losses of less than 230 men. Certainly, some fighter units did lose a great deal of their personnel; the 24th *Sentai*, for example, lost 70 per cent of its men, and the 11th *Sentai* lost 55 per cent.

By mid-August the airmen's psychological and physical fatigue was palpable in their failure to retain the initiative and properly back the formations of the Sixth Army. This allowed the VVS, with its fresh reserves, to achieve a significant superiority in men and resources, and to take the initiative despite heavy losses. The air component of the 1st Army Group paid for its victory with human losses that were proportional to those of its enemy: 100 dead pilots, fifty-nine missing in action, and 102 wounded.[293] Later publications give the number of dead as 174 (eighty-eight in combat, eleven killed by anti-aircraft fire, sixty-five missing in action, and ten killed in air raids or died in hospital), while the number of wounded is put at 113.[294] Thus human losses show a relative parity, with the VVS RKKA losses being about 30 per cent greater than those of the Japanese. However, these numbers were less favourable to the Japanese. As discussed above, the number of trained Japanese pilots was not only considerably less than the number of aircraft made in the Empire of the Rising Sun, but was out of step with the objectives and tasks set before the Imperial Air Force.

In fact, the real reason for the outcome of the air war over the Khalkhin-Gol River is best sought neither in the quality of available aircraft (where combat potential margins proved to be narrow), nor in the numerical superiority of the VVS (which was made up for in the early days by better Japanese training), but in the catastrophic shortage of crews for Japan's air force. In their almost 30 years of existence to that date, Japan's air schools and colleges had trained a mere 1,700 pilots, a very inadequate number for a superpower that had planned as recently as 1936 to built 3,600 combat aircraft. The number of pilots lost during the hostilities represented a relatively high proportion and caused a supply crisis for a long time to come. Apart from that, seventeen *chutai* commanders or more senior officers died in combat, this inevitably having an impact on the outcome of the decisive air battles in late August and the first half of September.

Aircraft losses by the close of the conflict had reached relatively balanced tallies: 250 Soviet versus 164 Japanese combat and auxiliary machines. Of these, respectively 207 and 90 combat types were lost in action. Regardless of the 2.3:1 ratio (with fighters it reached 2.4:1, with strike types being 2.5:1 – and the Soviets' use of SB bombers and I-16 fighters for reconnaissance must be borne in mind here), Japanese sortie numbers were roughly half those of the Soviets, something particularly noticeable after mid-August.[295] This sharply reduced the effectiveness of the Japanese air element, ceding air superiority to the 1st Army Group.

Naturally, it is normal for air combat loss analyses to be based on confirmed numbers. Yet keeping statistical tallies turned out to be difficult for experts who monitored the conflict closely. This was due to the propaganda effect in official military communiqués on the outcomes of engagements. In fact, this is a research problem in every conflict. In this case, the difficulties arise from the practice of inflating enemy losses hugely. Soviet claims put Japanese losses at between 450 and 646 (of which 564 were fighters), whereas Japanese statistics put Soviet losses at between 1,260 and 1,340 (ninety-eight of them on the ground). Such figures belong in the sphere of fiction. For one thing, the total number of I-16 fighters of various marks that served in the three Soviet fighter regiments in the battle area in 1939 came to 311 – the Japanese claims would have one believe that they had destroyed more than twice that number. The ratio between admitted Soviet losses of this type and Japanese claims of victories against it stands at 1:8.

Soviet pilots pose for a newspaper photograph: propaganda was one of the main weapons in this conflict. *(MoD Archives, Bulgaria)*

The pattern on the other side of the front line was similar: the ratio between announced Soviet victories and losses acknowledged by the Japanese was 9:1. The overall ratio between claims and acknowledged losses was balanced at some 6:1. The number of aces and the number of their reported victories was also at approximately this level of veracity. One must not blame pilots' fantasies for this. The environment into which they were introduced was entirely different from anything known hitherto. Though some analysts draw analogies with the final year of the Great War, any comparison has to be rather abstract.

The first difference was in the sheer numbers of aircraft employed. Some 850 to 900 machines were used by the Soviets, with 350-400 more being fielded by the Japanese. These numbers are not all that impressive, yet one must not forget that the operational zone was a maximum of no more than 80km in length, and approximately the same in depth. Most battles involved some 300 aircraft gathered at once over this area, something unknown in the history of warfare. This tense environment, and the relatively well-matched armament as regards calibre (the effect of the more powerful Soviet armament was negated by the less stable platforms), together with the doubled speed of engagements, certainly led to problems in determining victories and losses. Moreover, the aircraft were more reliable and able to take much more punishment than before. Some I-16s landed with sixty to eighty hits, and SB-2s could take hundreds. Very often pilots watched their rounds disappear into an adversary, followed by his sharp avoiding manoeuvre; this left them with

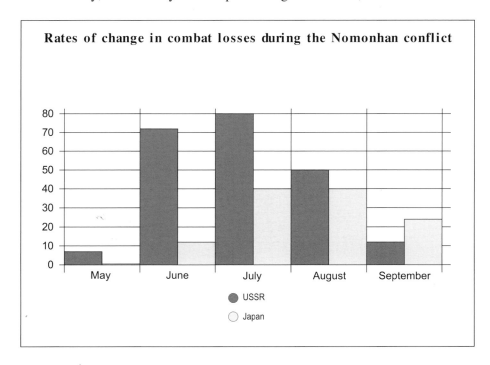

an impression of having destroyed him, whereas he may well have stayed in battle after fleeing the dogfight. Hence, analysts are left to do their own reckonings using the officially admitted figures by both sides.

The same conclusions may be drawn by comparing the data on page 27 with the number of combat aircraft sent to replace missing *sentai* aircraft (113 Ki-27s, twenty-six Ki-30s, six Ki-21s, eleven Ki-15s, fourteen Ki-4s and ten Ki-36s).[296] The same reasons called for the transfer from the USSR of not more than 300 aircraft of the basic types in the conflict.

Between 21 May and 15 September, Soviet aviation undertook 18,509 aircraft sorties by fighters and 2,015 sorties by bombers, used 990,266 ShKAS rounds, 75,057 PV-1 rounds, 57,979 20mm gun shells, and more than 78,360 bombs of various grades weighing a total of some 1,298 tonnes.[297] Three-quarters of the sorties aimed at securing air superiority, 17 per cent were for sealing battle areas and close air support, and 7 per cent were for aerial reconnaissance.

At the same time, Japanese airmen performed almost half this number of combat sorties, used 1.6 million rounds, and dropped 970 tonnes of bombs.[298] The basic method employed in battles was stepped-force introduction, but a feature of the conflict was the frequent use of simultaneous arrivals, leading to mass air battles. Using Spanish experience, Soviet air commanders delivered more frequent and more successful raids on enemy airfields as part of trying to secure air superiority. Using some 4 per cent of the air resource expended in the conflict for raids on base airfields, they secured 15 per cent of the overall Japanese aircraft losses.

It is clear that the aims of *Komkor* Georgiy Zhukov's successful advance called for significant reserves and a great amount of ordnance. Soviet logistic aviation made a great contribution to transporting this, using fifteen TB-3s and five Douglas aircraft for the purpose. They carried 2,235 tonnes, of which 1,350 tonnes were ordnance, the balance made up by troops. The same aeroplanes ferried back 5,056 wounded.[299]

Confirmed losses by major aircraft type in the Nomonhan conflict

Aircraft type	I-16	I-153	I-152	SB	TB-3	R-5Sh	Ki-27
Shot down in aerial combat	88	16	56	45	1	2	62
Lost for other reasons	24	6	4	8	1	1	34
Total	112	22	60	53	2	3	96

Aircraft type	Ki-10	Ki-30	Ki-21	Ki-15	Ki-36	Ki-4	BR.20
Shot down in aerial combat	3	11	3	7	3	1	–
Lost for other reasons	0	7	3	6	3	14	1
Total	3	18	6	13	6	15	1

The remains of a downed Polikarpov I-152. *(Svetoslav Spirov collection)*

Another advantage the Soviets had was in the calibre of their weapons. While Lt Gen Giga's pilots used rifle-calibre weapons and dropped mostly 15kg and 50kg bombs, the firepower of 20mm guns and 82mm NURS missiles (*Neupravlyaemie Reaktivnie Snaryady*, or Unguided Missile), the very rapid-firing ShKAS machine guns, and the mass use of 100kg and 250kg bombs lent enormous firepower to the Soviet air grouping. This has led some analysts of the events of the summer of 1939 to conclude that, had the 2nd *Hiko Syudan* had the same force strengths, means and reserve depth as the VVS RKKA, the Japanese land forces would never have been encircled and routed. Most Japanese pilots who took part in the conflict do not share this view, however. Despite their years in China, and the great losses they inflicted on the enemy, these pilots returned from the battlefield as defeated as their land force comrades. This largely determined their subsequent behaviour as a whole in Manchuria, and underwrote the peace on the eastern borders of the Soviet Union in the years of its supreme effort against the Nazi aggressor.

Tactically, the Ki-27 turned out to be the true master of the sky above the conflict area. A machine imbued with remarkable manoeuvrability, which could execute a tight 86-metre-radius turn in just 8.1 seconds, it remained to the last a dangerous adversary to Soviet airmen of all air services. Even the latest I-16 tip 10 was not much use against it. The type featured an M-25V engine pushed to 750hp and two additional fuselage-mounted ShKAS machine guns with 650 rounds each, in addition to the 900 rounds for each wing machine gun. It had air brakes, armour behind the pilot, and protected fuel tanks (mandatory fit from the I-16 tip 10 mark). Yet the sole visible advantage of the 'Ishak' in combat was its structural strength, which allowed it to take more punishment and power dive out of dogfights. The great delivery of rounds per second was negated by its poor stability; the engine proved to be a poor performer at altitude, allowing adversaries to climb away from dogfights; the armour could often be pierced; and the fuel tank fireproofing was of poor quality, allowing leaks after the first hits.

The I-15bis, which served as a mainstream fighter until the conflict's end, could only fight as part of mixed groups, its performance sentencing it to be a victim rather than an equal contender. The I-153 'Chayka' failed to live up to expectations; it was underdeveloped and embodied archaic ideas of the priorities of aerial warfare. The biplane had clearly had its day, and Japanese pilots did not take the type as a serious adversary. Neither was it more manoeuvrable, as had been hoped for. Its controls were heavier than those of the I-15bis, quickly tiring pilots, and the cockpit was draughty because of poorly fitting undercarriage seals. The upper wing bracing, the shape of which gave the aircraft its name ('Chayka' in Russian means 'Gull'), was also criticised for limiting forward visibility and hampering aiming. The wing turned out to be weak, as shown by seven cases of failure that led to non-combat fatalities. Before the August offensive, even experienced pilots converting to the type demonstrated lack of confidence and wariness of it. They continued to prefer the 'Ishak' as a mount against Japanese aces.

The 'Ishak' improved after being lightened. Its 32kg weight of engine-start batteries, oxygen equipment, radio (where fitted) and pneumatic air brake actuators (ineffective in fast and manoeuvrable dogfights) were stripped away. This, alongside the swapping of the M-25 engine with the M-62, improved I-16 performance significantly. Due to the oil tank position, the new engine initially had no pressure regulator and worked only at maximum revolutions, depriving it of a significant lifespan. After modifications to the lubrication system at the Zavod 21 factory, the problem was resolved and the I-16 tip 18 could face its Japanese adversary in Mongolia on almost even terms.

The Mongolian conflict showed the limited utility of aircraft designed to a philosophy of manoeuvrability in aerial combat for contemporary war. High speed, a strong structure and powerful armament turned out to be decisive for victory. Searing firepower, and armour plating that could withstand hits from Japanese 7.7mm rounds, put paid to Bushido's traditional views on samurai honour. Far East warriors were no longer concerned about loss of face should they have their cockpits and fuel tanks protected, as realism and common sense gained ground as a result of the conflict's lessons. A year after the sky over Mongolia grew quiet, the Ki-44 'Shoki' appeared, Japan's first fighter to feature an armour-plated pilot's seat and protected fuel tanks. Yet, as often happens in military establishments, the Japanese war machine did not respond properly and this powerful and rapid fighter was displaced by the Nakajima Ki-43 'Hayabusa', which shared its earlier and smaller brother's shortcomings.

Soviet and Mongolian supreme commanders appreciated the pilots' heroism highly. Of the seventy Heroes of the Soviet Union, twenty-three were pilots.[300] Smushkevich, Gritsavets and Kravchenko received this distinction for the second time. Some Heroes were awarded the honour posthumously. Sergey Gritsavets perished on 16 September, a day after the armistice between the USSR and Japan, during an I-152 ferry flight to the airfield near Orsha in Byelorussia. The 100th SABR was awarded the Order of Lenin, and the 22nd, 56th and 70th IAPs

59th *Sentai* pilots after the end of hostilities. *(MoD Archives, Bulgaria)*

were awarded the Order of the Red Banner. The 22nd IAP airmen were declared to have attained the best results. The unit became an elite one, its airmen managing 7,514 combat sorties in the eighty-five combat days from 22 June to 15 September, and destroying 262 Japanese aircraft, two static balloons, and much other equipment and men[301] (according to Soviet propaganda). Results claimed by Japanese fighters had been also impressive: 1st *Sentai*, 245 confirmed and ninety-five probable victories; 11th *Sentai*, 530 confirmed and fifty probable victories; 24th *Sentai*, 214 confirmed and fifty-six probable victories; 64th *Sentai*, fifty-two confirmed victories; 33rd *Sentai*, forty-one confirmed and eight probable; and 59th *Sentai*, eleven confirmed victories.[302]

The victory the Soviets achieved undoubtedly solved some strategic problems along the eastern borders of the enormous Communist state. To some extent, it may be argued to have saved it from defeat in the critical year of 1941. However, lack of the requisite self-criticism in the analysis of the results of the Mongolian campaign, including the lessons learned in the air and those linked with the knowledgeable Command and Control of its genuine potential, were amply repaid in the war against Finland and in the difficult years of the World War that followed it. These latter events, however, form the topic of other descriptions of the use of aviation in war.

Khalkhin-Gol remains in history as not only the name of a border river that has seen one of the many human conflicts at close quarters, but also as a place that first saw the massed use of air power to attain decisive objectives in a high-intensity local military conflict. This is where total aerial confrontation began.

Polikarpov I-15bis with additional grey lined camouflage

Polikarpov I-15bis , 70 IAP, Tamsak-Bulak airfield

Polikarpov I-15bis , 70 IAP, Tamsak-Bulak airfield

Kawasaki Ki-10-II, 33 S*entai* 3 *Chutai,* early September 1939

Polikarpov I-16 tip 10, 70 IAP

Polikarpov I-16 tip 10 with doubled number insignia

Polikarpov I-16 tip 10, 22 IAP

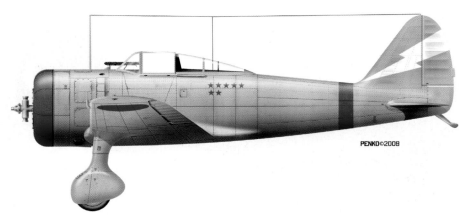

Nakajima Ki-27b, 11 *Sentai* 1 *Chutai*. Flown by Kendgi Shimada, Mandjuria 1939

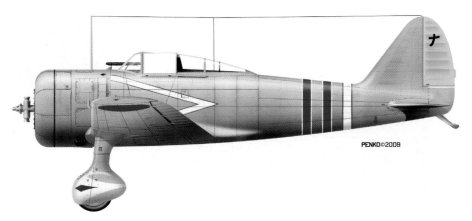

Nakajima Ki-27b, 1 *Sentai* 1 *Chutai*, Mandjuria 1939

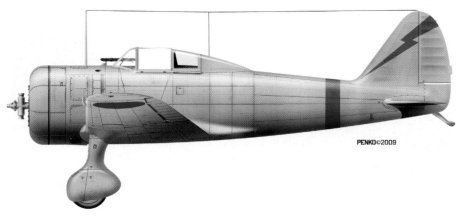

Nakajima Ki-27a, 11 *Sentai* 2 *Chutai*, Mandjuria 1939

Polikarpov I-153, 70 IAP. Flown by deputy Squadron Leader Victor Gusarov

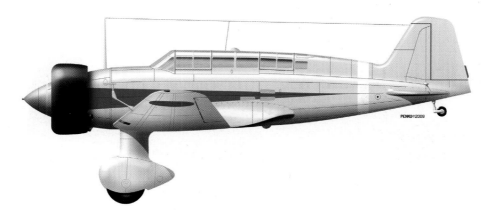

Mitsubishi K-15, 15 *Sentai*, Mandjuria July 1939

Polikarpov R-5SSS, summer 1939

Polikarpov R-Z from an unknown reconnaissance air regiment, May 1939

Nyeman R-10 from an unknown reconnaissance air regiment, 1939

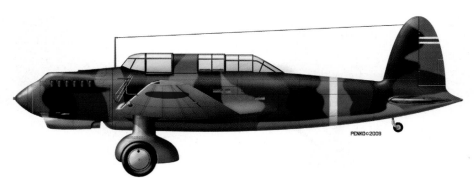

Kawasaki Ki-32, 75 S*entai*

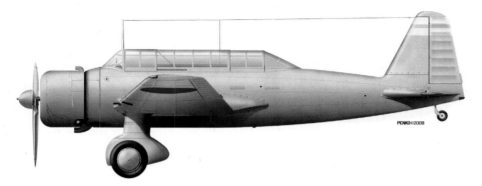

Kawasaki Ki-30, 16 *Sentai* 1 *Chutai*, Hailar airfield, May 1939

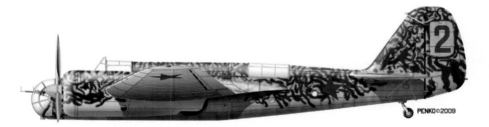

Tupolev SB-2 M-103, 49 SBAP, Mongolia 1940

Tupolev SB-2 of 2 Squadron 49 SBAP 100 Airbrigade

Fiat BR-20 of 12 *Sentai*

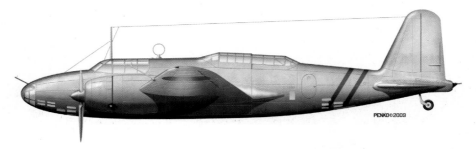

Mitsubishi Ki-21, 60 *Sentai* 2 *Chutai,* Mongolia 1939

Tupolev TB-3, 4 TBAP 19 transport-medical squadron, named 'Major Egrov's group'

Appendix 1

Aircraft used in the conflict

The Nakajima Ki-27 prototype. *(MoD Archives, Bulgaria)*

A captured Nakajima Ki-27 undergoing trials at the Soviet Air Testing Centre. *(MoD Archives, Bulgaria)*

Ki-27 (Army Fighter Type 97)

Engineer Yasushi Koyama designed the Ki-27a fighter (Army Fighter Type 97) in 1936 at Nakajima. A prototype and ten pre-production aircraft followed the experimental example. The first flight took place on 15 October 1936, tests ended successfully in late 1937, and the new fighter entered production.

The machine was an all-metal monoplane with a fixed undercarriage and enclosed cockpit, whose middle section opened by sliding back. The fuselage was a semi-monocoque structure skinned with duralumin. An auxiliary fuel tank sat behind the engine and ahead of the instrument panel. A hatch below

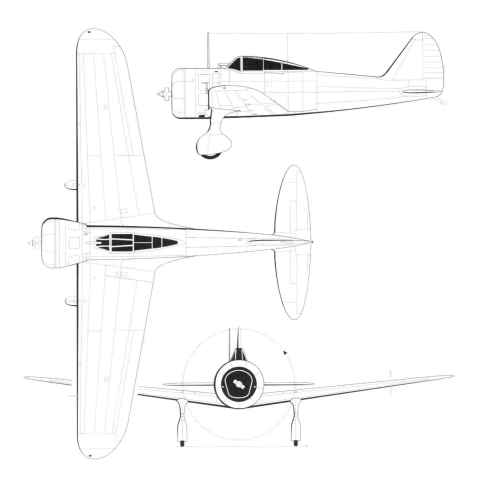

Ki-27-II p

The Nakajima Ki-27b at frontline airfield. *(MoD Archives, Bulgaria)*

the cockpit offered access to a compartment used for technical inspections, which could also accommodate light loads for ferry flights. The fixed parts of the empennage were also skinned in duralumin, while the rudder and elevators were cloth-covered.

The wing was an all-metal structure with a thin profile and duralumin skinning. The ailerons were cloth-covered, and the flaps were mechanically actuated. The wing contained four fuel tanks.

The undercarriage was fixed and spatted to reduce drag. The struts had air/oil oleos and there were mechanical wheel brakes. The tail strut was fixed and had spring/oil damping.

The Ki-27's navaid and light fit allowed night-flying, and it also had oxygen equipment. Officers' aircraft also had radiotelephone transceivers, other machines having receivers only.

The engine was a nine-cylinder Nakajima Ha-I, a single-row air-cooled radial developing 650hp. It drove a two-bladed variable-pitch metal propeller with a diameter of 3.1m/10ft 2in. The engine had a reductor and supercharger.

Armament comprised two synchronised 7.7mm Type 89 machine guns located over the engine, each with 1,000 rounds. The trigger was fitted over the engine lever, and aiming was through an optical gunsight protruding through the cockpit coaming.

In all, 565 Ki-27as were produced. Improvements were made from the very beginning. The first step involved fitting the more powerful Nakajima Ha-Ib engine of up to 780hp output. Further changes were incorporated in the Ki-27b: improved cockpit glazing, the option of two underwing auxiliary tanks of 130 litres/22.6 gallons each or four 25kg/55lb bombs. Some 1,492 examples of this version were produced. In parallel, 255 dual-control combat trainers were also manufactured.

These fighters were in active service until the close of the Second World War. Some 1,330 of them were intended for kamikaze attacks, fitted with a single 500kg/1,100lb underslung bomb. The overall number of test and production examples came to 3,386 by the close of manufacture in 1942.

After thorough tests of a Ki-27a captured in 1939, Soviet experts concluded that the Japanese fighter was superior to the Soviet I-152, I-16 and I-153 in level manoeuvres, confirming the machine's reputation as a dangerous adversary.

Ki-27b data

Span	11.35m/37ft 4in
Length	7.53m/24ft 8in
Height	3.00m/9ft 10in
Wing area	$18.61m^2$/200.3sq ft
Empty weight	1,110kg/2,425lb
Typical gross weight	1,790kg/3,946lb
Engine type	Nakajima Ha-Ib
Engine output	780hp
Top speed at ground level	395kmph/213kt
Maximum speed	468kmph/252kt
Range	1,790km/1,112 miles
Rate of climb	920m per min/3,018ft per min
Ceiling	10,000m/32,000ft
Crew	One
Armament	Two 7.7mm synchronised Type 89 machine guns and 100kg/245lb bombs

Ki-10 (Army Fighter Type 95)

The Ki-10 fighter (or Army Fighter Type 95) was designed in 1934 at Kawasaki by engineers Takeo Doi and Isami Imachi. The first four prototypes were ready for testing by early 1935. The machine was an all-metal biplane with a fixed undercarriage and open cockpit. The fuselage was a duralumin-skinned semi-monocoque structure; a similar approach was applied to the fixed parts of the empennage. The elevators and rudder were cloth-skinned metal structures.

The one-piece upper wing carried the ailerons, whereas the lower wing was divided into a centre section and outer wings. The two wings were braced by N-shaped struts and cabling. Initial production aircraft had timber leading edges, later machines having duralumin. Behind this, the wings were cloth-covered.

The split-axle undercarriage had oil and spring damping and carried mechanical brake linkages. Though the structure was spatted and faired, these items were usually removed on forward airfields. The tailskid was free-swivelling.

The Ki-10 was fitted with aids and lights for night-flying. The design had foreseen oxygen equipment, and leaders' aircraft had radio sets.

The engine was the twelve-cylinder Ha.9-Iia (a Japanese licence-manufactured BMW.9). This water-cooled 860hp twelve-cylinder V-engine drove a three-bladed metal propeller of 2.9m/9ft 6in diameter with a ground-variable pitch.

Armament comprised two synchronised 7.7mm Type 89 machine guns fitted over the engine and stores of 450 rounds for each of them. The firing button was located over the engine lever, and aiming was through an optical gunsight on the windscreen.

The first production Ki-10-Is began entering service in December 1935. Some 300 of these first-series machines had been built by late 1937. Experience, including that from combat in China, dictated design changes to boost manoeuvrability and longitudinal stability, so important for firing precision.

Takeo Doi offered the updated Ki-10-II in mid-1936, the version entering production in October 1937. This had 51cm/21in extra upper span, a 35cm/14in tail cone extension and a taller fin. Some 280 Ki-10-IIs were manufactured before construction of Japan's last biplane fighter ended in December 1938. Some of them served in the 33rd *Sentai* during the Nomonhan conflict.

A Ki-10-II captured by the Chinese was tested by Soviet specialists in mid-1938, flying mock combat with I-15s, I-16s, R-10s and DB-3s. Honours were found to be equal with the Soviet biplane fighters, being slower than the I-16 yet offering more concentrated firing. The Japanese fighter was no threat to the DB-3, but it was dangerous to the R-10. Evaluations continued until September 1938, when the captured machine was damaged beyond repair.

Ki-10s were on air defence duty until 1942, remaining as Japanese Air Force trainers until 1944. Update attempts were made, but failed to reach fruition. A total of 588 aircraft were manufactured.

Ki-10-II data

Span	10.02m/32ft 11in
Length	7.55m/24ft 10in
Height	3m/9ft 10in
Wing area	23m²/247.6sq ft
Empty weight	1,360kg/3,000lb
Typical take-off weight	1,740kg/3,836lb
Engine type	Kawasaki Ha.9-Iia
Engine output	860hp
Maximum low-altitude speed	376 kmph/208kt
Maximum speed	400kmph/216kt
Range	1,100km/680 miles
Rate of climb	1,000m per min/3,280ft per min
Ceiling	11,500m/37,730ft
Crew	One
Armament	Two 7.7mm synchronised Type 89 machine guns

Ki-10 captured by Russians. *(MoD Archives, Bulgaria)*

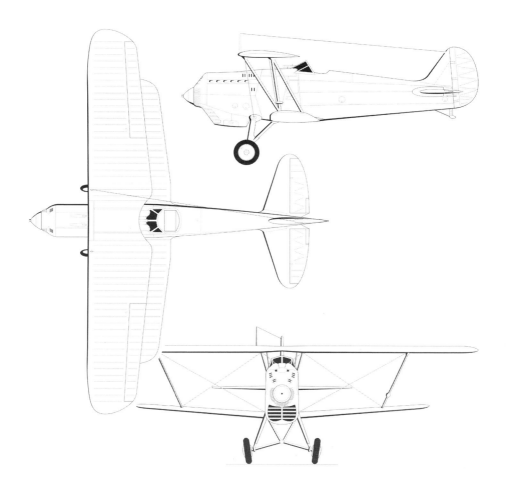

Ki-10-II p

Polikarpov I-16

The I-16 fighter was designed in 1934 under Nikolay Nikolayevich Polikarpov. The first prototypes were successfully tested that same year, with more than 1,400 I-16 tip 4 and tip 5 having been manufactured by late 1936.

The fighter was a mixed-structure monoplane with a retractable undercarriage and enclosed cockpit. Later versions had open cockpits and 8mm armour behind the pilot's seat. The fuselage was a wooden semi-monocoque with plywood skinning covered with smooth doped cloth. The tailplane and fin were cloth-covered metal structures.

Wings had metal structures divided into a centre section and outer wings. The leading edge was duralumin-covered, the remainder cloth-covered. The ailerons, cloth-covered metal structures, occupied the entire trailing edge, drooping by 15° to double as flaps on landing.

The undercarriage was of a pyramidal layout, with oil/gas damping. It was retracted into open wells in the centre section by manual means, actuated by a handle on the starboard side of the cockpit. Brakes were pedal-actuated. The tailskid was steerable and had rubber damping.

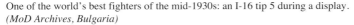

One of the world's best fighters of the mid-1930s: an I-16 tip 5 during a display. *(MoD Archives, Bulgaria)*

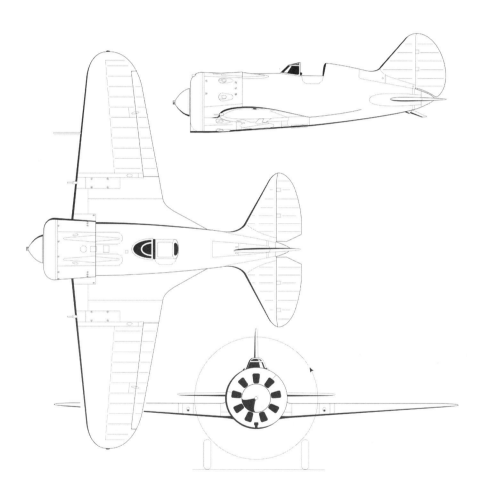

I-16 tip 10

The navigational and lighting fit allowed partial night operation. Oxygen and radio were foreseen by the designers, but Soviet equipment was of poor quality and none was fitted.

All I-16 versions had nine-cylinder single-row air-cooled radial engines rated at 1,100hp for take-off. They drove a 2.8m/9ft 2in two-bladed metal propeller with ground-variable pitch; versions from the I-16 tip 10 onwards had flight-variable propeller pitch.

Armament comprised two wing-mounted and two engine-mounted synchronised 7.62mm ShKAS machine guns with stores of 500 rounds for each (some versions after tip 12 had 20mm guns or 12.7mm machine guns). The firing button was positioned on the joystick. Aiming was through the optical and mechanical OP-1 gunsight positioned in the windscreen. It was also possible to carry up to 500kg/1,100lb of bombs or fit 82mm rocket-propelled grenades.

The initial I-16 tip 4 and tip 5s began arming combat units in early 1935, and these units entered action in 1936. Further versions followed very quickly, seeing action in Spain and later China, and over the Khalkhin-Gol River in due course.

The I-16 was a fighter calling for careful piloting by highly qualified personnel. Though considered obsolete by late 1939, production continued until early 1942. Active duty continued until late 1943, when it was withdrawn from service (the Spanish Air Force used the type until the early 1950s). The fighter underwent many update programmes affecting all 10,292 units manufactured.

I-16 tip 5 (*Svetoslav Spirov collection*)

I-16 data

Parameter	I-16 tip 5	I-16 tip 10	I-16 tip 17	I-16 tip 18
Span	9m/29ft 6 in	9.004m/29ft 6 in	9.004m/29ft 6 in	9.004m/29ft 6 in
Length	5.985m/19ft 7.5in	6.074m/19ft 11in	6.074m/19ft 11in	6.074m/19ft 11in
Height	3.25m/10ft 8in	3.25m/10ft 8in	3.25m/10ft 8in	3.25m/10ft 8in
Wing area	14.54m²/156.5sq ft	14.54m²/156.5sq ft	14.54m²/156.5sq ft	14.54m²/156.5sq ft
Empty weight	1,118kg/2,465lb	1,327kg/2,926lb	1,425kg/3,142lb	1,433kg/3,159lb
Typical gross weight	1,508kg/3,325lb	1,716kg/3,783lb	1,810kg/3,990lb	1,830kg/4,034lb
Engine type	M-25A	M-25B	M-25B	M-62
Engine output	730hp	750hp	750hp	800hp
Top speed at ground level	390kmph/211kt	398kmph/215kt	385kmph/208kt	413kmph/223kt
Maximum speed	445kmph/240kt	448kmph/242kt	425kmph/229kt	461kmph/249kt
Range	540km/335 miles	525km/326 miles	417km/259 miles	485km/301 miles
Rate of climb to 5,000m/16,400ft	850m per min/ 2,800ft per min	882m per min/ 2,900ft per min	668m per min/ 2,200ft per min	1,034m per min/ 3400ft per min
Ceiling	9,100m/29,900ft	8,470m/28,700ft	8,240m/27,000ft	9,300m/30,500ft
Crew	One	One	One	One
Armament	Two 7.62mm	Four 7.62mm	Two 7.62mm, two 20mm	Four 7.62mm

Polikarpov I-15bis (I-152)

The I-15bis fighter was designed in 1935 under Nikolay Nikolayevich Polikarpov, and was an update of the earlier I-15, regarding which Soviet military opinion was split. Production approval was given after the experimental example had been tested, manufacture commencing in early 1938.

The fighter was a mixed-structure, fixed-undercarriage, open-cockpit biplane. Its fuselage had a metal spaceframe structure of welded steel tubing, clad in duralumin sheeting forward and cloth behind. The fin and tailplane were cloth-covered metal structures.

The wings had metal-jointed timber structures. The upper one, with a duralumin centre section and timber outer wings, was fixed to the fuselage by N-shaped struts. It had cloth-covered duralumin ailerons. Upper and lower wings were braced by I-section struts and steel cabling. Both wings had duralumin leading edges and cloth skinning behind.

The undercarriage was of the cantilever type, with oil and air damping. It had spats, and the brakes were mechanical. The tail strut was controllable through the rudder pedals.

The navigational and light fit allowed partial night-flying. Oxygen equipment was foreseen by the designers, as was radio, but in the event few machines were equipped with either.

The M-25B engine was a single-row nine-cylinder air-cooled radial developing 775hp on take-off. It drove a twin-blade metal fixed-pitch propeller of 2.8m/9ft 2in diameter. The engine had an improved NACA cowling and was rated for higher altitudes than the M-25A.

Armament comprised four synchronised 7.62mm PV-1 machine guns fitted ahead of the cockpit and sharing a store of 3,050 rounds. The firing button was fitted to the top of the joystick. Aiming was through a mechanical or optical gunsight (the latter of the OP-1 type) fitted through the windscreen. Up to 150kg/330lb of bombs, each up to 50kg/110lb, could be fitted.

The I-152 was obsolescent even at the start of its life. Despite this, 2,408 machines were built between early 1938 and late 1939, seeing action in Spain, China, the Khalkhin-Gol River and the early stages of the Great Fatherland War, as the Soviets termed their participation in the Second World War. The fighter's combat career ended in 1943, and the following year it was withdrawn from training squadrons. It flew on in Spanish service until 1950.

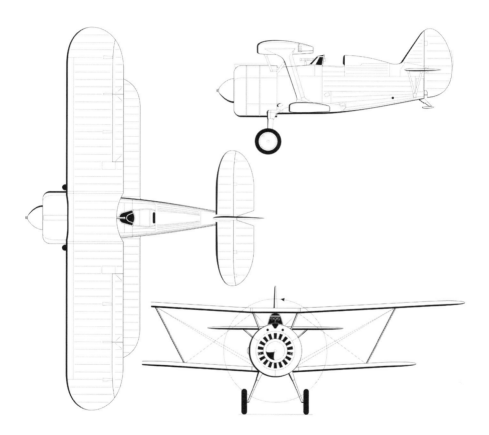

I-15bis

I-15bis (I-152) data

Span	10.2m/33ft 5in
Length	6.27m/20ft 7in
Height	3m/9ft 10in
Wing area	22.5m^2/242.2sq ft
Empty weight	1,310kg/2,888lb
Typical take-off weight	1,730kg/3,814lb
Engine	M-25B
Engine output	775hp
Top speed at ground level	327kmph/176kt
Maximum speed	379kmph/205kt
Range	520km/323 miles
Rate of climb	625m per min/2,050ft per min
Ceiling	9,800m/32,150ft
Crew	One
Armament	Four 7.62mm synchronised PV-1 machine guns and up to 150kg/330lb bombs

An I-152 in Spain. (*Svetoslav Spirov collection*)

Polikarpov I-153

The I-153 fighter was developed by Nikolay Polikarpov alongside the I-152. The two experimental machines, fitted with M-25B engines, began testing in August 1938. Aerodynamically and structurally similar to the I-152, the machine took account of Spanish combat experience.

The fuselage was still a metal spaceframe. It had an open cockpit with 8mm armour plating behind the pilot's seat. To boost speed, the undercarriage retracted to the rear using a pneumatic system. Again to boost speed, the upper wing was redesigned to a 'gull' type, the twinned centre section being made of duralumin. Other than that, the wings retained their timber structures clad with plywood and cloth. Their joints with the fuselage were faired.

All I-153s had a single-row nine-cylinder air-cooled radial engine developing 1100hp on take-off. It drove a twin-bladed metal propeller of 2.8m/9ft 2in diameter, initially of fixed pitch, later with flight-variable pitch. The engine cowling was streamlined, with a reduced diameter, as on the I-16.

The fighter carried diverse armament. The initial fit comprised four synchronised ShKAS machine guns and 2,500 rounds. Later, 12.7mm machine guns were fitted, while some machines received twin 20mm synchronised guns, as later used on the La-5 and La-7 fighters. Apart from bombs, some I-153s were armed with unguided RS-82 rocket-propelled grenades.

The I-153's combat career began over the Khalkhin-Gol, where Soviet theatre commanders saw it as a rather useful fighter. During its series production, between early 1939 and late 1941, 3,437 aircraft of the type were manufactured. The fighter saw active service until late 1943, flying on in Finnish service until 1944, the year that Soviet flying schools retired it.

The Polikarpov I-153 'Chayka'. *(MoD Archives, Bulgaria)*

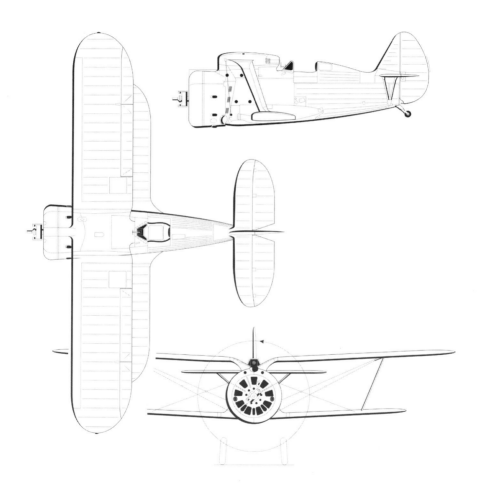

I-153 Chajka

I-153 data

Span	10m/32ft 10in
Length	6.18m/20ft 3in
Height	3m/9ft 10in
Wing area	22.14m²/238.3sq ft
Empty weight	1,348kg/2,972lb
Typical gross weight	1,765kg/3,891lb
Engine type	M-62
Engine output	800hp
Top speed at ground level	364kmph/196kt
Maximum speed	426kmph/230kt
Range	560km/348 miles
Rate of climb	910m per min/2,985ft per min
Ceiling	11,000m/36,000ft
Crew	One
Armament	Four 7.62mm synchronised ShKAS machine guns and up to 200kg/440lb bombs

I-153 with winter equipment. (*Svetoslav Spirov collection*)

Ki-36 in recce flight. (*Svetoslav Spirov collection*)

Tatikawa Ki-36 (Army Type 98)

The 'Direct Co-Operation' Tatikawa Ki-36 (Army Type 98) multi-role aircraft was designed in March 1938 by the Tatikawa Hikoki KK Design Team of the Tatikawa Aeroplane Company under the leadership of company chief designer Ryokichi Endo. Testing began on 20 April the same year and confirmed expectations: the machine offered excellent control and manoeuvrability. Take-offs and landings were possible from small, unprepared strips.

Prototype testing led to approval of series production, which began in November 1938. The Tatikawa Ki-36 was a cantilever low-wing monoplane of all-metal structure, covered by a mix of light alloy and fabric. Its wing comprised a centre section and cantilevered outer wings, and had a characteristic sweepback to improve downward visibility. The rudder and elevators had large areas to ensure high manoeuvrability. The two-man crew was enclosed by a long 'greenhouse' canopy and both men had good fields of view, that of the observer being improved by clear-view panels in the floor.

Landing gear was of the fixed tailwheel type, the main units being enclosed in spats. Navaids and lights allowed limited night operations. A radio transceiver and photographic equipment were fitted.

The prototype's engine was the Hitachi Ha-13 nine-cylinder single-row air-cooled radial providing 450hp. This drove a twin-bladed metal fixed-pitch propeller of 2.8m/9ft 2in diameter. Production machines had more powerful Hitachi Ha-13a engines developing up to 510hp for take-off.

Ki-36s were armed with one 7.7mm machine-gun offset to starboard and firing through the cowling, aiming being through a telescopic sight passing through the canopy. A rearward-firing 7.7mm Type 89 machine gun was available to the observer. Underwing racks could accommodate up to ten 12.5kg/28lb or 15kg/33lb fragmentation bombs.

The Ki-36 was first deployed with considerable success in China. Used on forward airstrips, it was exceptionally useful to Army commanders. The machine also scored successes over the Khalkhin-Gol. Mainly conducting reconnaissance at tactical depth, it also took part in striking targets near the front line.

By 1943 the machine had seen action against the Allies in the Pacific, thereafter being confined largely to China. It was also considered suitable for kamikaze use in the closing stages of the war, being modified to carry internally a bomb of up to 500kg/1,100lb.

When production ended in January 1944, 1,334 had been built, 862 by Tatikawa and 472 by Kawasaki. The type's combat career ended on the Civil War fronts in China, where it flew until 1948. It was also used as a trainer.

Ki-36 data

Span	11.8m/38ft 8in
Length	8m/26ft 3in
Height	3.64m/11ft 10in
Wing area	20m²/215.28sq ft
Empty weight	1,247kg/3,307lb
Typical gross weight	1,660kg/3,660lb
Engine type	Hitachi Ha-13a
Engine output	510hp
Dash speed	348kmph/188kt
Cruise speed	236kmph/127kt
Range	1,235km/767 miles
Rate of climb	448m per min/1470ft per min
Ceiling	8,150m/26,700ft
Crew	Two
Armament	7.7mm Type 89 synchronised pilot's and observer's machine guns and 150kg/330lb bombs

Ki-32 (*Svetoslav Spirov collection*)

Kawasaki Ki-32 (Army Type 98)

The Kawasaki Ki-32 (Army Type 98) single-engine twin-seat light bomber was designed in 1936 at the Kawasaki Aircraft Engineering Company under the leadership of Isamu Imati and Shiro Ota. It was the last bomber in the Imperial Army to be powered by a liquid-cooled engine. The first of eight Ki-32 prototypes took to the air in March 1937, but right from the start of testing the aircraft revealed serious detuning problems caused by engine unreliability, which led to the project being set aside.

The growing need for light bombers capable of striking from horizontal flight or from dives reinstated the project in military planning, and in July 1938 it went into production, the first aircraft coming off the assembly lines later the same year.

The Kawasaki Ki-32 was an all-metal mid-wing monoplane with a wide-track fixed cantilever undercarriage featuring open-sided spats and a bomb bay in the fuselage. Wing and tail surfaces were finely tapered.

The two-man crew (pilot and radio operator/bomb aimer) was enclosed and provided with excellent visibility in all directions. The navigational and lighting fit allowed night operations. The aircraft was fitted with radio transceivers.

The Army Type 98 was powered by a Kawasaki Ha-9-IIb V-12 liquid-cooled piston engine rated at 850hp for take-off, 775hp at sea level and 950hp at 3,800m/12,500ft. This drove a three-blade variable-pitch metal propeller.

Ki-32s were armed with one 7.7mm machine gun offset to starboard and firing through the cowling. Aiming was through a telescopic sight passing through the canopy. A rearward-firing 7.7mm Type 89 machine gun was fitted in the observer's compartment. The bomb bay accommodated 300kg/660lb of warload, supplemented by 150kg/330lb of bombs on external racks. The bombs could be dropped both in horizontal flight and in dives of up to 60°.

Delivery of the Kawasaki Ki-32 commenced in July 1938, production ending in May 1940. A total of 854 were built over this period. Its debut was in combat during the second Sino-Japanese conflict, and the type also saw action at the very close of the Khalkhin-Gol conflict. Popular among flyers for its good manoeuvrability, it remained in front-line service until the beginning of 1942. The type then found employment in training units.

Ki-32 data

Span	15m/49ft 2in
Length	11.65m/38ft 2in
Height	2.9m/9ft 6in
Wing area	34m²/366sq ft
Empty weight	2,181kg/4,808lb
Gross weight	3,762kg/8,294lb
Engine type	Kawasaki Ha-9-IIb
Engine output	850hp
Dash speed	423kmph/228kt
Cruise speed	300kmph/162kt
Range	1,965km/1,221 miles
Rate of climb	460m per min/1,510ft per min
Ceiling	8,920m/29,260ft
Crew	Two
Armament	Two 7.7mm Type 89 synchronised machine guns and 450kg/990lb bombs

Testing engines was a very important duty of ground personnel, especially for the Imperial Air Force's sole water-cooled aircraft. *(MoD Archives, Bulgaria)*

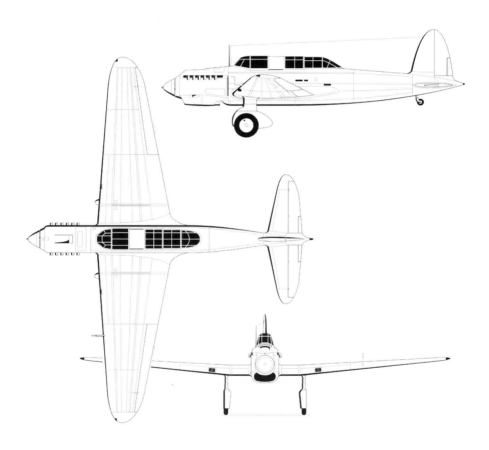

Ki-32

A Ki-30 on a recce mission over disputed territory. *(MoD Archives, Bulgaria)*

(Svetoslav Spirov collection)

Ki-30 (Army Type 97)

The Army Type 97 Ki-30 was a single-engined, multi-seat land-based light bomber designed by a Mitsubishi design team consisting of engineers Kawano, Mizumo and Ohki. Design began in 1936 with the task of creating an all-new light bomber suited to modern warfare.

The first prototype, powered by the Mitsubishi Ha-6 fourteen-cylinder air-cooled radial engine (developing 825hp), took off on its maiden flight on 28 February 1937 from Kagamigahara airfield. A second prototype, differing from the first solely in being powered by the Nakajima Ha-5 engine, was completed during the same month. It was the first Japanese aircraft of its kind fitted with a double-row air-cooled radial engine, split flaps, an internal bomb bay, and a variable-pitch three-bladed propeller.

Originally the all-metal, mid-wing monoplane was to have had a retractable main undercarriage, but fixed gear with spatted main wheels was chosen instead. Control surfaces were fabric-covered. The wing was mounted at a point above the line of the aircraft's belly so as to make a fully enclosed bomb bay possible. The pilot sat just above the leading edge of the wing, and the rear gunner/radio operator just behind the trailing edge. Both were under a long, extensively framed 'greenhouse' canopy offering excellent all-round vision. Oddly, there was no onboard intercom, pilot and gunner communicating through a primitive Gosport tube.

The Ki-30 was armed with one 7.7mm machine-gun offset to starboard and firing through the cowling. It was aimed using a telescopic sight through the canopy. There was a rearward-firing 7.7mm Type 89 machine gun in the observer's compartment. The bomb bay accommodated 300kg/60lb of warload, supplemented by 150kg/330lb of bombs on external racks. These could be dropped in level flight or in dives of up to 60°.

Sixteen service test examples were completed by January 1938, all powered by the Ha-5-Kai radial. Only two other changes were made: the forward-firing 7.7mm machine gun was moved from the port undercarriage leg to the left wing, and the outboard main wheel covers were removed to ease operations from muddy, unpaved forward airfields. Once these first sixteen planes were built and tested, the new aircraft was put into production as the Army Type 97 Light Bomber (Ki-30) in March 1938.

The Ki-30 swiftly established a reputation as one of the Japanese Air Force's most reliable machines once it was committed to combat over China in the spring of 1938. Losses were low as it nearly always operated under cover of escorting Ki-27 fighters. The same was proved by combat during the Nomonhan conflict, where the Ki-30 was the Japanese air group's main strike aircraft.

When the Pacific War begin in December 1941, the Type 97 was committed to operations in the Philippines once Japan gained local aerial superiority, but it quickly became clear that it was no match for modern Allied fighters. By the end of 1942 the aircraft were relegated to training, and others were transferred to the Royal Thai Air Force, which had already used the Ki-30 as early as January 1941 against the French in Indochina. In 1945, together with other obsolete aircraft, the Ki-30 was used as a kamikaze carrier while Japan desperately tried to stave off defeat.

The parent company built 618 production machines through April 1940, and the First Army Air Arsenal at Tatikawa built sixty-eight more by the time production ceased in September 1941. Including prototypes and service-test types, a grand total of 704 Ki-30s were built.

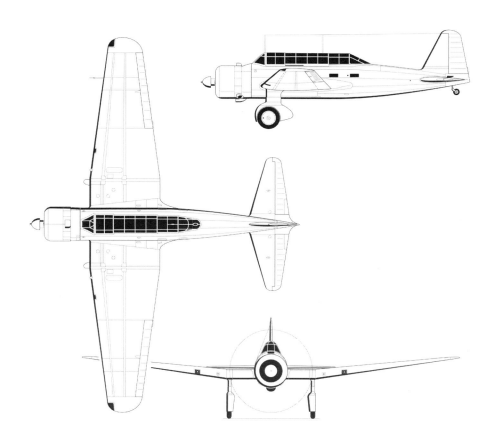

Ki-30

Ki-30 data

Span	14.55m/47ft 9in
Length	10.34m/33ft 10in
Height	3.64m/11ft 10in
Wing area	30.58m²/329.17sq ft
Empty weight	2,230kg/4,916lb
Gross weight	3,322kg/7,324lb
Engine type	Nakajima Ha-5-Kai
Engine output	950hp
Dash speed	432kmph/233kt
Cruise speed	380kmph/205kt
Range	1,965km/1,221 miles
Rate of climb	490m per min/1600ft per min
Ceiling	8,570m/28,120ft
Crew	Two
Armament	Two 7.7mm Type 89 pilot's and observer's synchronised machine guns and 450kg/990lb bombs

Mitsubishi Ki-21 (Army Type 97)

The Army Type 97 Heavy Bomber Model 2A (Mitsubishi Ki-21) was designed by a Mitsubishi design team headed by engineers Ozawa and Nakata. Their task was to meet an Imperial Japanese Army requirement of early 1936 for a four-seat bomber.

The K-21 was a mid-wing monoplane of all-metal construction. The design incorporated retractable tailwheel landing gear, a ventral bomb bay and two radial engines in nacelles at the leading edge of each wing. The fuselage was an oval-section semi-monocoque structure with stressed skin. The wing was split into three sections, with flaps and light alloy skinning. The ailerons were cloth-covered. The metal empennage was also cloth-covered. The undercarriage was retracted and extended using a hydraulic system. The Ki-21 had 825hp Mitsubishi Ha-6 radial engines.

The bomber was first flown on 18 December 1936. After initial testing, the manufacturer continued to improve the machine, making a further four prototypes that demonstrated better qualities. They had two 850hp Nakajima Ha-5-Kai fourteen-cylinder two-row radial engines. The Army had no hesitation in ordering the aircraft into production under the designation Army Type 97 Heavy Bomber Model 1A, company designation Mitsubishi Ki-21-Ia. Service delivery started in late 1937, and the first of the production aircraft began to enter service in the summer of 1938.

The Mitsubishi Ki-21. *(MoD Archives, Bulgaria)*

Initial machines had only three 7.7mm machine guns for self-protection from enemy fighters. Despite this, the Ki-21-Ia proved itself significantly better suited to combat than the imported Italian Fiat BR.20 bombers in the same class. Its equipment allowed night operations, helping avoid losses when striking targets beyond the combat radius of escorting fighters. The bomber entered the Nomonhan conflict on 27 June 1939. One of the six aircraft lost during the encounter force-landed in Soviet-held territory, becoming the trophy of Soviet commanders.

The bombers continued to be improved based on experience and were used in the Pacific theatre. Ki-21s were manufactured until September 1944 by Mitsubishi (1,713) and Nakajima (351), remaining on strength until mid-1945.

Ki-21 data

Span	22.5m/73ft 10in
Length	16m/52ft 6in
Height	4.85m/15ft 11in
Wing area	69.6m^2/749sq ft
Empty weight	6,070kg/13,382lb
Gross weight	10,610kg/23,390lb
Engine type	Nakajima Ha-5-Kai
Engine output	950hp
Dash speed	486kmph/262kt
Cruise speed	380kmph/205kt
Range	2,700km/1,678 miles
Rate of climb	360m per min/1180ft per min
Ceiling	10,000m/32,800ft
Crew	Five to seven
Armament	Five 7.7mm Type 89 machine guns (nose, ventral, tail, port and starboard) and one 12.7mm Type 1 machine gun in dorsal turret, plus 1,000kg/2,205lb bombs

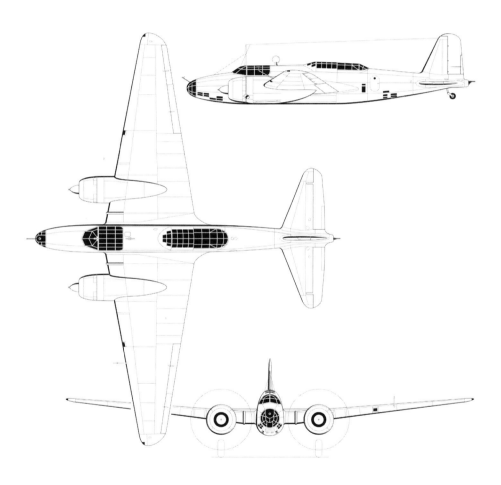

Ki-21

The Mitsubishi Ki-21. (*Svetoslav Spirov collection*)

A Japanese Fiat BR.20 of the 12th *Sentai*. (*MoD Archives, Bulgaria*)

Fiat BR.20

The Fiat BR.20 bomber was designed by renowned Italian aeronautical engineer Celestino Rosatelli in 1935. The project aimed to create a high-speed strike aircraft while taking account of Italian industrial potential. The result was a technically conservative machine.

The BR.20 was an all-metal twin-engined low-wing monoplane. The fuselage was a welded steel tube spaceframe, with approximately half covered in duralumin and half with cloth. The tail surfaces utilised the then-fashionable twin-fin configuration.

The wing was all-metal, with flaps and ailerons. It carried the two twin-row eighteen-cylinder air-cooled Fiat A.80RC.41 engines, each developing 1,030hp. They drove three-bladed metal propellers with automatically variable pitch. Hydraulics retracted the main undercarriage legs into the engines' nacelles. The tailwheel had a spat.

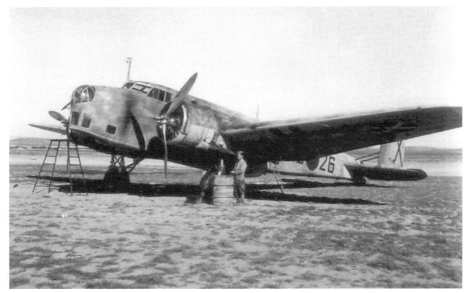

Fiat BR.20 in General Franco service. (*Svetoslav Spirov collection*)

The bomber's armament comprised four 7.69mm SAFAT machine guns with 500 rounds each. The bomb load was up to 1,600kg/3,500lb, with the largest store being a 800kg/1,750lb high-explosive bomb. Aiming this was through a rather primitive sight used by the bomb-aimer who occupied the nosecone. Apart from him, the crew comprised a pilot, navigator and two machine gunners. Technological simplicity allowed the first experimental Fiat BR.20 to be completed and enter flight testing by 10 February 1936. The machine had no significant shortcomings and entered production that September. The first batch of twenty had been accepted by the military by February 1937.

Later the same year, six of the type were sent to Spain for combat testing. Somewhat later, the Japanese Government contracted with the manufacturers for the supply of seventy-two bombers, which were received in 1938; thirty-six entered 12th *Sentai* service under the Type I designation. Spares shortages amid active combat rapidly reduced the availability of airworthy machines.

Soviet intelligence in China first noted the type in early 1939. Japanese crews quickly learned that the Italian machine's armament was unable to repulse fighters effectively. This and other shortcomings also came to the fore during the Nomonhan conflict, after which the type was retired from service.

The Fiat BR.20 bomber continued to be developed and produced until mid-1943. A total of 580 were built, being active until the close of hostilities in Italy towards the end of the war.

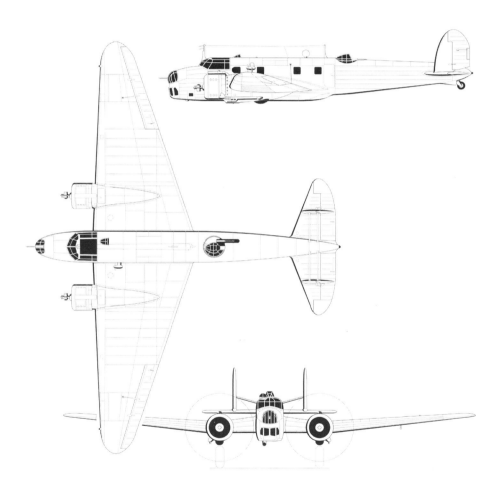

Fiat BR.20

Fiat BR.20 data

Span	21.56m/70ft 9in
Length	16.17m/53ft
Height	4.75m/15ft 7in
Wing area	74.07m²/797.3sq ft
Empty weight	6,400kg/14,110lb
Gross weight	9,900kg/21,830lb
Engine type	Two Fiat A.80RC.41
Engine output	1,030hp each
Dash speed	432kmph/233kt
Cruise speed	349kmph/188kt
Range	3,000km/1,860 miles
Rate of climb	285m per min/935ft per min
Ceiling	7,600m/25,000ft
Crew	Five
Armament	Five 7.69mm SAFAT machine guns and 1,600kg/3,500lb bombs

Ki-15 (Army Type 97)

The Ki-15 was designed at Mitsubishi by engineers Fumihilo Kono, Tomio Kubo and Syokiti Mizumo for aerial reconnaissance. Work commenced in 1935, and the type emerged as an all-metal twin-seat low-wing monoplane with a fixed undercarriage. The fuselage was a semi-monocoque structure with an oval section broader at the lower end. The smooth duralumin skin was stressed. Of the empennage, only the rudder was cloth-covered. The all-metal wing comprised a centre section and two cantilever outer wings of trapezoid planform. The latter's joints with the centre section were where the fixed, spatted undercarriage was fitted. The landing gear, including the tail prop, had oleo-pneumatic damping. Wing devices included ailerons and landing flaps.

For early Ki-15s the designers selected the single-row nine-cylinder air-cooled Nakajima Ha-8 radial engine developing up to 750hp. Offering sufficient altitude capabilities, it drove a fixed-pitch, twin-bladed metal propeller.

The two-man crew occupied an enclosed cockpit offering good visibility. They had oxygen equipment, cameras and radio transceivers. The sole armament at their disposal was a 7.7mm machine gun defending the aft hemisphere and operated by the observer.

The Ki-15 prototype flew in May 1936. Though a remarkable top speed of 480kmph/265kt was attained, the original engine proved disappointing. Nevertheless, the recce aircraft entered production as the Type 97 and in early 1938 the first Ki-15-I-equipped squadron entered action in China. Combat sorties showed that the new type was practically untouchable.

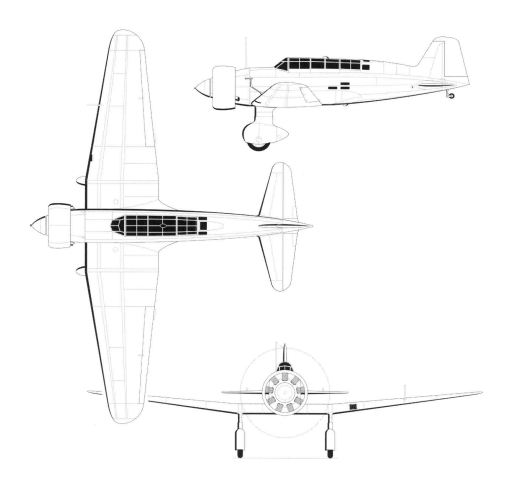

Ki-15-I p

Ki.15-I in civil insignia. (*Svetoslav Spirov collection*)

Despite this, update efforts continued apace, and late 1938 saw the service entry of a modified version. The main change in this, the Ki.15-II, was the fourteen-cylinder twin-row radial Ha.26-I engine developing 900hp. The new engine not only allowed a top speed of 510kmph/275kt, but also had significantly improved forward visibility due to the smaller diameter of the forward fuselage.

One *chutai* fielding Ki.15-Is saw action in the Nomonhan conflict. The machines were highly effective, being difficult targets even for I-16 tip 10 fighters. All the same, the Japanese admitted seven losses, a relatively high share of the total.

Ki.15-Is and IIs continued to see action until late 1942. Until 1944 they served as trainers, with kamikaze raids being the ultimate chapter in the history of this remarkable aircraft.

Ki-15-II data

Span	12m/39ft 5in
Length	8.7m/28ft 6in
Height	3.24m/10ft 7in
Wing area	20.36m²/219sq ft
Empty weight	1,592kg/3,500lb
Gross weight	2,481kg/5,470lb
Engine type	Nakajima Ha-26
Engine output	900hp
Dash speed	510kmph/275kt
Cruise speed	380kmph/205kt
Range	2,300km/2,175 miles
Rate of climb	745m per min/2,445ft per min
Ceiling	11,500m/37,700ft
Crew	Two
Armament	One 7.7mm Type 89 machine gun

Tupolev TB-3

The TB-3 heavy strategic bomber was designed by the Tupolev bureau in late 1929. After tests of the experimental ANT-6 finished on 28 April 1932, an initial batch of ten was constructed. The following year saw the formation of the first heavy bomber brigades.

The TB-3 was an all-metal four-engined monoplane with a fixed undercarriage and no braking system. Skinning was corrugated and the cockpits were open. The initial engine was the M-17F. Self-protection was afforded by 7.62mm DA machine guns fitted in five turrets and having 100 discs of 63 rounds each. The normal bomb load was 2,000kg/4,400lb.

From 1934 the type underwent numerous refits to improve aerodynamics and utilise more powerful M-34 engines. The propellers remained timber for some time, with a fixed pitch and a diameter of 3.18m/10ft 5in. These were eventually replaced by four-bladed units of 4.4m/14ft 5in diameter. By the close of 1938, 819 aircraft of various versions had been manufactured, becoming emblematic of Soviet 1930s air power.

TB-3 strategic bomber over Europe. (*Svetoslav Spirov collection*)

TB-3

From October 1933 the USSR had three brigades equipped with 143 TB-3s in the Far East. These were capable of striking Tokyo, the Japanese having no equal defence.

The type saw action in China, the Nomonhan conflict, the Winter War against Finland and the Great Patriotic War. Curiously, it also saw civil aviation duty, being especially useful in Polar regions where it saw service until the early 1950s.

TB-3 data

Span	41.80m/137ft 2in
Length	25.10m /82ft 5in
Height	8.50m /27ft 9in
Wing area	234.50sq m /2522,37sq ft
Empty weight	12,290kg /27,013lb
Gross weight	18,877kg /41,492lb
Engine type	Four M-34FRNs
Engine output	900hp each
Dash speed	300km/h /166kt
Cruise speed	182km/h /101kt
Range	2,000km /1,110miles
Rate of climb	175m per min /574ft per min
Ceiling	5480m /18,000ft
Crew	Four
Armament	Four 7.62mm DA machine guns and 3,000kg / 6600lb bombs

Nyeman R-10

Groups of designers under Ing. Nyeman began work on the R-10 tactical recce aircraft in 1934. Their task was to produce a modern, high-speed monoplane to supplant the obsolescent R-5. Initially designated the HAI-5, it was to have an all-timber structure with smooth ply skinning, and the empennage was to be of similar construction. The pilot and observer were to sit in enclosed cockpits. The wing had rather swept-back outer sections, which were removable for overland or ship transport.

Armament was in line with the type's core purpose. To reduce drag, the bomb load of up to 400kg/900lb was concealed within a fuselage bay with serial-release racks. Bomb aiming and dropping was remote, a first in Soviet practice. The ShKAS machine gun was within an entirely enclosed swivelling turret aft of the wing, significantly improving the field of fire. Anther machine gun of the same type, with 500 rounds, was fitted in the starboard wing for forward firing,

Nyeman R-10 (*Svetoslav Spirov collection*)

aimed through an OPB gunsight. Subsequent versions had improved machine gun protection. The aircraft carried cameras mounted on a swivelling frame.

The single-strut undercarriage was retractable by thirty-three turns of a manual crank operated by the pilot and assisted by a pneumatic servo. Belly landings were designed to be entirely safe.

The M-22 engine was initially fitted to the experimental aircraft, but was seen as hopelessly obsolescent and was replaced by the M-25A. The engine drove a twin-bladed propeller of fixed pitch.

After hasty re-engining of the prototype, the first flight took place in late June 1936, and testing finished on 24 October of the same year. A speed of 388kmph/209kt was attained. Before the end of testing the decision was made to launch series production of the type.

The first production machine came off the lines on 1 May 1937 and by the close of 1938 100 had been manufactured. By May 1939 the Far Eastern First Independent Red Banner Army had forty-five R-10s. While they did conduct aerial reconnaissance during the Nomonhan conflict, their basic purpose was to prove themselves in action.

Subsequently the type saw action in the Polish campaign, the Winter War in Finland and the initial period of Eastern Front operations. Its combat career came to a close in mid-1944. Until the end of production in 1940, a total of 493 M-25A- or B-powered machines had been manufactured.

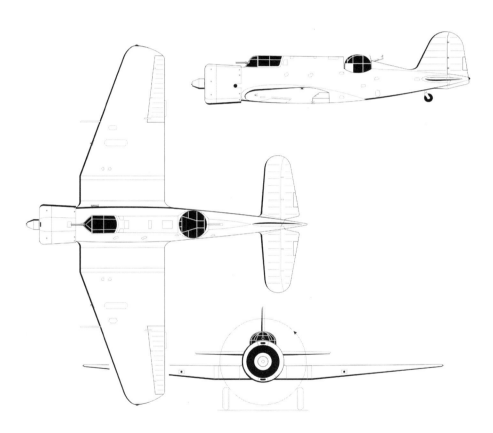

R-10

R-10 data

Span	12.20m /40ft
Length	9.40m /30ft 8in
Height	3.80m /12ft 5in
Wing area	26.80sq m /216,3 sq ft
Empty weight	2,197kg /4,830lb
Gross weight	2,877kg /6,324lb
Engine type	M-25B
Engine output	730hp
Dash speed	370km/h /205kt
Cruise speed	340km/h /190kt
Range	1,300km /813 miles
Rate of climb	417m per min /1368ft per min
Ceiling	6,700m /21,980ft
Crew	Two
Armament	Three 7.62mm ShKAS machine guns and 400kg/880lb bombs

Tupolev SB-2

Design of the SB-2 high-speed bomber began in January 1934 at Arkhangelskiy's design group under Tupolev's leadership. The experimental machine was ready by October the same year when testing commenced. After

A SB-2bis with a late modification of M-103 engines. (*Svetoslav Spirov collection*)

The SB-2bis was the major Soviet front-line strike bomber. *(MoD Archives, Bulgaria)*

successful proving flights, production commenced in early 1936.

The SB was an all-metal three-crew mid-wing monoplane powered by two engines and featuring a retractable undercarriage. Its fuselage was of relatively thin oval section and was split into two parts. The nose was glazed and had a vertical slot for machine gun aiming. The wing, fitted at an angle of incidence of 2 degrees, comprised a centre section and two outer wings. The entire airframe was skinned in VV soft alloy sheeting. The single-strut undercarriage had oleo-pneumatic damping and was retracted using hydraulics. The mainwheels had brakes. The navigator sat in the nose, and behind him was the pilot's compartment, while the gunner sat aft of the wing. The navigational fit allowed night operations but the crew had no radio.

The bomb bay was amidships and could accommodate a single 500kg/1,100lb bomb. There were three 7.62mm ShKAS machine guns, one in the navigator's compartment and dorsal and ventral ones aft, operated by the gunner. The three shared a total of 2,260 rounds.

Production SB-2s used water-cooled M-100 engines developing 860hp and driving two-bladed metal props. From March 1938 the SB-2bis had M-103s developing 960hp and driving three-bladed propellers. The new version also had a strengthened structure and boosted armament, the warload reaching 1,500kg/3,300lb. Series production rose to thirteen aircraft a day.

The SB became the main strike aircraft of the Workers' and Peasants' Red Army Air Force (the VVS RKKA). Its combat christening was in Spanish skies, where it was initially untouchable by fighters. Later it saw action in China. The first combat use of the SB-2bis was during the Nomonhan conflict.

The SB was actively used during the Second World War until mid-1943. Its last sorties were, however, by Bulgarian pilots over Macedonia in November 1944 (using Czech-licensed B.71s).

Overall Soviet production between 1936 and 1941 was 6,831 SBs of various versions. Another 110 were manufactured in Czechoslovakia.

An SB-2 cockpit. *(MoD Archives, Bulgaria)*

SB-2bis data

Span	20.33m/66ft 8in
Length	12.57m/41ft 3in
Height	3.48m/11ft 5in
Wing area	56.7m^2/610.3sq ft
Empty weight	4,768kg/10,514lb
Gross weight	7,880kg/17,372lb
Engine type	Two M-103s
Engine output	960hp each
Dash speed	450kmph/243kt
Cruise speed	375kmph/202kt
Range	1,600km/1,000 miles
Rate of climb	580m per min/1900ft per min
Ceiling	9,300m/30,500ft
Crew	Three
Armament	Five 7.62mm ShKAS machine guns and 1,500kg/3,300lb bombs

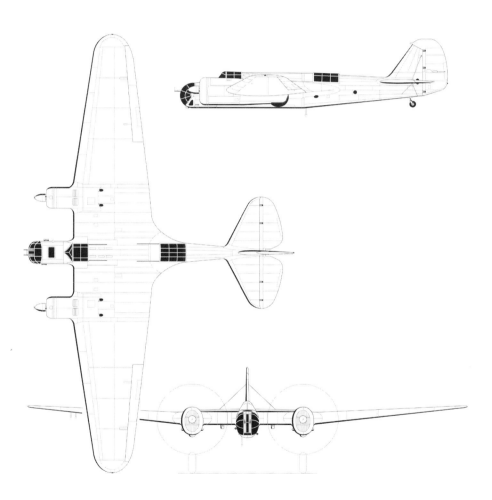

SB-2

The R-5, the principal Russian recce aircraft. *(MoD Archives, Bulgaria)*

Polikarpov R-5, R-5SSS, R-Z

The R-5 light bomber/recce aircraft was designed by Nikolay Polikarpov's bureau in 1928. Works tests took place in early 1929, the machine then entering series production. The aircraft embodied the concept of a multi-role mass combat type with adequate performance for its time and low manufacturing and maintenance costs.

The R-5 was a single-engined two-seat biplane of mixed structure and fixed undercarriage. Its fuselage was of timber frame construction; only the stressed elements were made of metal, the engine frame, the undercarriage struts and the control system. Skinning was ply. The wing was a cloth-covered timber structure. The upper and lower wings were braced by N-shaped struts and patent tape. The empennage was also timber, covered with cloth. The only metal skin covered the M-17B engine. This was a water-cooled unit with a moving radiator whose position was governed by airspeed. Landing gear was typical for its time and had pedal-controlled brakes.

The R-5 had a fixed synchronised 7.62mm PV-1 machine gun fitted ahead of the pilot, and two DA machine guns of the same calibre fitted in a turret in the observer's cockpit. For recce missions, the type could carry up to 300kg/660lb of bombs in addition to a relevant photographic and radio fit. In the bomber role, the load rose to 500kg/1,100lb of bombs.

R-5s rapidly took centre stage in the Soviet air forces of the early 1930s. Their low price and modest requirements made them indispensable in locations where others would have experienced problems. The type was also used by civil aviators. This universal appeal drove efforts to modernise it and to enable it to fulfil specialist tasks.

A float naval version was designed in 1931. A year later, a single-crewed torpedo carrier was flown. From 1933 the R-5Sh entered production, as a striker (*shturmovik*) with greater offensive firepower. More powerful M-17F

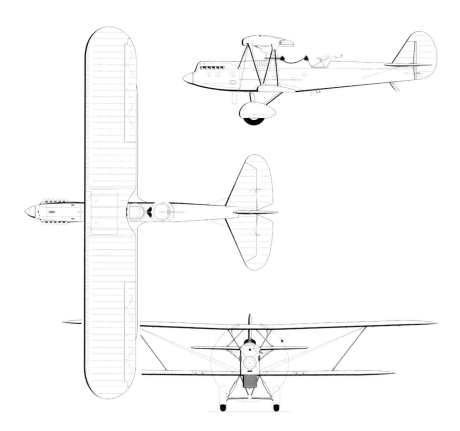

P-SSS

engines were fitted from 1934. Aerodynamics and control surface exterior finish were improved, while the older machine guns were replaced by new ShKAS units. This resulted in the R-5SSS, the three letters standing for high-speed, high rate of climb and high firing rate.

There was no way, however, of overcoming the limitations imposed by the 1920s layout, which called for more radical design solutions. A further modification featured a cut-back wing area, the significantly more powerful M-34RN engine and a semi-enclosed cockpit. The fuselage was also resized. This was the 1937 version, the R-Zet, the ultimate Soviet biplane recce aircraft. It was rather more demanding of its pilots, who now had to have solid experience. Between 1928 and 1939 some 4,914 R-5s, 620 R-5SSS and 1,031 R-Zets of various versions were manufactured. They not only participated in all armed conflicts of the 1930s, but also saw action until the close of the Second World War. Civil versions of this remarkable aircraft remained in use until the early 1950s.

Top: R-5 mechanic started up engines. *Above:* R-Zet in refueling process. (*Svetoslav Spirov collection*)

R-5 data

Parameter	R-5	R-5Sh	R-5SSS	R-Zet
Span	15.3m/50ft 2in		15.5m/50ft 10in	
Length	10.56m/34ft 8in			9.72m/31ft 10in
Height	2.62m/8ft 7in	3.25m/10ft 8in		3.5m/11ft 6in
Wing area	50.2m²/540.4sq ft			42.52m²/457.7sq ft
Empty weight	1,965kg/4,330lb	2,240kg/4,940lb	2,180kg/4,800lb	2,182kg/4,800lb
Gross weight	2,805kg/6,185lb	3,410kg/7,520lb	3,289kg/7,250lb	3,200kg/7,055lb
Engine type	M-17B		M-17F	M-34RN
Engine output	680hp		715hp	850hp
Dash speed	244kmph/132kt	202kmph/109kt	249kmph/134kt	316kmph/170kt
Cruise speed	210kmph/113kt	192kmph/104kt	221kmph/119kt	266kmph/144kt
Range	800km/500 miles		1,000km/620 miles	
Rate of climb	295m per min/ 970ft per min	245m per min/ 800ft per min	315m per min/ 1,030ft per min	425m per min/ 1,400ft per min
Ceiling	6,100m/20,000ft	4,440m/14,570ft	6,640m/21,800ft	8,700m/28550ft
Crew	Two			
Armament	One 7.62mm PV-1, two 7.62mm DAs, 400kg/900lb bombs	Three 7.62mm PV-1s, two 7.62mm DAs, 500kg/1100lb bombs	Three/seven 7.62mm ShKAS, 500kg/1,100lb bombs	Two 7.62mm ShKAS, 500kg/1,100lb bombs

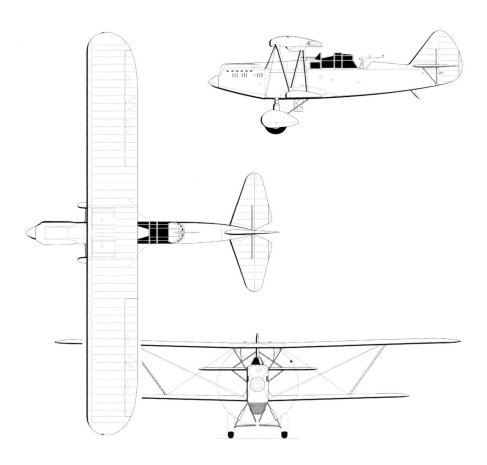

R-Zet

Appendix 2

Claimed Soviet fighter victories in the Nomonhan conflict

Name	Victories (shared)	Unit
Antonenko, Alexei Kasyanovich	0 (6)	Naval Air Forces Group
Chistyakov, Viktor Feofanovich	3	22 IAP
Danilov, Stepan Pavlovich	8	56 IAP
Geibo, Iosif Ivanovich	2 (1)	70 IAP
Gerasimov, Nikolai Semyonovich	1	70 IAP
Gerdev, Nikolai Prokofyevich	11 (3)	70 IAP
Grinev, Nikolai Vasilyevich	4 (6)	22 IAP
Gritsavets, Sergey Ivanovich	12	70 IAP
Kalachev, Vladimir Nikolayevich	6 (2)	22 IAP
Kleshchev, Ivan Ivanovich	1	
Kovats, Petr Semyonovich	3	
Krasnoyurchenko, Ivan Ivanovich	5	22 IAP
Kravchenko, Grigorii Panteleyevich	20	22 IAP
Kutsevalov, Timofei Fyodorovich	4 (5)	56 IAP
Kuz'menko, Konstantin Mefodievich	4 (10)	22 IAP
Lakeyev, Ivan Alexeyevich	1 (3)	
Mashkovskii, Stepan Filippovich	3 (1)	56 IAP
Matveyev, Aleksandr Andreyevich	2 (5)	70 IAP
Medvedev, Dmitrii Aleksandrovich	3	22 IAP
Moshin, Aleksei Fedorovich	2 (3)	56 IAP
Motyl, Ivan Miroslavovich	1	
Murmilov, Aleksandr Andreevich	4 (5)	22 IAP
Naidenko, Vasilii	5	22 IAP
Noga, Mitrofan Petrovich	9 (2)	70 IAP
Petuhov, Sergei Mikhailovich	2	
Pologov, Pavel Andreevich	1	
Pyankov, Aleksandr Petrovich	3 (8)	22 IAP
Rakhov, Viktor Georgiyevich	8 (6)	22 IAP
Smushkevich, Yakov	4	
Skobarihin, Vitaliy Fedorovich	5 (6)	22 IAP
Smirnov, Boris Aleksandrovich	4	70 IAP
Stepanov, Andrei Mihailovich	3	70 IAP

Stepanov, Yevgenii Nikolayevich	1	22 IAP
Suvirov, Viktor Ivanovich	3	22 IAP
Timofeev, Sergei Ivanovich	5 (7)	
Trubachenko, Vasilii Petrovich	5 (3)	22 IAP
Viktorov, Nikolai Nikiforovich	5	70 IAP
Vorozheykin, Arseniy Vasilyevich	6 (13)	22 IAP
Vuss, Vasilii Nikiforovich	4 (4)	22 IAP
Yakimenko, Anton Dmitriyevich	3 (4)	22 IAP
Yamanov, Valerian Aleksandrovich	4	56 IAP
Zaitsenko, Sergei Danilovich	1	22 IAP
Zaitsev, Aleksandr Andreyevich	6	70 IAP

Appendix 3

Claimed Japanese fighter victories in the Nomonhan conflict

Name	Victories	Unit
Anma, Katsumi	5	
Aoyagi, Yutaka	10	11th *Sentai*
Asano, Hitoshi	22	1st *Sentai*
Ashida, Masao	13	
Eto, Toyoki	2	
Fukuda, Tokuro	11	
Furugori, Goro	20	11th *Sentai*
Hanada, Mamoru	17	
Hanada, Tomio	25	11th *Sentai*
Hasegawa, Tomoari	19	
Hayashi, Takeomi	2	
Hida, Hitoshi	7	
Hirose, Yoshio	2	
Hisashichi, Noguchi	9	
Hosono, Isamu	21	1st *Sentai*
Ina, Akira	9	
Inouye, Misao	8	
Ishii, Takeo	18	
Ishizawa, Koji	11	
Ishizuka, Tokuyasu	12	
Ito, Riichi	16	
Iwahashi, Jyozo	20	11th *Sentai*
Iwase, Koichi	10	11th *Sentai*
Kanai, Moritsugu	7	
Kanamaru, Teizo	3	
Kanbara, Daisuke	9	11th *Sentai*
Kani, Saiji	9	
Kato, Shoji	23	11th *Sentai*
Kimura, Saburo	19	
Kimura, Yutaka	9	
Kira, Katsuaki	9	
Kobayasho, Taro	10	

Kodama, Takayori	11	
Kuroe, Yasuhiko	2	2 *Chutai*/59th *Hiko Sentai*
Kuroki, Tameyoshi	3	
Kurono, Shoji	12	
Masuzawa, Masatoshi	10	

Lt Masatoshi Masuzawa (centre) was one of the best pilots of the 1st *Sentai*. (*MoD Archives, Bulgaria*)

Matsuura, Toshio	10	
Minami, Takashi	14	
Miyamaru, Shoshio	1	
Motojima, Muneyoshi	16	
Motomura, Koji	14	
Nishihara, Goro	12	
Okuda, Jiro	14	
Otsuka, Zenzaburo	22	11th *Sentai*
Saito, Chiyoshi	21	24th *Sentai*
Saito, Shogo	25	24th *Sentai*
Sakai, Iori	8	
Shibata, Rikio	14	
Shimada, Kenji	27	11th *Sentai*
Shimamura, Miyoshi	8	
Shindo, Norio	13	
Shinohara, Hiromiti	58	11th *Sentai*
Shiromoto, Naoharu	11	
Sudo, Tokuya	10	
Suzuki, Eisaku	11	
Suzuki, Syoichi	17	
Takagaki, Haruo	15	

Takahashi, Katsutaro	2	
Takeshi, Shimizu	4	
Takiyama, Yamato	9	
Tarui, Mitsuyoshi	28	1st *Sentai*
Togo, Saburo	22	11th *Sentai*
Yajima, Yoshihiko	16	
Yonaga, Hyoe	16	
Yoshiyama, Bunji	20	11th *Sentai*

Bibliographical notes

1 Широкорад, А., „Русско-Японские войны 1904–1945 гг.', Harvest, Minsk, 2003, p 480

2 Котельников, В., „Было дело на Хасане', „Авиамастер' No 2 2003, p 12

3 Op. cit., p 17

4 Ibid., p 18

5 Op. cit., p 15

6 Ibid., p 18

7 Чудодеев, Ю. В. (ed.), „В небе Китая', Hayka, Moscow, 1980, p 4

8 Кривель, А., „Слышишь, Халхин-Гол!', Издательство политической литературы, Moscow, 1989, p 64

9 Коломиец, М., „Бои у реки Халхин-Гол', Стратегия КМ, Moscow, 1999, p 22

10 Шишов, А., „Россия и Япония. История военных Конфликтов', Вече, Moscow, 2000, p 477

11 Op. cit., p 473

12 Коломиец, М., ibid., p 18

13 Op. cit., p 19

14 Жуков, Г., „Воспоменания и размышления', Издательство Агенции печати „Новости', Moscow, 1983, p 137

15 Кондратьев, В., „Халхин-Гол – война в воздухе', Библиотека журнала „Техника молодёжи', Серия „Авиация', Moscow, 2002, p 5

16 Скороморохов, М., „Тактика в боевых примерах', Военное издательство, Moscow, 1985, p 5

17 Ibid., p 127

18 Ворожейкин, А., „Истребители', Военное издательство, Moscow, 1961, p 81

19 Коломиец, М., op. cit., p 21

20 Vejřík, L., „Vzestup a pád orlů Nipponu 1931-1941 (Prolog)', Svět křídel, Cheb, 1994, p 191

21 Шишов, А., ibid., p 485

22 Кондратьев, В., „Дебют в Китайском небе', „Авиамастер' No 4 2001, p 22–26

23 Котловский, А., А. Шпигунов, „«Чато» Поликарпова. Самолет и модель', „Авиация и время' No 2, 2000, p 49–52

24 'Polikarpov Fighters', In Action, Part 1, Squadron/Signal Publications, Carollton, Texas, 1995, p 29

25 Op. cit., p 43

26 Семёнов, Г., „Товарищ Сергио', Прапор, Khar'kov, 1982, p 220

27 Косминков, К., „Истребители в небе Китая и Монголии', „Крыля Родины' No 10, 1990, p 21–23

28 Ibid.

29 Бюшгенс, Г. (ed.), „Самолетостроение в СССР 1917–1945. Книга 1', Издательский отдел ЦАГИ, Moscow, 1992, p 159

30 Кондратьев, В. „Дебют в Китайском небе', p 22–26

31 Косминков, К., op. cit., p 21–23

32 Ibid.

33 Иванов, С., „СБ – гордость советской авиации', часть 2, Белорецк, 2001, p 17–18

34 Котельников, В., '«Зет» – наследник Р-5', „Авиамастер', No 2 1997, p 9–13

35 Котельников, В., „Воздушный линкор 2-го Класса', „История авиации', No 1 2002, p 18–27

36 Савин, В., „Крылатый сверхсрочник', „Моделиск-Конструктор' No 3 1989, p 17–24

37 Фирсов, А., „Два меча самураев', „Крыля Родины', No 9 1998, p 22–27

38 Котельников, В., '«Аист» римских легионеров', „Авиамастер', No 2 2002, p 18–35

39 Bridgman, L., Fighting Aircraft of World War II, Jane's, London, 1994

40 Коломиец, М., op. cit., p 23

41 Шишов, А., ibid., p 479

42 Коломиец, М., op. cit., p 24

43 Широкорад, А., ibid., p 508

44 Коломиец, М., op. cit., p 26

45 Hata, I., Y. Izawa, C. Shores, Japanese Army Air Force Fighter Units and their Aces, 1931-1945, Grubb Street Press, London, 2002, p 14

46 Кондратьев, В., „Халхин-Гол', ibid., p 7

47 Op. cit.

48 Hata et al., ibid., p 244

49 Baeza, B., 'L'incident du Nomonhan', Aviones 1996/1997, p 41

50 Кондратьев, В., „Халхин-Гол', op. cit., p 7

51 Семёнов, Г., „Товарищ', ibid., p 194.

52 Hata et al., op. cit., p 219

53 Яковлев, В., К. Боброва, Г. Шмаков, „Крылатый богатырь', ДОСААФ, Moscow, 1984, p 82

54 Кондратьев, В., „Халхин-Гол', ibid., p 7

55 Baeza, op. cit., p 41

56 Широкорад, А., ibid., p 512

57 Vejřík, L., „Vzestup', op. cit., p 193

58 Кривель, А., ibid., p 41

59 Hata et al., op. cit., p 15

60 Кривель, А., ibid., p 41

61 Шишов, А., op. cit., p 487

62 Кривель, А., ibid., p 44
63 Baeza, 'L'incident', op. cit., p 8
64 Яковлев et al., ibid., p 85
65 Hata et al., op. cit., p 197
66 Кондратьев, В., „Халхин-Гол', ibid., p 9
67 Кривель, А., Op. cit., p 44
68 Широкорад, А., ibid., p 514
69 Щербаков, А., „Крылатым доверьте небо!', Издательство
    политической литературы, Moscow, 1976, p 67
70 Чудодеев, Ю. В. (ed.), „В небе Китая', op. cit., p 12.
71 Яковлев et al., ibid., p 80
72 Жуков, Г., op. cit., p 192
73 Соколов, Б., „Неизвестный Жуков – портрет без ретуши', Родина-
    плюс, Moscow, 2000, p 118
74 Семёнов, Г., ibid., p 186
75 Щербаков, А., op. cit., p 87
76 Baeza, 'L'incident', ibid., p 8
77 Op. cit.
78 Vejřík, L., „Vzestup', ibid., p 197
79 Семёнов, Г., op. cit., p 194
80 Шишов, А., ibid., p 488
81 Кондратьев, В., „Халхин-Гол', op. cit., p 10
82 Ворожейкин, А., ibid., p 37
83 Op. cit., p 41
84 Ibid., p 45
85 Кондратьев, В., „Халхин-Гол', op. cit., p 12
86 Coox, A., Nomonhan: Japan against Russia, 1939, Stanford University
    Press, Stanford, California, 1985, p 266
87 Иванов, Ю., „Камикадзе – пилоты смертники', Русич, Smolensk, 2001
88 Polak, T., „Esa mezivalecneho obdobi', Aero Plastic Kits Revue, p 46-
    96, p 64–67
89 Кондратьев, В., „Халхин-Гол', ibid., p 12
90 Яковлев et al., op. cit., p 93
91 Ворожейкин, А., ibid., p 56
92 Baeza, 'L'incident', op. cit., p 10
93 Coox, A., Nomonhan, ibid., p 268
94 Шингарёв, С., „Под нами Халхин-Гол', „Московский рабочий',
    Moscow, 1979, p 39
95 Coox, A., Nomonhan, op. cit., p 936
96 Кондратьев, В., „Халхин-Гол', ibid., p 14
97 Coox, A., Nomonhan, op. cit., p 266
98 Яковлев et al., ibid., p 96.

99 Шингарёв, С., „Под нами', op. cit., p 50
100 Семёнов, Г., ibid., p 205
101 Кондратьев, В., „Халхин-Гол', op. cit., p 14
102 Baeza, 'L'incident', ibid., p 10
103 Кондратьев, В., „Халхин-Гол', op. cit., p 15
104 Яковлев et al., ibid., p 97
105 Шингарёв, С., „Под нами', op. cit., p 56–57
106 Ibid.
107 Кондратьев, В., „Халхин-Гол', ibid., p 15
108 Шингарёв, С., „Под нами', op. cit., p 52
109 Кондратьев, В., „Халхин-Гол', ibid., p 15
110 Baeza, 'L'incident', op. cit., p 10
111 Ibid.
112 Op. cit.
113 Coox, A., Nomonhan, ibid., p 271
114 Op. cit., p 274
115 Шингарёв, С., „Под нами', ibid., p 61
116 Vejřík, L., „Vzestup', op. cit., p 179
117 Яковлев et al., ibid., p 99
118 Coox, A., Nomonhan, op. cit., p 275
119 Baeza, 'L'incident', ibid., p 10
120 Семёнов, Г., op. cit., p 211.
121 Яковлев et al., ibid., p 103
122 Кондратьев, В., „Халхин-Гол', op. cit., p 16
123 Семёнов, Г., ibid., p 214
124 Baeza, 'L'incident', op. cit., p 10
125 Шишов, А., ibid., p 489
126 Яковлев et al., op. cit., p 106
127 Coox, A., Nomonhan, ibid., p 277
128 Коломиец, М., op. cit., p 32
129 Шишов, А., ibid., p 493
130 „Военный энциклопедический словарь', Военное издательство,
    Moscow, 1984, p 791
131 Широкорад, А., op. cit., p 518
132 Кондратьев, В., „Халхин-Гол', ibid., p 17
133 Шингарёв, С., „Под нами', op. cit., p 87
134 Ворожейкин, А., ibid., p 93
135 Яковлев et al., op. cit., p 107
136 Коломиец, М., ibid., p 39
137 Яковлев et al., op. cit., p 111
138 Hata et al., ibid., p 240
139 Яковлев et al., op. cit., p 111

140 Baeza, 'L'incident', ibid., p 10
141 Котельников, 'Аист', op. cit., p 18–35
142 Baeza, 'L'incident', ibid., p 10
143 Ворожейкин, А., op. cit., p 98
144 Иванов, Ю., „Камикадзе', ibid., p 17–18
145 Ворожейкин, А., op. cit., p 150
146 Hata et al., ibid., p 196
147 Кондратьев, В., „Халхин-Гол', op. cit., p 20
148 Котельников, В., „Воздушный', ibid., p 18–27
149 Яковлев et al., op. cit., p 116
150 Hata et al., ibid., p 196
151 Кондратьев, В., „Халхин-Гол', op. cit., p 21
152 Baeza, 'L'incident', ibid., p 11
153 Яковлев et al., op. cit., p 116
154 Шингарёв, С., „Под нами', ibid., p 99–100
155 Яковлев et al., op. cit., p 120
156 Семёнов, Г., ibid., p 221
157 Ворожейкин, А., op. cit., p 170
158 Шингарёв, С., „Под нами', ibid., p 101
159 Семёнов, Г., op. cit., p 201
160 Baeza, 'L'incident', ibid., p 11
161 Яковлев et al., op. cit., p117–118
162 Baeza, 'L'incident', ibid., p 11
163 Кондратьев, В., „Халхин-Гол', op. cit., p 22
164 Иванов, Ю., „Камикадзе', ibid., p 17–18
165 Baeza, 'L'incident', op. cit., p 11
166 Шингарёв, С., „Под нами', ibid., p 111
167 Baeza, 'L'incident', op. cit., p 11
168 Кондратьев, В., „Халхин-Гол', ibid., p 23
169 Якубович, Н., „Там вдали у реки...', „Крыля Родины' No 10 1998, p 15–17
170 Кондратьев, В., „Халхин-Гол', op. cit., p 24
171 Baeza, 'L'incident', ibid., p 11
172 Кондратьев, В., „Халхин-Гол', op. cit., p 24
173 Hata et al., ibid., p 191
174 Кондратьев, В., „Халхин-Гол', op. cit., p 24
175 Семёнов, Г., ibid., p 225
176 Op. cit., p 231
177 Широкорад, А., ibid., p 520
178 Яковлев et al., op. cit., p 121
179 Шингарёв, С., „Под нами', ibid., p 101
180 Яковлев et al., op. cit., p 122

181 Hata et al., ibid., p 212

182 Op. cit., p. 260

183 Широкорад, А., ibid., p 520.

184 Hata et al., op. cit., p 240

185 Coox, A., Nomonhan, ibid., p 933

186 Кондратьев, В., „Халхин-Гол', op. cit., p 25

187 Ворожейкин, А., ibid., p 212

188 Vejřík, L., „Vzestup', op. cit., p 234

189 Кондратьев, В., „Халхин-Гол', ibid., p 26

190 Шингарёв, С., „Под нами', op. cit., p 110

191 Широкорад, А., ibid., p 521

192 Кривель, А., op. cit., p 51

193 Шингарёв, С., „Под нами', ibid., p 121

194 Hata et al., op. cit., p 229

195 Ibid., p 234

196 Op. cit., p 206

197 Жуков, Г., ibid.

198 Шингарёв, С., „Под нами', op. cit., p 121

199 Baeza, 'L'incident', ibid., p 9

200 Яковлев et al., op. cit., p 123

201 Ibid.

202 Baeza, 'L'incident', op. cit., p 9

203 Hata et al., ibid., p 218

204 Жуков, Г., op. cit., p 199

205 Кондратьев, В., „Халхин-Гол', ibid., p 27

206 Op. cit.

207 Шишов, А., ibid., p 502

208 Шингарёв, С., „Под нами', op. cit., p 114

209 Яковлев et al., ibid., p 126

210 Op. cit., p 127

211 Шингарёв, С., „Под нами', ibid., p 124

212 Коломиец, М., op. cit., p 56

213 Широкорад, А., ibid., p 524

214 Шингарёв, С., „Под нами', op. cit., p 116

215 Кондратьев, В., „Халхин-Гол', ibid., p 27

216 Семёнов, Г., op. cit., p 235

217 Жуков, Г., ibid., p 200

218 Котельников, В., „Воздушный', op. cit., p 18–27

219 Кондратиев, В., „Краски Халхин-Гола', „Авиамастер' No 6 2002, p 40–45

220 Кондратьев, В., „Халхин-Гол', ibid., p 28

221 Шингарёв, С., „Под нами', op. cit., p 123

222 Жуков, Г., ibid., p 207

223 Coox, A., Nomonhan, op. cit., p 683–684

224 Ibid., p 684

225 Шингарёв, С., „Под нами', op. cit., p 126

226 Яковлев et al., ibid., p 129

227 Ворожейкин, А., op. cit., p 226

228 Шингарёв, С., „Под нами', ibid., p 128

229 Кондратьев, В., „Халхин-Гол', op. cit., p 31

230 Широкорад, А., ibid., p 527

231 Coox, A., Nomonhan, op. cit., p 672

232 Широкорад, А., ibid., p 528

233 Op. cit.

234 Яковлев et al., ibid., p 130

235 Широкорад, А., op. cit., p 538

236 Coox, A., Nomonhan, ibid., p 672

237 Широкорад, А., op. cit., p 536

238 Яковлев et al., ibid., p 130

239 Vejřík, L., „Vzestup', op. cit., p 239

240 Шингарёв, С., „Под нами', ibid., p 131

241 Coox, A., Nomonhan, op. cit., p 685

242 Широкорад, А., ibid., p 534

243 Baeza, 'L'incident', op. cit., p 11

244 Широкорад, А., ibid., p 534

245 Baeza, 'L'incident', op. cit., p 11

246 Hata et al., ibid., p 190

247 Широкорад, А., op. cit., p 535

248 Кондратьев, В., „Халхин-Гол', ibid., p 32

249 Baeza, 'L'incident', op. cit., p 11

250 Кондратьев, В., „Халхин-Гол', ibid., p 33

251 Baeza, 'L'incident', op. cit., p 11

252 Широкорад, А., ibid., p 536

253 Coox, A., Nomonhan, op. cit., p 688

254 Яковлев et al., ibid., p 131

255 Кондратьев, В., „Халхин-Гол', op. cit., p 34

256 Hata et al., ibid., p 259

257 Шингарёв, С., „Под нами', op. cit., p 132

258 Baeza, 'L'incident', ibid., p 20

259 Яковлев et al., op. cit., p 131–132

260 Шишов, А., ibid., p 507

261 Op. cit.

262 Ворожейкин, А., ibid., p 271

263 Baeza, 'L'incident', op. cit., p 21

264 Ворожейкин, А., ibid., p 270

265 Baeza, 'L'incident', op. cit., p 21

266 Кондратьев, В., „Халхин-Гол', ibid., p 35

267 Широкорад, А., op. cit., p 540

268 Ibid., p 550

269 Coox, A., Nomonhan, op. cit., p 755

270 Ворожейкин, А., ibid., p 273

271 Кондратиев, В., „Краски', op. cit., p 40–45

272 Широкорад, А., ibid., p 550

273 Baeza, 'L'incident', op. cit., p 20

274 Ibid., p 21

275 Широкорад, А., op. cit., p 538

276 Hata et al., ibid., p 22

277 Широкорад, А., op. cit., p 538

278 Hata et al., ibid., p 22

279 Кондратьев, В., „Халхин-Гол', op. cit., p 36

280 Широкорад, А., ibid., p 539

281 Walg, A., 'Wings Over the Steppes', Air Enthusiast November 1996/April 1997

282 Vejřík, L., „Vzestup', op. cit., p 242

283 Coox, A., Nomonhan, ibid., p 882

284 Op. cit.

285 Baeza, 'L'incident', ibid., p 22

286 Ворожейкин, А., op. cit., p 278

287 Baeza, 'L'incident', ibid., p 22

288 Ворожейкин, А., op. cit., p 285–292

289 Coox, A., Nomonhan, ibid., p 884

290 Baeza, 'L'incident', op. cit., p 22

291 Кондратьев, В., „Халхин-Гол', ibid., p 41

292 Соколов, Б., „Неизвестный', op. cit., p 146

293 Ibid.

294 Кондратьев, В., „Халхин-Гол', op. cit., p 41

295 Широкорад, А., ibid., p 551

296 Vejřík, L., „Vzestup', op. cit., p 244

297 Кондратьев, В., „Халхин-Гол', ibid., p 41, 51

298 Vejřík, L., „Vzestup', op. cit., p 245

299 Широкорад, А., ibid., p 552

300 Шишов, А., op. cit., p 517

301 Яковлев et al., ibid., p 135

302 Hata et al., op. cit., p 23

Index

Airborne
Neil Williams
One of Britain's best-known
pilots - in his own words
240 pages, paperback
Illustrated throughout
9 781906 559212 £10.95

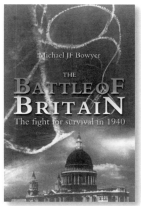

The Battle of Britain
The Fight for Survival in 1940
Michael JF Bowyer
The Battle of Britain day-by-day,
detailing squadrons, aircraft,
locations and people.
240 pages, paperback
Over 120 b&w photographs
9 780859 791472 £10.95

Eagles of the Third Reich
Men of the Luftwaffe in WWII
Samuel W Mitcham Jr
The leaders and pilots
of the Luftwaffe.
320 pages, paperback
51 b&w photographs and 8 maps
9 780859 791496 £10.95

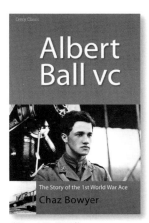

Albert Ball VC
Chaz Bowyer
Fascinating story of the Royal
Flying Corps' first celebrity ace
with 44 kills.
280pp soft cover
Over 75 b&w photographs
9 780947 554897 £10.95

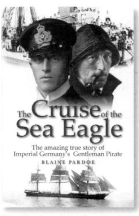

The Cruise of the Sea Eagle
The story of Imperial Germany's
Gentleman Pirate
Blaine Pardoe
Felix von Luckner, the Imperial
German navy raider of WW I.
272 pages, paperback
Approx 30 b&w photographs
9 780859 791205 £10.95

Echoes in the Air
True aviation ghost stories
Jac k Currie
A compilation of researched
aviation ghost stories, famous
and newly discovered,
accompanied by illustrations,
diagrams and photographs.
240 pages paperback
Illustrated throughout
9 780859 791632 £10.95

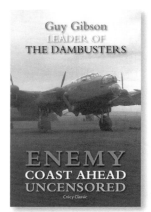

**Enemy Coast Ahead –
Uncensored**
Leader of the Dambusters
Wing Commander Guy Gibson
One of the most outstanding
accounts of WWII.
288 pages, soft cover
b&w photographs and
illustrations throughout
9 780859 791182 £10.95

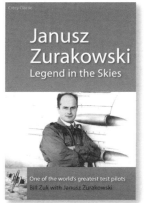

Janusz Zurakowski
Legend in the Skies
Bill Zuk and Janusz Zurakowski
A rare combination of skilled
engineer, painstaking test pilot
and unparalleled display pilot.
336 pages, soft cover
Over 75 b&w photographs
9 780859 79128 1 £10.95

Pure Luck
Alan Bramson
An authorised biography of
aviation pioneer Sir Thomas
Sopwith, 1888-1989
Foreword by HRH The Prince of
Wales
288 pages, soft cover
Over 90 b&w photographs
9 780859 791069 £10.95

Fist from the Sky
Peter C Smith
The story of Captain Takashige
Egusa the Imperial Japanese
Navy's most illustrious dive-
bomber pilot
272 pages, soft cover
Over 75 B+W photographs
9 780859 79122 9 £10.95

**The Luftwaffe Fighters'
Battle of Britain**
Chris Goss
An insight into the experiences of
the German fighter and bomber
crews from the attacker's
viewpoint.
208 pages, soft cover
Over 140 photographs
9 780859 791519 £10.95

Sigh for a Merlin
Testing the Spitfire
Alex Henshaw
The enthralling account of Alex
Henshaw's life as a test pilot
with the Spitfire.
240 pages, soft cover
b&w photographs throughout
9 780947 554835 £10.95

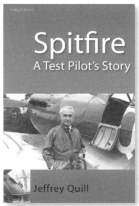

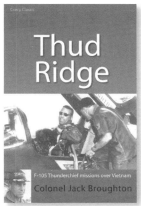

Spitfire
A Test Pilot's Story
Jeffrey Quill
The autobiography of an
exceptional test pilot and RAF
and Fleet Air Arm fighter pilot.
336 pages, soft cover
b&w photographs throughout
9 780947 554729 £10.95

Thud Ridge
Jack Broughton
F-105 Thunderchief missions
over the hostile skies of North
Vietnam
288 pages, soft cover
79 photographs plus maps and
plans
9 780859 791168 £10.95

Winged Warfare
William Avery ('Billy') Bishop
VC, DSO MC
A unique autobiographical and
contemporary account of one of
the highest scoring fighter aces
of World War I.
224 pages, soft cover
integrated b&w photographs
9 780947 554903 £10.95

Stormbird
Hermann Buchner
Autobiography of one of the
Luftwaffe's highest scoring
Me262 aces.
272 pages, soft cover
140 b&w photographs and 16
page colour section
9 780859 791404 £10.95

We Landed By Moonlight
Hugh Verity
Secret RAF Landings in France
1940-1944
256 pages, soft cover
b&w photographs throughout
9 780947 554750 £10.95

 Crécy

Order online at **www.crecy.co.uk**
or telephone +44 (0) 161 499 0024
Crécy Publishing 1a Ringway Trading Est,
Shadowmoss Rd, Manchester, M22 5LH
enquiries@crecy.co.uk